CHIEF BENDER'S BURDEN

CHIEF
BENDER'S
BURDEN

THE SILENT STRUGGLE
OF A BASEBALL STAR

TOM SWIFT

University of Nebraska Press   Lincoln & London

Library of Congress Cataloging-in-
Publication Data

Swift, Tom.
Chief Bender's burden : the
silent struggle of a baseball star /
Tom Swift.
p. cm.
Includes bibliographical references
and index.
ISBN 978-0-8032-4321-7 (cloth :
alk. paper)
1. Bender, Charles Albert,
1883–1954. 2. Baseball players—
Pennsylvania—Philadelphia—
Biography.
3. Indian baseball players—United
States—Biography. 4. Philadelphia
Athletics (Baseball team)—
Biography. I. Title.
GV865.B45S95 2008
796.357092—dc22
[B]
2007033591

Set in ITC New Baskerville by
Kim Essman.

For Carrie

I'm blessed to round the bases
while holding your hand

A story worthy of a Dickens or a Stevenson lies back of the marvelous [Charles Bender's] stolid skill . . . and of the stoicism that heard unheeded the roar of the crowd. It is the story of a life set apart by race distinction, of nerves hardened by many slights cast upon a sensitive spirit.

Philadelphia Press, October 18, 1910

Chapter One. The baseball sailed into Wally Schang's mitt in a blur. One pitch. Then a second. Pop. Pop. Sixty and a half feet away, a lanky man reached back, rotated his hips, and whipped his right arm forward. The catcher quickly returned the ball, rocked, and prepared to receive another. Pop. As he delivered his pitches, Charles Albert Bender's body remained closed, his arm hidden, until the last moment, and by the time he reached the release point he was coming over the top. Pop. Thin calves masked the strength in the long legs with which he leveraged his power. On the follow-through, his glove trailed behind his back like the tail end of an airplane and his throwing hand looked like it was pulling down a window shade. Pop. Bender kicked so high—the signature aspect of his motion—that as he strode toward the plate a batter could see the bottom of his left foot. On this occasion, however, there was no batter. On October 8, 1914, one day before the start of the World Series, Bender and his teammates were in Shibe Park, preparing.

Pop.

The anticipation in Philadelphia, throughout the city's pubs, barbershops, factories, and department stores, was palpable. The Philadelphia Athletics had raced out to a comfortable margin in the American League pennant race, and their fourth league title in five seasons was clinched early. Unthreatened after June, the Athletics won by 8½ games over the

Boston Red Sox, and no other team was closer than 19 games out. Perhaps because the regular season was anticlimactic, or possibly because the Athletics were on such a historic run, whatever the reason, Philadelphia fans were revved for this party as though they were about to celebrate another successful Revolution.

Demand for tickets was greater for this Series than any previous October. Reserved seats went on sale earlier in the week, and Joseph Banks, a plump eighteen-year-old in a bow tie, was the first in line. Banks plopped down a wood block twenty-six hours before tickets went on sale at Gimbels department store. Eventually, the crowd behind his makeshift seat was so thick along Ninth Street that business owners complained and asked that the line be shifted over to Ludlow, down an alley between Gimbels and Leary's bookstore. Most were men and boys in hats and ties. Two boys, Abe Heisman and Ed Hill, stood immediately behind Banks. Their enviable places in line would later fetch far more than they ever earned in allowance. About five hours after tickets went on sale more than five thousand had been sold. By midafternoon a sign was posted announcing that the supply had been exhausted. Thousands turned away in disgust. A number of scalpers, or speculators as they were called, had gobbled up tickets. Several were arrested in the days before the game. Scandal.

As Bender popped Schang's mitt, the ticket hysteria continued. Fans lined up outside Shibe Park with the hope they could obtain bleacher seats. Sales would start at ten o'clock the next morning. By midnight the line would be almost four blocks long. Through the night thousands waited outside the park for the gate to open. Several times the crowd almost overflowed, and dozens of Philadelphia's finest struggled to maintain order. Prominent sportswriter James Isaminger lamented the only problem on Philadelphians' minds: "Shibe Park should have been built of rubber," he said, "so it could be stretched out for this World's Series."

This was a well-constructed team. In 1905 the Athletics had reached the World Series, but that club had peaked. Manager Connie Mack, with control over personnel, began a rebuilding process. By the end of the decade the American League's resident genius had collected a number of young, malleable players that he molded into a balanced and bright baseball team. The Athletics had the league's most dynamic offense, a solid group of outfielders, a deep pitching staff that included seven ten-game winners, and one of the game's premiere position players, second baseman Eddie Collins. Collins and third baseman Frank Baker were the best players in the league at their respective positions. When joined with Jack Barry, a fine shortstop, and first baseman Stuffy McInnis, who had such a soft mitt and quick feet he broke into the big leagues as a shortstop, the quartet became famous, dubbed by one writer as "The $100,000 Infield."

Bender's presence was no small element in the confident brew Philadelphians were sipping. By this time Philadelphia was aware that the Athletics had the preeminent World Series figure on their side. Newspaper inches often were filled with speculation about pitching assignments for such big games, but there wasn't doubt as to which man Mack would send to the mound for Game 1. "Bender, when it comes to pitching an individual game, has no equals," sportswriter F. C. Lane said in *Baseball Magazine.* "In a short series like the World's Champions' contests, no pitcher in the business can excel Bender." The day of the game, the *Philadelphia North American* ran a picture of Bender in mid-windup. The caption was concise: "Greatest money pitcher in baseball."

The opponent, the Boston Braves, was further reason for optimism. The Braves had a starless pitching staff and a pedestrian lineup. The National League had lost the past four World Series and didn't appear to have any dominant teams. The American League was fashioning a superior brand of baseball, and no team played it better than the one with the blue "A" stitched into their white and blue pin-striped wool uniforms. Conventional wisdom said the only team that could beat the Athletics was the Athletics. Early in the season newspapers gave reports of inflated egos, and Charles Bender's confidence at this point was evident. According to a story published in the *Boston Daily Globe* written by Boston manager George Stallings three months after the fact, in the final game of the regular season, with the Braves scouting the Athletics from the stands, Bender walked up to Johnny Evers, Boston's diminutive on-field leader, who was sitting in the last row of the grandstand. Bender tapped Evers on the shoulder and Johnny looked around.

"Oh," Bender said. "I thought you were a gambler that I was looking for. There he is down there. I see him now."

Bender walked over to the person he said he was seeking, a stout man,

Stallings said, that had "no more resemblance to Johnny than a billboard has to a calling card." Evers said he didn't think Bender actually laid down money. Rather, he was just being brash.

Philadelphia had won so much so often that overconfidence was certainly possible. There was also rare turmoil in the clubhouse, as the Federal League was in the field that season and actively courting Athletics stars. The team divided along monetary lines: some players believed they deserved more money than Connie Mack was willing to pay and others remained loyal to Mack, accepting the line about limited means. Tension had built over the course of the year. But the Athletics had managed the situation throughout the six-month season and there was no reason to believe they couldn't play through a seven-game series. The A's had dispatched the Chicago Cubs in 1910, and the New York Giants in 1911 and 1913. In other words, Philadelphia had been there before and beaten more-heralded teams, outplayed more-talented lineups, outwitted more-respected managers. Boston was a lucky winner in a weak league. On the surface, this wasn't a Series. It was a coronation.

"Perhaps before the series ends," Isaminger said, "Boston fans will believe that Connie Mack has an infernal machine."

They called him Chief. Of course. Nearly every man of Native descent who stepped onto a ball field during the first half of the century was called Chief. The moniker, some have likened it to calling a black man "boy," was a tidy way for whites to place a race of people under their thumb. As scholar Jeffrey Powers-Beck said, the tag was a means to "appropriate" Bender in the "manner of the cigar-store Indian or the Wild West Show Indian." Historian John P. Rossi called the epithet "a perfect reflection of the naïveté and racism of the age." Bender resented the constant bigotry. "I do not want my name to be presented to the public as an Indian, but as a pitcher," he said almost a decade before. The newspapermen didn't listen.

There was scarcely a time when Bender was written about when his race was not prominently mentioned. Bender didn't win games. He scalped opponents. Bender wasn't a talented pitcher with an impressive repertoire. He pitched in his best Indian way. Bender wasn't a player with guile. He was Mack's wily redskin. The prejudiced descriptions were almost unyielding. Consider a lead sentence following Bender's effort in Game 4 of the 1911 World Series: "Charles Albert Bender, a child of the forest, pitched the Athletics to victory . . ." After Bender's sterling performance in the 1905 World Series, *Sporting Life* writer Charles Zuber said that "Bender, according to reports, is a typical representative of his race, being just sufficiently below the white man's standard to be coddled into doing anything that his manager might suggest, and to the proper exercise of this influence on the part of manager Connie Mack much of the Indian's success as a twirler is due. Like the Negro on the stage, who . . . will work himself to death if you jolly him, the Indian can be 'conned' into taking up any sort of burden."

Bender was often portrayed as a caricature and was the subject of myriad cartoons—many exhibits of narrow-mindedness. After he threw one of the most dominating games of the early years of the American League, Bender was depicted wielding a tomahawk and wearing a headdress as though he was a happy warrior. Other examples made him appear as a predator. During his rookie season, as the Athletics were traveling by train en route to St. Louis, Bender's wallet was apparently stolen. The wallet contained one hundred dollars, no chunk of change for a nineteen-year-old in 1903. Although he was the victim, newspaper cartoonist Charles Nelan portrayed Bender, then a somber young Ojibwe man trying to fit in, as a redskin on the warpath. With white passengers looking on in horror, as though Bender might soon take their heads, he was depicted on all fours—looking for his "wampum belt" in an incident writer Charles Dryden said "entailed no end of trouble" as "all hands were routed from sweet dreams"—with facial features so distorted he looked something less than human. Never mind that Bender likely had more education than the average person who held the very newspaper in which such coverage appeared.

The incident was indicative. The press assumed Indians were stony and oblivious. The press thought the taunts and slurs had no effect on Bender. The press was wrong.

Baseball players of the time represented an ethnic mishmash, but the game was as racist as the public that supported it. African Americans, of course, were banned. American Indians were allowed on the field, but they were expected to withstand racially charged ridicule as part of a day's work. Bench jockeying was as much a part of the era as the sacrifice bunt, and the banter was not sanitized for political correctness. Back to the reservation! Grab heap much wampum! Nig! Often when Bender pitched, baseball fans wore out their lungs with renditions of Indian battle cries and war whoops. He often looked at such displays with a still face. Sometimes, as the mockery continued, he grinned. Or, after a particularly effective inning, he would make a half-circle coming out of the box and yell, "Foreigners! Foreigners!"

But some incidents could not be finessed with wit. In 1907 the Athletics were playing in Washington, and the swarthy Bender walked into a café run by an intolerant owner. Dressed well, he quietly asked for a beverage. The proprietor, standing near, remarked softly, "Screw, dig—you ought to know better."

Bender looked surprised. "I ordered a seltzer lemonade."

"Get out now. Go quietly. You're not allowed."

Bender was confused. He repeated his order.

"If you insist on trouble, all right." The proprietor gave a signal. Two waiters rushed over and then a bartender joined them. By the time the owner was done ranting several others had crowded around. Five minutes later Bender was tossed onto Pennsylvania Avenue, his clothes messed up. He brushed himself and walked away.

Many other whites saw Indians as exotic novelties, and Bender was their noble savage. It became en vogue to nickname teams the Braves or Indians. The club Bender was about to face was one example. As Powers-Beck pointed out, teams all over the country began calling themselves Indians and recruiting American Indian players as gate attractions. In describing such teams' fortunes the press had easy, colorful verbs, and readers gobbled them by the spoonful.

Children who loved to "play Indian"—*How to Play Indian: Directions for Organizing a Tribe of Indians and Making Their Teepees in True Indian Style* was published some dozen years before—often approached Bender when he was in public and greeted him by mimicking Indian gestures. Bender didn't become angry with them, but supposedly he always signed his name on their baseballs and bats as Charles or Charley. Over time he acknowledged the nickname was indelibly linked to his baseball fame. He was called Chief so often—and so often with affection—that he allowed the name to be etched into his tombstone. Marie, his wife, too, identified herself as "Mrs. Chief Bender." But whether on the field doing his job . . . in his home reading a newspaper . . . on his way to the market . . . at nearly every point at which Charles Bender engaged the world he was viewed through a lens filtered by prejudice.

Perhaps the unrelenting duress is what caused Bender's face to often seem devoid of life. In several surviving photographs his stare advances the notion that he knows something you don't—and that something isn't good. Maybe, though, the empty looks were offered to cameras simply because of an aversion to having his picture taken. "One day an intrepid sharpshooter defied the Chief's warning," William E. Brandt wrote in a 1930 edition of the *Saturday Evening Post.* "Chief, who was warming up at the time, gave his control a little practice by bouncing a ball against the camera's eye, thus ending picture taking for the day."

Contemporaries called Bender among the brightest players in baseball. This was because of the way he approached hitters, often breaking from convention, using whatever he could think of—including a pitch he may have invented—to get them out. Bender's demeanor also had something to do with the impression others formed. Especially in the early years of his career, he was seen more often than he was heard. His mouth moved deliberately beneath his long straight nose. His words were few but they were articulate. His height—six-foot-two-inches carried erect, like a military man, but with ease, like a diplomat—commanded respect. Plus, with his stern expression and focused eyes, he was one of those guys who just looked smart.

He always seemed in control, and that was part of his game, too. Billy Evans, a prominent umpire during Bender's career and later a baseball executive, called Bender "a master workman" who "knows how to pitch." Evans said Bender "takes advantage of every weakness, and once a player shows him a weak spot he is marked for life by the crafty Indian." Bender cared more than most that his pitches found a piece of home; perhaps that was because he knew more than most how much the rest of life is outside human control.

His face's default setting was serious. But by 1914 Bender had forged a more demonstrative and playful identity. His trademark smile was never wider than when he was trying to work out of jam. Perhaps as a way to endear himself, or maybe just because he liked to make others smile, too, he would needle people. According to the *Philadelphia Press*, after throwing warmups to catcher Ira Thomas at Shibe Park during an afternoon in which he was scheduled to pitch, he went to the dressing room, put on a double-breasted suit and a fuzzy, soft felt hat, and took up a crooked-handled cane. In this outfit he boarded a car at Twenty-second Street and Lehigh Avenue on its way downtown.

He placed his crooked stick carefully between his knees, then passed one gloved hand first above and then below the other. When the car stopped before it was about to turn onto Arch Street, he moved his hands back and forth, a dozen quick, deceptive movements while maintaining a wild smile.

"Is that man crazy over there?" whispered a woman to the person in the next seat.

"Don't know," the person replied, smiling, "but it looks that way to me."

Bender's costume and his gyrations had everyone thinking he was nuts, everyone except a friend who had boarded the car with him. As Bender detrained at Twelfth and Arch he turned around and grinned, while his friend announced, "That's Chief Bender!"

The game was scheduled for two o'clock the next day, at which time Bender would step onto the small hill at the center of the diamond and simultaneously stand on a pinnacle of sorts. Baseball wasn't just popular; it was part of being an American. Though the country was not highly educated—most people lived on farms and few graduated from high school—fans enjoyed the intellectual stimulation baseball provided. Games started in the afternoon. Men in the crowd smoked cigars and cigarettes. Players wore flannel uniforms with no names or numbers, and mitts that fit snugly around their hands. During this so-called Deadball Era fans were offered their first whiff of ballpark hotdogs and first sang "Take Me Out to the Ball Game." A one-handed catch was something to see. When a ball landed in the stands, fans tossed it back. The men on the field were special, but they were not out of reach.

The first decade of Bender's career coincided with an explosion in baseball attendance. Americans ate box scores for breakfast; even those rarely, if ever, afforded the chance to see a game looked for every scrap of news about favorite teams and players. And by the start of the 1914 World Series that was an easier task than it ever had been. As social historian Patty Loew has shown, advances in telegraphy efficiently connected newspaper offices around the country. The incorporation of the Associated Press in 1900 and United Press International in 1907, coupled with increased advertising revenue and faster presses, allowed editors to expand baseball coverage. Readers consumed these bigger, better newspapers—most cities had more than one—under electric lights, a new luxury. Increasingly, baseball stars became national celebrities.

An American Indian wasn't supposed to reach this point. Bender had obliterated the stereotypes, dispelled the misplaced bromides: Indians are lazy. Indians are not competitive. It wouldn't have been difficult to find other men and women defying the warped ideas about what could be done by a man of Bender's pigmentation, though it would have taken some work to find one doing so on such a grand stage. Even American Indian people who had never seen him pitch were inspired by Bender's success. He had effectively turned over the actuarial tables.

As he threw to Schang, Bender couldn't have foreseen what would soon happen. When things are going your way you don't think the world will ever turn. But there is a limit to how long a man can carry the burden of race on his shoulders. By this time it was clear that the institutions and mores of the day, white created and controlled, had forced Charles Bender to straddle a blunt color line. He knew two different worlds but didn't sit comfortably in either one, and such dissonance exacts a toll. It's possible to see with the distance time provides, but at that moment Bender couldn't have known his life quest, seemingly in hand, would soon slip through his fingers. He may have thought he had that universal need most never have to look for—his place in the world, his home—but that was a mirage.

Mack had ordered his players to rest for several days after clinching the pennant, but the manager always allowed Bender to prepare for games as he pleased. At this point in his career—Bender had turned thirty that spring—Mack conceded his pitcher knew best how to ready himself. A few days before the Series, Mack gave him three innings in a game

9

against the New York Highlanders and Bender allowed only one hit and looked strong. He was coming off a regular season during which he had won fourteen straight games. He had more than twice as many shutouts (seven) as he had losses (three). During the previous five regular seasons he had gone a combined 91-31. Charles Albert Bender was the go-to pitcher on the best team assembled. He was at the height of his powers. On the eve of the World Series he was primed as no other pitcher at the time could have been.

Pop.

Bender had thrown to Schang for fifteen minutes by the time he delivered his final preparatory pitch. He then threw the ball to the ground. Before heading into the clubhouse to have his arm massaged by the team trainer, Bender smiled at Philadelphia Athletics captain Ira Thomas. He was ready.

"I'm right," he said.

At some point in the next twenty-four hours that self-assessment would change.

Chapter Two. The historical record does not offer clarity about what Charles Bender did in the hours that followed his World Series eve bullpen with Wally Schang in Shibe Park. In fact, there are competing stories about Bender's activities the night before the first game. The particulars, however, may be less important than their likely cause—the caustic caldron of emotion that must have percolated inside his head.

Beneath his raven-black hair and quiet, copper face, did he feel guilt about his affluence and prestige? Few American Indians of the time received such adulation. Did he feel alone? Not many could have understood his lot. Did he feel shame? He had been told repeatedly over a period of years that his ancestry was considered inferior. In fact, his education had been predicated on that very notion. Did he resent the clash of emotions he was forced to face? Did he feel hatred toward those who created a world without affording him a natural place in it? Bender's precise thoughts are unknowable. But it's no psychological leap to consider that from time to time he probably felt twinges of all of the above.

Not surprisingly, he kept his mind busy. Sometimes the liniment he reached for was found in a bottle. At some point in life he became a smoker. He also pursued a staggering number of constructive hobbies and activities. In many ways, Bender was a Renaissance man. He hunted, fished, and golfed, and at one time organized a bowling team. In 1903 he

Charles Bender, one of the best trapshooters in the United States, shot because he was fascinated by the sport and because "it gets my mind off all other matters for the time being."

had picked up billiards and by 1904 newspapers were already mentioning how good he was at the game. He was said to be an excellent swimmer. He could paint and sing. In the off-season during his first years in the big leagues he worked in a jewelry store and became an expert appraiser, often supplying fellow ballplayers with diamonds.

During his baseball career and for years after, Bender also was recognized as among the best trapshooters in the country. He shot live birds as well as clay pigeons and was so good he was paid by an ammunition company to go on product demonstration tours. It was written Bender had a standing offer for a lucrative full-time job whenever he was ready to leave baseball. He was such an adept shooter that at one point he faced the Pennsylvania state champion in a one-on-one competition for a thousand dollars. In 1917, Bender and Charles Newcomb—at the time the reigning national amateur trapshooting champion—were supposedly hired to help train potential World War I aviators in the art of shooting.

Bender began shooting as a boy, but it wasn't until he was an adult that he entered sanctioned competitions, and he often placed at or near the top of leader boards. After he left the big leagues, he led a barnstorming tour of famous ex-ballplayers, including Christy Mathewson, who traveled the country, competing against trapshooters from gun clubs in various cities. It was often written in newspapers that Bender was one of the best marksmen in the country.

He wasn't just good. The sport also gave him deep pleasure. "Perhaps you have already suspected it," Bender said in *Baseball Magazine*, "but to make sure that there be no mistake about it, let me tell you in plain English: I am a gun bug."

Bender's next hunting trip was rarely far into the future. In fact, one time two of his favorite pastimes intertwined. As the story goes, the Athletics were training in Marlin, Texas, one spring morning when Bender spotted a big black buzzard hovering over the practice field. He grabbed his rifle and brought the bird down, supposedly saying that the Athletics were not so moribund as to attract such creatures. (The next day Bender found a sheriff awaiting him at the field. It took all Connie Mack's tact and diplomacy, noted *The Sporting News* years after the fact, to save Bender from the clink.)

Bender tried to master every task in which he was engaged. As a pitcher, he strove to be the best. As a trapshooter, his approach was no different. His lean, rugged frame standing steady, his head tilted to his gun, he learned by applying his bright and insatiably curious mind. "With every visit to the traps, the fascination grows," he said. "The practice at the traps not only provides a certain amount of physical exercise, but it also trains the eye and mind." He was a natural. Like good pitchers, good shooters must have even temperament and the ability to concentrate for protracted periods. Good vision also helped, and Bender's determined brown eyes observed things others missed.

The *Carlisle Herald* published an essay Bender wrote in which he said his shooting enhanced his pitching. "Trapshooting alone will not make a pitcher," he said, "but the quick calculation of the angle of flight of the target, its elevation and the effect of wind in deflecting not only the target, but also the charge of the shot, are not without value to the moundsman. . . . The exercise you get in clay-bird shooting is not violent, yet it is not exactly the mollycoddle kind, for the handling of a shotgun throughout the 100-bird program, taking the mild pounding of a like repetition of recoil and the other activities of a half day at the traps are just about enough for the average man."

What was it about firing a gun that was so attractive? "It would be pretty hard to give the biggest reason why trapshooting appeals," he said. "There are so many reasons and almost any combination of these reasons would hold a man in the game once he had experienced the fascination of shattering a clay saucer that was getting away from him at a rate that made a bird's flight look lazy." The nature of the sport also was appealing. Standing alone, often in a quiet field, success or failure self-determined, shooting was a way to escape. As he toed the line there weren't the heckling crowds he found when he toed the slab.

"Another thing I like about trapshooting," Bender said, "is that it gets my mind off all other matters for the time being."

Bender took life one shot at time, one pitch at a time, but by the night before the 1914 World Series the triggers must have been impossible to avoid. Perhaps before this particular crucial contest the flash point was the pressure of the game itself. More likely, it was something innocuous that made him smolder in ways he rarely exposed to the outside world. Sometimes it's not the momentous events that break a man, but rather the small cuts that collect over time.

"Mr. Mack thought I was the coolest pitcher he ever had. Cool," Bender said, "on the outside, maybe, but burning up inside. I was nervous, just like anyone else—maybe twice as nervous—but I couldn't let it out. Indians can't."

When the battle is internal it's during the ordinary moments that silent arrows shoot through the mind. Maybe, soon after the sun lowered on the horizon, perhaps after eating one of Marie's meals in their Philly row home, a Pennsylvania Railroad engine whistled in the still evening air. Indeed, maybe something so frustratingly ordinary prompted Bender to contemplate how improbable it was that he ever threw a major league pitch—and the cruel conundrum the world thrust upon him before he ever did.

Woo-woo! Woo-woo! A locomotive roared toward the platform in the dark of night as Charley Bender looked on in amazement. He was seven years old and didn't understand that a train remained on its tracks. All he knew was that he hadn't before seen such a light.

"I thought the big reflector . . . was the moon driving down the track to destroy us," he said years later.

Terrified, Charley dashed. He ran from his family, broke from the reservation agent, and headed for the nearby prairie grass. He looked for scrub brush, someplace, anyplace that could serve as a hiding spot.

He likely had to run some. Charley's home at this time, the White Earth Reservation in the northwest section of Minnesota, like much of the state's topography, formed as glaciers receded, which left behind many lakes and small hills. The prairie stretched wide and was covered with short grasses dotted by oak trees, making the area favorable for grazing cattle and bison. Streams ran west through this glacial lakebed to the Red River, which emptied into Hudson Bay. The expanse of land that surrounds the Red River contained some of the richest soil on earth.

White Earth was so named for the white glacial loess found beneath the surface soil. Charley Bender was not born on the reservation, but his family moved there before his earliest memory. Various facts about his first years are sketchy. For one, Bender's birthday is fuzzy. His birth certificate, registered in 1942 by a half-sister who was eight years older than Charles, says May 3, 1883. Other sources list May 5, 1883. But based on the federal Indian census and on Bender's school records, the correct year, almost certainly, is 1884.

Many sources list Charley's birthplace as Brainerd, one of several errors often repeated in the various biographical sketches published throughout his baseball career. According to research on Bender's early years conducted by Robert Tholkes, within a year of Charley's birth the family lived in an area close to Partridge Lake, twenty miles east of Brainerd. No town existed on the site, and the township in which the area is situated was not organized until 1900. So it is most accurate to say that the most accomplished American Indian baseball player in history was born in Crow Wing County in northern Minnesota.

Bender's father, Albertus Bliss Bender (often referred to as William), was one of the early white settlers in Minnesota, a homesteader-farmer of German-American descent. Born in Maine (according to his death certificate; he may have in fact been born in Massachusetts), as a child Albertus lived with an aunt and an uncle, but apparently left at a young age because of poor treatment by these adoptive parents. Eventually, he was working in a logging camp in northern Minnesota, where, according to scholar Paulette Fairbanks Molin, he learned to speak some Ojibwe and where he met Charley's mother. Albertus tried to support his family by logging, hunting and fishing, but was somewhat of an itinerant and was not likely a stable presence in the Bender household.

Charley's mother, Mary Razor Bender, was short and had dark hair. Believed to have been a member of the Mississippi Band of the Ojibwe, her Indian name was Pay shaw de o quay. Mary was educated in Ojibwe cultural ways, but not in white schools and didn't know much English. She enjoyed kids and spent most of her adult life raising them. She gave birth to at least eleven children, perhaps as many as fourteen. Not only were Albertus and Mary a mixed-race couple, they possibly did not officially marry until an 1889 ceremony, by which time Mary already had six children. Apparently, during at least one point in their marriage they lived apart, and by the time the last of their children had been raised Albertus and Mary separated for good.

Mary was described in a biographical sketch written about her later years as a "freehearted woman, a helpful neighbor, a skilled blueberry picker, and a gifted quilt-maker and knitter." She tanned her own leather, dried pumpkins and blueberries, and enjoyed pot-roasted woodchuck, which she shared with neighbors. She made maple syrup and taught a friend, Dorothy Butler Dally, to knit. In return, Dally wrote letters to Mary's grown children on her behalf.

According to the sketch, Mary often had a box of snoose wrapped in a clean handkerchief, and if she ran out she would stand by the side of the road and stop a neighbor, Tom Gardner, or some pulp truck driver and ask for more. "Gardner learned that if he offered a full box Mary would keep it all so he carried a mostly empty box just for her." Mary acted as a midwife to neighborhood mothers and gave the prayer at the funeral of a baby who died of diphtheria. She dressed the baby and laid her out in her casket.

Charley was the fourth child born and the third son (after Frank and John). Anna followed Charley, and soon after the family moved to the White Earth Reservation, where Albertus built a log house and a small farm on Mary's 160-acre allotment. In the 1880s the Bender family settled on its allotted land in what is now Gregory Township in Mahnomen County. Eventually, the Benders' combined reservation allotments totaled twenty-three eighty-acre sections.

The Benders had to be self-sufficient, and they made do by hunting and canning. They were not unusual. During these early years of Charley's childhood White Earth was destitute. In the preceding two decades the federal government, through a series of treaties, tried to concentrate Minnesota Anishinaabeg on the White Earth Reservation. The General Allotment Act of 1887 threatened reservation land, as it mandated that tribal land be divided and allotted to individual citizens, not tribes. The government wanted American Indians to acquire private property, abandon communal life, and join in white culture and commerce.

As scholar Melissa Meyer chronicles in *The White Earth Tragedy*, White Earth Anishinaabeg may very well have adapted had they been afforded a fair playing field. But allotment policy was not given a realistic chance to succeed. By 1893 there was rampant exploitation of timberland and farmland; the Anishinaabeg lost many allotments, including some of the most valuable—at the edge of the prairie there were thick forests of red and white pine—through illegal means. "The examiners," Meyer said, "furnished correct figures to a lumber syndicate, while reporting only minimum estimates to the government."

Strip people of their resources and then require them to adapt—that's essentially what the Anishinaabeg were required to do. Instead of acknowledging the fraud, the "backwardness" of American Indians was seen as the reason they could not assimilate. Indians, went the thinking, were simply unable to adapt to "progress," and so policymakers were able to turn land over to private white interests and still sleep at night. The reality, Meyer said, was that corporate interests won out over the needs of the White Earth people. The Anishinaabeg were fleeced.

The Benders, Tholkes wrote, were among those who missed out on the reservation's valuable timberlands. Instead, their prairie land was hilly and marshy. Albertus's starter farm likely produced vegetables and included some livestock. Possibly enough was raised, at least during periods Albertus was tending to matters, to feed the family, though Mary's government subsidies almost certainly were crucial.

In other words, Charley Bender learned about adult realities earlier than a child should. Things were so meager that by the time he stood on the platform waiting for the train he had already been employed, taking a job as a farmhand for a dollar a week. He didn't have much time for games as a kid, but he did indulge in one boyhood hobby—throwing stones at gophers. He was said to have excellent aim.

"And that," he said years later, "is how I laid my foundation as a pitcher."

The bicultural aspect of Mary and Albertus's relationship is not a minor detail in Charles Bender's story. At the time, few were colorblind. According to Meyer, Anishinaabe women who married white men broke a clan line, and children without Anishinaabe fathers had no institutionalized role in the tribal hierarchy. These children were not ostracized, but as long as they remained at White Earth, the best Charley and others like him could hope for was to find work—perhaps as farmers or real estate brokers—in a place that didn't have a robust economy. In other words, at a young age he must have known his future belonged in another place.

By the time Charley became of school age, reservation families such as the Benders often sent their kids to boarding schools as a matter of course. There were four on-reservation boarding schools, and Charley went to one of them for a short time, but these schools often were overcrowded. Perhaps Charley didn't stay for that reason. Bicultural families were more inclined to regard formal education—white education—as important, so maybe that was behind Albertus and Mary's thinking. After all, some of the White Earth students who had attended and already returned from off-reservation schools commanded the best jobs. Or, given the number of Bender children, and the possibility that Albertus was estranged, Mary may not have had the money to consider anything else.

"There were so many of us at home and so little to feed us," Bender said, "that Mother didn't mind giving me up."

Whatever the reasoning, the Rev. Joseph Gilfillan, head of White Earth Episcopal mission, may have made the plans that led to Charley's departure. Gilfillan regularly sent students to the Lincoln Institution near Philadelphia, and Mary McHenry Cox, director at Lincoln, likely arranged to take Charley and other children to the school.

The train that scared Charley into hiding was there for that reason. A reservation agent searched a long time in the brush before finally finding him. Eventually, the boy took a seat on the train, along with his older brother, John, and his younger sister, Anna, and the three of them headed east. To school. To a new world.

When Mary Bender placed Charley and his siblings on the train she didn't know when she would see them again. The hope was that the sacrifice then would lead to a payoff later, that her children would receive a quality education and eventually find gainful employment that afforded them fulfilling lives. But that hope was like wishing on a star in the White Earth night.

Charley traveled east caught in a net that swept up generations of young American Indians, who shouldered efforts that, for all intents and purposes, were designed to extinguish a people's culture. The boarding school Charley would soon attend was not a typical school in any twenty-first-century manner of thinking. Instead of being nurtured with love and guided to stretch his mind, Charley would live his formative years without his parents in a strange and frosty place. The isolation was by design. He would not be allowed to visit home, even during the summer, and visits from parents were seldom, especially from parents such as the Benders, who would not have the means to travel that far. Proponents of this strategy argued that the more the students stayed away from the reservation the easier the task of "civilizing" them. Only when children had been separated from what was familiar to them—their tribes, languages, traditions, and anything else central to their identity—were schools able to instill proper values and aspirations. Or at least white definitions of those terms.

The aim was to provide students such as Charley with practical education. As Brenda J. Child explained in *Boarding School Seasons*, it was widely assumed such an approach suited the "native mentality." Rudimentary training would help "solve the nation's so-called Indian problem by training the growing number of impoverished and landless Indians for wage labor." In other words, the government looked at Charley Bender, and thousands of other boys and girls, and saw young people incapable of heady pursuits. They wouldn't be doctors, lawyers, or World Series heroes. They would be farmhands and factory workers.

Charley would soon be taught to be ashamed of his ancestry. His schools would promote the idea there was no one of value at home. If he disobeyed, if he didn't kowtow, he would be dealt with harshly. Charley would learn early to follow the line. Otherwise, his mouth might be washed with soap—or worse. Physical abuse was not uncommon. Which was but one form of neglect. Food preparation was seldom given high priority, and so cooks, who did not have to fret over regulations, served Charley and his fellow students bland, unfortified food. Living conditions often were unsanitary: drains backed up and faucets leaked; toilets were often not equipped with luxuries such as toilet paper; and students washed themselves communally. Not surprisingly, many contracted measles, influenza, tuberculosis, meningitis, or the mumps. The schools spread disease like wood spreads fire, and adequate medical attention was scarce.

Take children away from everything they know. Strip them of their identity. Work them. Hard. Starve them. And place them into an incubator of disease. An effective strategy—if the aim is to decimate a race of people.

"Ironically, policies and practices of the assimilation years dismantled the economies of self-sufficient people who had for generations successfully educated their children in cultural knowledge, values and economic tradition best suited to the woodland environment," Child said. "A new educational agenda from Washington, which mandated forced acculturation away from that source of learning, would create unprecedented sources of stress for the Ojibwe families and jar their distinctive cultural foundation."

It's not mere speculation to say Bender grew up without a home of his own—that was the very idea. As the train chugged east it would have been impossible for Charley to know what was in store for him. As he looked upon new lands there's no way his young mind could understand that the experiences that were to follow would force him to eventually contemplate matters central to his identity—matters few adult minds have to reconcile.

The Lincoln Institution opened in 1866 to house orphaned white Protestant sons of Civil War soldiers. It was used for that purpose for about sixteen years, but in the early 1880s, after the school had outlived its mission, management changed course. Within two years Lincoln received a contract from the government and was reopened as an off-reservation boarding school. By the time Charley Bender began his studies at the school, Lincoln represented the merger of two institutions—the reformed Lincoln and the Educational Home, which had housed orphaned and impoverished white and Indian children operated by the Protestant Episcopal Church.

The school was funded by the Indian Department, later the Bureau of Indian Affairs, and after the merger used the Educational Home's staff and facilities. The two facilities were separated by gender. At Lincoln, girls received instruction in sewing, cooking, and ironing, and other training for domestic work. Charley and other boys, housed at the Home, a rectangular four-story structure with a steeple, painted, glazed, farmed, and performed manual labor. At one point, Bender was assigned to work in the laundry room.

The school superintendent was Mary McHenry Cox, a headstrong woman who was not the most endearing person Charley Bender would ever meet. Cox presided over a school that promoted itself as espousing a Christian ethic, yet had been accused of cruelty to students. The school was at different times investigated by the state as well as by the Society for the Prevention of Cruelty to Children.

Compared with some other boarding schools, not much has been written about the Educational Home, and the record of Charley's time there is far from complete. Bender was one of twelve White Earth children who enrolled on July 15, 1891; by 1894 two dozen of the 103 students at the school—ages ranging from seven to twenty-two—were from Charley's home reservation. (Charley Roy, who pitched in seven games for the Philadelphia Phillies in 1906, was also supposedly in this group.) The reason for such a large White Earth group is not clear. Rev. Gilfillan's ties with the institution may have been a factor. Another, Tholkes suggested, may have been that in 1889 the White Earth Indians had been promised subsidies in exchange for land sold to white lumber interests. Portions of these subsidies could have been used for Charley and others to attend the Home.

The school roster included both the children's English and Indian names. Bender was listed as Mandowescence, a boyish nickname translated as Little Spirit Animal. As an adult, Bender always maintained that "on or off the reservation" his name was Charles; it's unlikely he ever received an adult Ojibwe name.

The school prayer offered an idea of what Charley Bender should learn and how he should live: "Be watchful over them for good; provide for their necessities; make them dutiful and submissive to authority; preserve them from sickness and accidents; and turn their youthful steps unto thy testimonies . . . so as these children grow in years, they may grow in wisdom for the good of society and the prosperity of true religion."

Charley spent half the school day in class, the other half at work. He was given basic education and began learning the fundamentals of various trades so that he too could one day be a shoemaker, tailor, baker, or blacksmith. In the evening he listened to sermons and, presumably, engaged in prayer. On Sundays he went to Sunday school, where he and fellow students studied the Christian Lord, learned psalms and parables, and received sermons about Christian virtues and un-Christian vices.

Cox believed proper recreation was found in music, which was more "enlightening and civilizing" than athletics, and each week Charley learned a hymn. Because school officials viewed the song and dance rituals of native peoples as heathen activities, students were often taught civilized, safe music. (In his later years, Bender was a regular speaker at banquets and known to sing a song or two, a talent he may have acquired at the Home.) The superintendent also noted that many schools and colleges had taken sports to excess, playing them on a daily basis. Appalling. Boys at the Home were allowed to play only on holidays.

Despite the lack of opportunity, and even though Bender was not old enough or skilled enough to play with the local club teams, it was at the Educational Home that he first started to develop affection for baseball, at one point learning to make baseballs from core to cover.

"We were great copycats, and since we didn't have baseballs, we'd make our own, getting some leather at a shoe shop, fashioning it as it should be, and using that to cover a core made of a rubber ball with some twine wrapped around it," he said. "Oh, yes, we made our own bats, too—went out in the woods and cut them."

The first American Indian pitcher Bender saw was Jake Jamison, but another member of the local team, Louis Bruce, was his hero. Bruce was older than Bender and the idol of many boys at the Home. He later had a tryout with the Philadelphia Athletics, but never stuck with a big-league club.

"At that time—I was eight—I had an idea that I wanted to be a catcher, but the idea lasted only until I got hit between the eyes with the ball," Bender said. "After that I decided to do the throwing. In those days we didn't have mitts like they have now. My catcher's glove was a dress glove with the fingertips cut off.

"It is surprising that more of those Indian boys did not grow up to become major league players. They really had the ability."

How did the Educational Home influence Charles Bender's life? Bender always smoothed over his early educational experiences, if he talked about them at all. Years later he didn't express fond memories of his first off-reservation boarding school, but he didn't complain, either.

"I worked in the laundry to help pay my way," he said. "I learned to play ball watching the older boys."

But, undoubtedly, something important had happened at the Home. Charley had come from a family that, while bicultural, was enmeshed in the American Indian struggle. He had begun an education that intended to point him in the opposite direction, and his next school setting would send him further down that road.

It's logical to assume that at the Home Bender first began to think about how he should live his life. The result would not square with traditional Indian ways. He had turned a corner—and there was no going back.

Which didn't mean he wouldn't try to go back. The Educational Home's intention was to make it unlikely that Charley and the others would return to the traditional life. In a portion of the 1894 annual report, the secretary to the school's board of managers noted that "of the returned pupils (then numbering 180) not more than four have gone back to the old life." Children typically remained at the school at least until the age of twelve. Charley Bender was at the Educational Home for five years when he was returned to White Earth for reasons that are not clear. When the time came, Cox handed him a lunch and some money and sent him in the direction of Minnesota. Bender later recalled that another Indian boy from the state, Seymour Fairbanks, traveled on the same train.

By this time, Bender had started to develop his love of shooting. While at the Home, he spent nine months of the year in school and much of the other three roaming fields with a fishing pole or gun in his hands while living with Pennsylvania farmers. He and his friends spent time at a nearby river shooting bullfrogs. Before he left Philadelphia he bought a gun for a few dollars at a hardware store.

The ride back to White Earth lasted days. Bender said that when the train made stops he and Fairbanks hopped out and did some shooting. Charley had fun until the train stopped at the Detroit Lakes depot and he didn't have enough money for the stagecoach fare. Fairbanks paid Bender's way as far as the reservation, but once he stepped out he had a long walk from there. The thought was that he was heading home. It's true he headed for his parents' house. But the trip home was an altogether different journey—the kind that lasts a lifetime.

Though he couldn't have understood any of that then, as he walked down the road, his gun resting on his shoulder.

Chapter Three. Charley Bender had just turned twelve when he was released from the Educational Home and sent back to White Earth. He had been out of touch with his family for five formative years, and he returned to a situation that had not improved and possibly regressed after land sales began in 1889. Drunkenness on the reservation was still widespread, and the economy was no stronger. Charley found that his family had continued to grow, that he was one of nine children who scrambled to find food at the dinner table. Put it together and, as Robert Tholkes noted, the house in which Bender lived in June of 1896 must have been a stark contrast to his living conditions of the previous five years, which included time with the families of Pennsylvania farmers. The flooring of the Benders' log cabin would have been made of wood or earth. Temperatures in the one or two rooms would seldom have been comfortable. Elbow room would have been scarce. Maybe there was a lean-to kitchen attached. Undoubtedly, the place was dirty as such homes were difficult to keep clean. As Charley Bender looked around, it couldn't have taken him long to realize he wanted something more, and he would soon go looking for that something.

Right after he received a not-subtle push out the door.

Charley had been back to White Earth for no more than a few months during a busy summer on the family land. Like his siblings, he had been pushed to exhaustion one afternoon while working for his father, who was struggling to provide for a large family and not easily confused with a gentle human being. According to a story Bender told as an adult, Albertus sent Charley and his brother Frank down to the lake for fresh water. He handed Charley a pail, but his son did not exhibit enthusiasm for the chore.

"Get along," his father said, according to Bender's recollection.

When Charley didn't move quickly his father used non-verbal motivation—by firmly planting his shoe in Charley's backside. The bucket flew out of Charley's hand as the boy fell on his face.

Frank walked over, picked up the pail, brushed Charley off, and put the bucket back in his brother's hand. The two sprinted toward the lake. As they neared the water, Frank turned to Charley.

"Are you going to stand for that kick in the pants from Father?"

Charley hesitated. Frank continued. "I wouldn't," he said. "Let's run away."

At that point, Charley could have sought his mother. He could have fought back, which likely would have only served to get himself beaten. Children react in any number of ways to abuse. Instead of being a sad story, Charley's father's kick in the rear served as a defining moment. People would push him down. But he wouldn't stay there.

Frank, five years older, took charge. The two started for Frank's godfather's home, miles away. The man wasn't happy to see the boys and made them sleep in his barn. But their father didn't come after them, and when Frank and Charley didn't feel wanted at the godfather's house they went to another White Earth farm and got jobs in the fields. While there, a teacher from the Carlisle Indian School, the renowned boarding school in Carlisle, Pennsylvania, came through looking for boys. Frank and Charley volunteered.

American Indian boarding school histories are littered with stories of runaways. Missing their parents, their homes, their culture, and stuck in a distant place that didn't exhibit sympathy for one drop of their ocean of loss, it was not unusual for boys and girls to flee. Charley Bender was a different kind of kid, and life handed him a different set of circumstances. He didn't run away *from* school. He ran away *to* school. Something inside propelled him to fashion a different life than the one he saw at his parents' house.

Charley and Frank took a bold step, but not a radical move. The climate on the reservation was such that children were encouraged to leave. There were few jobs at White Earth, and many believed prosperity could be found only in nearby towns, the Twin Cities or out east. Once young people had entered the dominant culture, as Charley had done when he attended the Educational Home, they began lives that did not easily translate to reservation life. But many returned to the reservation because that's what their parents wanted them to do. Booting his butt was perhaps the single best thing Charley's father ever did for him. In effect, his father was giving him permission—or at least the motivation—to leave.

"In the first place, if it had not been for a good, solid kick in the pants—I mean a real, honest-to-goodness kick in the pants from my dad—I would probably have been just another Indian around Brainerd," Bender said in his later years. "Except for this bit of fatherly 'advice' I would not have played big-league ball."

Bender's father would never hold a prominent place in his life. But there were other men, and Charley was about to meet the one whose life might well have had the greatest influence on his own.

Richard Henry Pratt was a tall man with a long nose whose convictions had the elasticity of cement. An idealist, he used controversial means to advance his views about American Indians. His ego was large, his work was just, and his beliefs were seldom wrong. Supporters—and a sympathetic biographer—called him the Red Man's Moses. Detractors viewed him as something of a mad scientist. As anthropologist Genevieve Bell's research has shown, Pratt was one of those people who generated a strong reaction: you loved him or you loathed him.

Born in Rushford, New York, in 1840, to devout Methodist parents, at one point when Pratt was a boy, after the family had moved to Logansport, Indiana, his father left the family to join the mass hunt for gold in California. And one day the elder Pratt looked into his pan and found some. But during his return trip to Indiana he was robbed and murdered. The family suddenly had to cope not only with profound loss but also with sudden financial hardship. Left with little alternative, before he was a teenager Richard Pratt withdrew from school and went to work. He held various jobs in common trades, possibly supporting his mother and brothers into adulthood.

When the Civil War began, Pratt's life shifted in another radically different direction. He enlisted in the Ninth Indiana Infantry and over time earned various ranks. He married Anna Laura Mason in 1864, and the couple, which would have four children, returned to Logansport in 1865. Pratt found employment in the hardware business, but the work didn't suit his nature. Instead, about two years later he reenlisted in the army. The lack of a childhood must have affected Pratt, and undoubtedly the bootstraps-up success he had despite his struggles instilled a type of self-assuredness only experience can provide. He would never have to strain to make an argument in favor of individual autonomy.

Pratt was stationed at Fort Gibson, Indian Territory, where he was put in charge of a unit of American Indian scouts, including Cherokee, Choctaw, Osage, and Tonkawa. These scouts were educated, English-speaking men who commanded his respect. And that was a foreign concept.

"Their intelligence, civilization, and common sense was a revelation," Pratt wrote years later, "because I had concluded that as an Army officer I was there to deal with atrocious aborigines."

About eight years later he took charge of Indian prisoners incarcerated at an old Spanish fort, Castillo de San Marco, later known as Fort Marion, in St. Augustine, Florida, and there Pratt decided to experiment. Rather than keep the prisoners continuously confined, he designed a program under which, eventually, they would be able to assimilate into the dominant culture. The prisoners were introduced to the basics of white education in a makeshift classroom, and after some time they worked at part-time jobs in the area. He emphasized vocational-type training—the prisoners split their days between the "school" and an outing program that included manual labor—and established what would become a prototype of the standard boarding school curriculum.

"We can never make the Indians real, useful American citizens by any systems of education and treatment which enforce tribal cohesion and deny citizenship associations," Pratt later wrote.

Pratt was open-minded enough to allow experience to form his attitudes. Eventually, Bell said, he came to believe education was the "great leveler," that through education and equal access, anyone could find a place in America. His worldview contained an insightful notion: American Indians had insufficient education, not flawed DNA.

In 1878 the prisoners' sentence was up, but Pratt didn't want to abandon the experiment, so he brought a group of American Indians to Hampton Normal and Agricultural School in Virginia. Hampton had been established in 1868, and the student body was African American. While at Hampton, Pratt acquired a passion—some say an obsession—for the acculturation of American Indians. However, though he had further developed his ideas about Indian education from Hampton president Samuel Chapman Armstrong, Pratt ultimately wasn't satisfied with the arrangement and he decided to start his own school.

Using his political connections, he was handed the keys to an old cavalry barracks at Carlisle, in western Pennsylvania. Called the Carlisle Indian Industrial School when it opened in 1879, Pratt later referred to his academy as the U.S. Indian School. Carlisle was the earliest off-reservation boarding school and the template for subsequent schools; twenty-five years after Pratt founded the school the government operated some two dozen nonreservation schools based on the Carlisle model.

In establishing Carlisle, Pratt had created a unique institution: a non-reservation school designed to assimilate American Indians into the white world. This novel concept would profoundly affect the lives of scores of human beings. And Charles Albert Bender would become one of the academy's most prominent products.

During his Major League career Charles Bender had a quintessential athletic build—a long, lithe body, thin but hearty. But when twelve-year-old Charley Bender enrolled at the Carlisle Indian School on September 5, 1896, he was a sliver. He passed through the school's red brick gates for the first time standing five-three and a half and weighing 101 pounds.

Charley joined the other new arrivals at check-in, the first step in a process to snuff out traditional culture. Among other things, this meant haircuts—traumatic to children from some tribes—and a ban on the use of tribal languages. For many American Indian children these first moments created obvious aggravation and anxiety. Native peoples had a long history of violent encounters with the military, and here they were essentially being forced to join the team. However, the process could not have been as startling to Charley Bender. Whereas many of his fellow classmates picked out white-sounding names that appeared on a blackboard they could not read, Charley was already Charley. If he received a haircut, it was not his first short shave. And as a member of a bicultural family, English was likely his first language. Certainly, by this time, it was the one he knew best.

Like the others, Charley's clothes were confiscated and he was given a dark blue uniform with red braided shoulders, a felt cap, clean underwear, long johns, and a hat and shoes. He was also handed a set of towels and a trunk in which to store personal items in a room he shared with boys, possibly of differing ages and tribes, he didn't know.

Charley was stripped and washed and underwent examinations by Carlisle medical staff. Many students had their pictures taken for the original before-and-after ad campaign. That is, Pratt had students photographed upon arrival and again after Carlisle had exuded its civilizing influence. The images were powerful marketing tools, but Charley was not necessarily in this group. By the time he stepped onto campus, Carlisle had become more selective, and Charley's transformation was already under way. With some fifty months of schooling under his belt, he entered Carlisle at the fourth-grade level, which was relatively advanced for the time.

He may have been uncomfortable in new surroundings, as any twelve-year-old half a country from his parents' house would be, but he knew about life at boarding school. Unlike some of the others, he chose to be there. This was his chance to find a place in the world.

Carlisle must have immediately seemed like a continuation of the philosophy advanced at the Educational Home—with fewer nuances. Pratt was not unsure of himself. His aim was a reflection of Manifest Destiny: as soon as native peoples were shown the merits of white American culture, white American culture would show that the road to happiness was paved by Christian scripture and capitalistic enterprise. Pratt was shouldering the white man's burden.

"They will never become civilized if they don't let their own way go down and let the white people's way come up," Pratt said. "Indian ways will never be good anymore."

By the time Charley Bender took his first glance at the institution the school was no longer on trial; it was established as the crown jewel of off-reservation boarding schools and a key cog in the wheel of assimilation. Pratt's directives would be crystal clear and not open to discussion. Charley would know as soon as he stepped on campus that he was there to acquire a new identity, one that would allow him to find a niche in the dominant culture and leave behind the kind of life he had been born into. This way of thinking would be taught to Bender without subtlety. Pratt had a famous and succinct phrasing for his philosophy: "Kill the Indian, save the man."

Often, Pratt's school did just that. "Before Carlisle, the public saw Indians as unredeemable savages, a threat to the nation, and an obstruction to progress," Bell said. "After Carlisle, all that changed. Carlisle came to symbolize the possibilities of assimilation; it presented a different sort of Indian education, and it gave the American public a new kind of Indian."

Charley Bender would be one of those, and after he arrived at Carlisle, he settled in. Soon he would learn what Richard Henry Pratt expected of him.

"Carlisle's mission is to kill *this* Indian, as we build up the better man," Pratt said. "We give the rising Indian something nobler and higher to think about and do, and he comes out a young man with the ambitions and aspirations of his more favored white brother. We do not like to keep alive the stories of his past, hence deal more with his present and his future."

In other words, Charley would be instructed to adopt the "ambitions and aspirations" of his "white brother" and reject a fundamental part of his identity. No easy fix for a young man. But he would try. His chances at a prosperous future depended on it, something he would learn soon after the first time he stepped into his dormitory room.

Chapter Four. When Charles Bender stepped out of his house on October 9, 1914, his future had arrived and he appeared to have fulfilled Richard Henry Pratt's promise for him. By the 1914 World Series, he was a success according to Pratt's benchmarks—he had a lovely wife, steady income, and a middle-class row home far away from the reservation. He also had more professional acclaim than Pratt could ever have imagined, as Bender was about to start Game 1 of the World Series, a plum role in the biggest show running, for the fourth time in five years. It's not known what time Bender left his house or how he traveled to that first game. But he and other Philadelphia Athletics lived within walking distance of Shibe Park, and it was not unusual for him to hoof it to work. Whether he strolled or rolled, as he moved down the road he began to pass pumped up fans on their way to the ballpark. What did he think about along the way? That's not a matter of record, but at some point he may have given at least passing glance to, of all things, a game of golf that took place three months before.

Bender's interest in the game was likely sparked during trips south for spring training. During those years Connie Mack didn't believe in pushing his players too hard in March and especially didn't want his veterans worn out before baseball's long slog. So he encouraged them to play golf. Lots of golf. Whatever the precise timeline, soon after Bender picked up a club he took to the sport in the same manner he took to baseball and trapshooting. That is, he learned everything he could and made rapid improvement.

Bender wintered in Atlanta during the 1910–1911 off-season, and every day, weather permitting, he played at least eighteen, sometimes thirty-six, holes at East Lake Golf Club. The March 1911 issue of *American Golfer* noted that Bender was still learning. "If the theory, that the more you hit at the ball the more exercise you get, is correct, then we predict that the Chief is now in tip-top condition and that another good season is coming to him." The same article said Bender was "a most enthusiastic golfer" and that "while he cannot yet be considered as good a golfer as he is a slabman, still, by constant practice, he has learned to make some wonderful shots from the rough and he has become a genius in pitching his ball from a sand trap (by hand)." By that spring the *Philadelphia North American* noted one morning that Bender "astonished" with his long drives.

As Jeff Purtell's research has shown, Bender honed his game on a championship course. East Lake was not a municipal par 3; it was described in *Golf: USGA Bulletin* that year as the "hardest course in the South." At East Lake, Bender may have crossed paths with Stewart Maiden, the Carnoustie-born golf pro whose swing years later was mimicked by Bobby Jones, the only player to complete golf's grand slam in a single season.

At the end of the 1911 baseball season Bender had improved his golf game, and after the World Series he and teammate Jack Coombs played a round at the Atlantic City Country Club with reigning U.S. Open champion John McDermott. McDermott, who had won the 1911 Open at the Chicago Golf Club, was the first U.S.-born player to win and the youngest in history. At some point in the twentieth century it became common to see Major Leaguers paired with professional golfers at celebrity pro-ams. But, as Purtell pointd out, this case may have been the first of star ballplayers seen playing with a world-class golfer.

The theory at the time was that golf enhanced a baseball player's ability. In 1913, *American Golfer* said that, "Big Chief Bender, the premier pitcher of all the Indian hurlers in captivity . . . will keep in shape by playing golf all winter." Bender often spent winter in the Atlanta area playing golf, and "it is the good condition that golf keeps him in during the winter which enables him to now pitch such good ball during the baseball season."

American Golfer wrote more than once of Bender's exploits. At one point he apparently appeared in a club championship final, possibly at the Aronimink Golf Club in Newtown Square, Pennsylvania. The magazine wrote he was a "very fine player" known to be a "bear with an iron." While discussing area players the magazine later wrote that another player had said that if one "really wished to see a long shot they should go out to Aronimink when Chief Bender . . . was performing with his cleek (1-iron)." Bender apparently was either a regular guest or a member of Aronimink. Which is no bit of trivia. Unlike baseball at the time, the golf establishment frequently did not allow non-Caucasians to play. (Ironically, in 1993 Aronimink withdrew its plans to host the PGA Championship because it couldn't extend membership to an African American before the start of the tournament.)

"Naturally, I like all outdoor games," Bender said, "but golf and trapshooting are my favorites, after baseball. I am not going to choose between these two, for I expect to continue to play golf, and I don't want to create hard feelings."

Christy Mathewson said Bender could "play golf well enough to make the best amateurs in the country hustle." In fact, in late September 1914 Bender and Jack Coombs had challenged Matty and Heinie Zimmerman to a golf match after the season—a duel, *Sporting Life* said, that would be between the two best golfers in the American and National leagues respectively. Bender's progress was so sharp that at one point *American Golfer* said he was "far and away the best golfer in the American League." (After Bender left the AL, the magazine noted his departure allowed Ty Cobb to realize his ambition of carrying that unofficial title.)

The reason Charles Bender may have been thinking about golf as he made his way to Game 1 of the 1914 World Series was because in early July of that year he had an unforgettable conversation at Englewood Golf Club in New Jersey while sitting with his friend, Grantland Rice. Rice would become the dean of American sportswriters—he authored the famous "Four Horsemen" description of the Notre Dame backfield and once wrote that "For when the One Great Scorer comes to mark against your name, He writes, not that you won or lost, but how you played the game"—and he was frequently Bender's golf partner. Bender later recalled that on this particular afternoon, he and Rice were joined by a man named Oswald Kirksey. Kirksey was a broker, but he was not interested in talking about stocks.

"Chief," Kirksey said, "I'll lay you $75 that the Boston Braves will win the pennant and the World's Series."

Rice and Bender must have stared back at Kirksey as though he had proposed that the three of them hop into his invisible rocket and head for the outer reaches of the universe. It was a preposterous bet. Boston began the 1914 season about as poorly as a team can, winning 3 of its first 19 games. Such a start didn't seem all that unusual, either. The Braves had finished last four years in a row, from 1909 to 1912, losing 100-plus games—there were only 154 on the schedule—under five managers and three owners. In 1913, the Braves more closely resembled a competitive team, but they still won only 69 games. This was hardly a juggernaut in a funk.

On June 5, 1914, the Braves lost to the Cincinnati Reds, which dropped their record to 12-28. They then began a climb toward respectability, but the ascent was interrupted by a five-game losing streak. When the games of July 15 were complete, the Braves were back in last place at 33-43. Meanwhile, John McGraw's New York Giants appeared to be cruising to a fourth straight pennant.

Boston had a nondescript lineup and three decent pitchers, none of whom had reliable track records. Kirksey was advancing a ridiculous notion, one that seemed more suited to come from a man who slept in a padded room than a respectable businessman at an upscale establishment.

"You're crazy," Bender said. "Why, the Braves are in last place."

They wouldn't, however, remain there. Perhaps as Bender approached the ballpark before the first game he saw reminders of that startling fact in the form of Boston's Royal Rooters, a group of ardent fans that came to Philadelphia by train for the first game. Led by former mayor John Fitzgerald—"Honey Fitz," the grandfather of John F. Kennedy—the rooters paraded in the street before the game.

The more known picture unfolded as Bender approached Twenty-first and Lehigh—at the time one of the most famous street corners in sports.

The first ballpark built of concrete and steel, Shibe Park covered a city block. The first base foul line ran parallel to Lehigh Avenue, right field to center field ran parallel to Twentieth Street, center field to left field was parallel to Somerset Street, and the third-base foul line parallel to Twenty-first. Ballparks before this time, built with wood, were not durable and often susceptible to fires. Shibe Park began a boom in ballpark construction; during a six-year period that began with Shibe Park's opening, thirteen of sixteen teams built new parks that lasted into the 1950s. The park ushered in an era and instantly became a baseball mecca.

For the first eight years after the Ben Shibe–owned Athletics entered the new American League in 1901, the team had played at modest Columbia Park. After it quickly became apparent that Columbia was not a serviceable Major League ballpark—between 1901 and 1908 Major League Baseball attendance doubled—Shibe decided he wanted something more than a larger facsimile of the standard baseball facility. Columbia Park's replacement, his thinking went, would be a grand structure, one that would remain impressive long after he had watched his last baseball game.

As a young man Shibe had driven a streetcar, and as a round, stern Philadelphia-born entrepreneur his interest in sports led him to manufacture and sell baseball and cricket equipment. (As partner in A. J. Reach & Company, he changed the game when he brought the cork-centered ball to the majors.) Initially, Shibe owned half the team; his son, John, was in charge of business matters while Connie Mack owned 25 percent and was in charge of on-field decisions. In 1913, Mack acquired the remaining 25 percent and became an equal partner, and by then they had built a baseball palace that was a monument to their legacy. Shibe Park became home to the Athletics on April 12, 1909, and existed in Philadelphia longer than the team it was built to house.

"We certainly were mighty proud of our park," Mack said years later. "We wondered whether we could ever fill those long rows of seats."

By 1914 that was no longer an open question.

The park was located in north Philly, well outside the center of downtown, in a somewhat rural section of town known as Swampoodle. The area was mostly vacant lots and woods and, in fact, during construction Shibe feared he may have gone too far north. At Twenty-second and

Lehigh was Philadelphia's Hospital for Contagious Diseases, also referred to as "the smallpox hospital." It was a curious decision to place a ballpark near a place people wouldn't pass without covering their mouths, but the land was cheap and Shibe knew the city would close the hospital not long after the park opened.

As Bruce Kuklick's research has shown, the location had other merits. The park was accessible using the city's transportation system, perhaps the best in the world at the time. Downtown businessmen had an easy trip to Lehigh using the Broad Street Trolley. From there, a short walk or another short trolley ride took them the rest of the way. The field was also close to railroad lines, which brought visiting teams to town and sent the Athletics to American League cities. Other trains carried commuters to the park from nearby suburbs. Some fans, or "kranks" as they were sometimes called, lived a trolley ride or walk away.

Those various means of transportation brought crowds to the streets outside the ballpark in the hours before the first pitch of the 1914 World Series. As Bender made his way, fans walked toward Shibe Park and passed storefronts that had been built into the side of the ballpark. Others strolled past the right-field bleachers, a furniture warehouse, and a public service department. A garage was located under the left-field stands, used mostly by players and team officials, and at one point it housed Shibe's son's collection of racing boats.

Fans looking up saw the ballpark's most prominent feature: an ornate façade in what was considered French Renaissance style, with thick white columns, arched windows, red-brown brick, and a domed tower that housed management, including Mack's plush office, which contained thick oak desks and leather-upholstered chairs. Walking into the park at the main entrance fans passed under casts of Mack and Shibe, and nearby, SHIBE PARK was etched into a corner arch. If the sights (vendors hawking A's pennants), the sounds (Get yer peanuts he-ah!), and smells (fresh popcorn) of anticipated baseball didn't tell them otherwise, fans might have thought they were about to enter an enormous church, pastors Mack and Shibe presiding.

Most fans at the 1914 World Series entered the park at the base of the tower and into a large semicircular lobby, which provided a ritzy entrance. After passing through one of the sixteen turnstiles fans walked through a pavilion and up a stairway to the main grandstand. Wide concourses stretched past the players' dressing rooms to the different sections of bleachers. This walk slowly revealed the sea of grass. It would take some work to exaggerate the difference between Shibe Park and the ballparks built before it. When it opened, that glimpse of the field was the first time fans experienced the sight of a modern ballpark. In a way, Shibe Park was baseball's original green cathedral. The park, *Sporting Life* said, "has inaugurated a new era in baseball." The *Evening Telegraph* immediately proclaimed Shibe Park "an enduring monument to the national past-time: baseball—the greatest game ever intended for all classes of people."

In 1914 general admission tickets were 25 cents, grandstand 75 cents, reserved $1. For the World Series, the teams were allowed to charge $5 for box seats, with other reserved seats at $3 and $2, and general admission bleachers for $1. In the hours before the game, the early-arriving fans took their seats in covered single-deck bleachers that extended down both foul lines and in uncovered bleachers in left field that stretched from the corner to the center-field flagpole. About fifty-five hundred steel folding chairs were found in the lower stands; about forty-five hundred in the upper. Some fans settled on the rows of wooden bleachers down the lines in right and left. The most inexpensive bleachers held thirteen thousand. This abundance of cheap seats, it has been said, was because Ben Shibe believed that those who "live by the sweat of their brow should have as good a chance of seeing the game as the man who never had to roll up his sleeves to earn a dollar."

But Shibe Park had its choice seats, too, and they were the ones located in the shade during the team's games. Those privileged with reserved tickets also found their seats well before game time. William K. Vanderbilt was among them. A prominent member of one of America's wealthiest families, Vanderbilt arrived on his yacht with a party of friends. George M. Cohan, Connie Mack's friend, had box seats for himself and twenty-one guests. After they finished with their parade, the Royal Rooters huddled in one section. A number of boxers and promoters were also on hand, and as they sat there some jokingly took bets on who would win a fistfight between Connie Mack and Boston manager George Stallings. Earlier in the week Stallings had threatened Mack physically when he didn't allow the Braves to practice in Shibe Park at the preferred time. It was like putting up your dukes to the school principal. "The trouble with Stallings is that the novelty of winning a pennant has disturbed his balance," Mack said. The story made for juicy copy and intensified interest in the Series.

Whether behind home plate or well beyond field level, fans saw a park with dimensions that stretched 378 feet from home plate to the left-field line, 509 feet to center, and 340 feet down the right field line. But those measurements were not the same as the actual field of play because of the practice, common in the day, of allowing overflow crowds onto the field, cutting off the playing area in front of the blank twelve-foot wall that stretched around the Shibe Park outfield. These fans were not innocent bystanders; some acted as a tenth man, surging forward to aid a home player's batted ball or back-peddling when the home outfielder needed more turf to make a play. Among the park's other attributes, there was an abnormally long distance from home to the backstop, ninety feet at one point. Shibe Park also may have had the tallest pitcher's mound in the game. Some sources have said it was an excessive twenty inches tall. If that figure was ever correct it almost certainly wasn't consistently so. In any event, the ample foul territory, the spacious outfields and tall mound meant that Charles Bender worked in a park that was friendly to men in his profession.

By the time the Athletics and Braves would take the field for batting practice, not only would the ballpark be booked, the row homes across the street from the outfield fence would hardly be visible. Fans used all available seating; looking out from home plate gave the appearance as though people were painted on walls.

Homeowners on Twentieth Street charged three bucks a head for the bleachers they had erected on their roofs. Four men and a boy clung to a telegraph pole overlooking the park on Somerset. Ten men occupied a precarious position throughout the game on top of a huge signboard that stood above an adjacent brick building. Rooftops were so heavily burdened fans in the park wondered when, not if, they would collapse.

Sensing the chance to earn extra cash, peanuts, and soda vendors extended their business to the roof bleachers. It was hard work climbing up stairs and ladders, and they quickly began to sweat. For a modern comparison, imagine the houses across from Wrigley Field if the Chicago Cubs returned to the World Series and the fire marshal had no regard for the fire code. The scene was similar: every inch in which a fanny could be placed a fanny was placed. All around, small boys strained to get a glimpse. One of them, Louis Ross, who had been turned away at the ticket window for the bleacher seats, broke his right wrist falling from a wall he had scaled using a fan's shoulders as a stepladder. Another youngster slipped from a telegraph pole and fell in the path of a huckster's wagon at Twenty-first and Somerset. Scraped and bruised, he was taken to a hospital.

Below the wall of humanity, crowds lingered, hoping to find a spot for themselves from which they could get a view of the field. Thousands would not. But they had to try. This was no ordinary baseball game. It was the World Series. The champion Athletics were heavy favorites.

And baseball's greatest clutch pitcher would soon arrive.

By the time Charles Bender entered the park, Oswald Kirksey's words must have seemed ominous. Not long after Bender, Rice, and Kirksey's lunch, on July 16 the Boston Braves started a six-game winning streak and moved up four spots in the standings, to fourth place. The Giants also won six straight, so the Braves remained in the background. But after losing a couple, Boston won 18 of 20 games and climbed its way into a tie with floundering New York. The Braves went from last to first in thirty-seven days.

For the next two weeks the two teams were neck-and-neck, but on September 8 the Braves grabbed the lead for good by winning the rubber game of a three-game series with the Giants in Boston. In the remaining four weeks, New York played average ball while the Braves lost only six more games.

Amazingly, after going 61-16 in exactly half of the 154-game season, the Braves didn't just win the pennant—they won it by 10½ games. It was such a historic run the word "Miracle" has been permanently affixed to the team's nickname.

Few minds of the time allowed for the possibility that a team sitting in last place at midseason could run away with a league, and Bender's and Rice's were not among those that did.

"I'll still take your money," Kirksey had said, smiling.

"I'll take the bet," Bender said, "but I'll not take your money, because you're nuts."

But when Bender walked under the grandstands behind third base toward the A's clubhouse door before Game 1 he no longer could have wondered whether Kirksey deserved a straightjacket.

Chapter Five. Oswald Kirskey's prediction was all that more credible because as Charles Bender walked through the A's clubhouse door into the carpeted room with heavy oak chairs and a pinochle table, something wasn't right. He found his steel locker but he did not feel ready to pitch. He felt ill.

This was not especially rare, as Bender had been sick often throughout his career. On several occasions headlines prominently dashed across Philadelphia sports sections read, "Bender ill and may be out for the rest of the year" or some variation of that news. Among other ailments, he suffered from muscular rheumatism, a condition that typically includes muscle pain, fatigue, and sleep disturbances. The historical record does not clarify Bender's specific symptoms—possibly a combination of burning and other painful sensations throughout his body—but Bender often struggled with arm fatigue.

During Bender's career prominent ballplayers received endorsement deals from companies that made candy bars, chewing tobacco, soft drinks, automobiles, and baseball equipment. Bender received an endorsement deal, too. His profile was seen in newspaper advertisements for a rheumatic remedy. Late in his career, Bender endorsed Mike Martin's Liniment, a rheumatic balm. "You just rub it in good or have somebody rub you good with Mike Martin's Liniment and right away all the soreness, aches and pains vanish away," Bender was quoted in an advertisement. "If you old fellows want to feel frisky, supple and fine, get a bottle of Mike Martin's Liniment and use it like Mike Martin tells you on the label."

Ailments caused Bender to miss swaths of several seasons, including some of his finest. It was not uncommon for him to start or finish a season receiving just a handful of starts over the course of several months. Details of his bouts with illness were not often elaborated on in the press. But according to the *Washington Post*, he was taken ill a short time after he joined the Athletics. Connie Mack wanted a doctor to look at him, but Bender waved him off.

"I'm sick but I don't need medicine," he said.

Mack left Bender's room for a few minutes and when he returned he looked around and found that Bender had vanished. Mack asked around. No one knew where Bender went. He didn't show all night. For two days and nights a search was made, but Bender couldn't be found. Mack, the *Post* said, was "almost frantic." At this point, he was about to alert the authorities when he peeked in Bender's room one more time. Bender was there, under a blanket.

"Where have you been?" Mack said.

"Sick."

"But you haven't been in your room at the hotel. Were you at a hospital?"

"No," Bender said, "I went away where it was quiet and where I could be alone. When an Indian is sick he doesn't want any noise around and he doesn't want medicine or doctors. He just wants to let nature take its course in curing him."

Given the nature of pitching and the lack of a stable rotation, it's impossible to know precisely how many games Bender missed because of poor health. Sometimes he had a tired arm, and at some point he endured the self-induced illness that comes from spending too much time in a pub. But he also suffered an inordinate number of health problems—separate from the hazards of his profession or his personal habits—that may have been the effects of rheumatism or similar ailments.

For Bender, 1904 was an especially difficult season. He was sick so often he started thirteen fewer games and pitched 66⅓ fewer innings that season than he had as a rookie the year before. Over that winter Bender recovered after having his appendix removed by Dr. Americus R. Allen in Carlisle. (Almost ten years later the appendix made headlines of its own when it was reportedly stolen. The removed appendix had been enshrined in Allen's office, and the *Carlisle Evening Sentinel* said, "The relic was second only in local interest to the old town pump, which was rooted out of existence for purely sanitary reasons." The pump was unsanitary; the removed appendix was not. A Cumberland County detective vying for election vowed that he would "restore the talisman." Carlisle's Board of Trade, the City Council, officials of the Carlisle Indian School, and directors of a local museum considered offering a reward for the return of the appendix in "any presentable condition.")

The operation was a success. As the team gathered to travel to spring training in March of 1905 Bender had a conversation with Philadelphia owner Ben Shibe. "I feel entirely well," he said. "I don't think I was ever better in my life. If I do not make good this year I will not be able to lay it to poor condition. I feel able to go in and pitch a full nine-inning game right off the reel. Since my operation I have mended rapidly and do not anticipate any such trouble as I had last year." That would not be the case. During the 1905 season Bender was sick for several weeks, but he was reluctant to leave the team in the midst of a pennant chase as the Athletics were leading a three-team race with Cleveland and Chicago. However, Bender's health became debilitating during a series in St. Louis, and he took a train to Detroit to rest at his wife's parents' house, where a doctor declared he was suffering from Brights disease, an inflammation of the kidneys, and likely was done for the season.

As often as he was sick, though, he bounced back. Three days after the announcement that he might be pitching from a hospital bed the rest of 1905, the *North American* noted, Bender cabled from Detroit to say that reports of his demise were exaggerated. Medical treatment and rest had Bender feeling better, and he would be pitching again in a week or two. Two days later, when the rest of the team arrived in Detroit to take on the Tigers, he was in uniform, practicing, and it didn't take long for Connie Mack to make use of him. Weldon Henley had started for the Athletics and the Tigers knocked him out of the box early. Bender came in relief and pitched eight innings, allowing one run. He threw seven straight scoreless frames at one point and had six strikeouts.

Illness was so much a part of his career that after the 1908 season

Bender considered leaving the A's. He had a rough season and he had begun to develop his trapshooting talent, earning a nice sum at certain events, both in prize money and by betting on himself. In February of 1909 he was quoted in newspapers as saying that he had decided to quit baseball.

"I have positively decided not to pitch any more," Bender said. "In the future I will devote my time to the match-shooting business, in which I have been a success. I have found that it greatly improves my health."

Mack didn't seem distraught: "I have done no business with Bender this winter. . . . He did very little work for us last year and it is immaterial to me whether he pitches for the Athletics this season."

Of course, Bender did pitch for the Athletics that season, and for the next five as well. But it was not the last time health problems would force him to remain in the dugout, as he would miss parts of several other seasons. He would always wait for the bug to leave his system, and usually it would, but never for good.

On the cool, moist Friday afternoon in which the Athletics intended to notch the first win on their way to a fourth World Series victory, one day after Bender had felt so right pitching to Wally Schang, he supposedly told manager Connie Mack he had an upset stomach and trouble with his gall bladder. He didn't know whether he could pitch. This was startling. Sure, Bender had been sick often in the past, but it was not like him to beg out of a start as crucial as Game 1 of the 1914 World Series.

Mack smiled. "Oh, you can beat those fellows," he said. "Just warm up and go to the box."

Before the game both Bender and Eddie Plank warmed up. Wearing high collars, team sweaters, and short-billed hats, they threw on the side. It was not uncommon for more than one pitcher to throw before a big game. Sometimes a manager wanted to see which man had better stuff. More often he wanted to keep his counterpart on his toes. In this case, Mack might also have been listening to Bender's claims. Whatever the manager's strategy, Plank actually threw longer and with more purpose than did Bender.

On the field there were about thirty photographers taking pictures of players. Billy Gibson and his troubadours sang ragtime songs to enter-

"When I warmed up I didn't have anything," Charles Bender said years later. "I told [Connie Mack] again, but he brushed my complaints aside."

tain the crowd. And starting lineups were announced through a megaphone. Bender pitched to Wally Schang for about five minutes and did not exert himself much. Something seemed amiss.

"When I warmed up I didn't have anything," Bender said years later. "I told [Mack] again, but he brushed my complaints aside."

The scope and nature of Bender's health is an aspect of his life about which concrete answers are not possible. But it's an area that's hard not to consider. Modern studies suggest that early parental support affects both mental and physical health in adulthood. A child reared without adequate adult support is more likely to become depressed, struggle with self-control, and lack self-esteem. Chronic physical conditions, including those that intensify with age, are also more common. Bender grew up with almost no parental support from age seven on, and it's not known how much he received before that time. Throughout adulthood he suffered from various maladies, including those considered chronic. The mind, after all, is part of the body. One who goes without a basic need is likely to fall sick, mentally or physically, from time to time.

In the moments before the game—as Bender walked from the pitcher's box over to the third-base line and, halfway between the plate and the bag, dragged his foot through the chalk line, leaving a mark more than twelve inches long—there was no clear explanation. Maybe Bender's periodic and prolonged bouts with various illnesses were nothing more than the case of a man with a predilection for poor health. Maybe his immune system had withered during years in government boarding schools. Or perhaps his outward symptoms were tied to the inner struggle that presented itself years earlier, not long after he crossed another kind of white line.

Chapter Six. In the distance, a bugle called. Six o'clock reveille. Fifteen minutes later, Charley Bender, then a petite Carlisle cadet, marched in formation to a dining hall segregated by age and gender. He, like all students, was well aware that his school was run by a military man. The students were organized into companies and addressed like soldiers. Not long after arriving, Charley had been told to listen for the bells, and by his early teens knew the bells told him when he was supposed to march. To class. To work. To breakfast.

Inside the dining hall there was a long white table bearing the Carlisle logo, written in red. Female students, wearing white aprons over uniform Victorian-style dresses and navy capes, served Charley and his fellow students. Like all meals, breakfast was prepared by student workers—with supervision, of course. The experiences of Carlisle students varied in some respects, but one thing was consistent: none of them were afforded one moment of privacy. As Charley sat at the table eating, a set of eyes watched to make sure he used proper manners. If, say, he wanted more milk for his oatmeal, he had to ask. About the only thing Charley and his classmates could do without permission was to lift spoon to mouth.

After breakfast, Charley marched across the three hundred–acre campus on his way to class. The landscape included elm and cherry trees, and several buildings that were whitewashed and arranged around a large rectangle of sidewalk. Initially there were only sixteen buildings on the site, but by Bender's time there were more than thirty. Student buildings had classrooms, study halls, and common areas. Among other landmarks, faculty and staff lived in houses behind some of the student dormitories, which were separated by gender (mingling between sexes was closely monitored), a guardhouse, athletics fields, a warehouse, a gymnasium, and workshops. A bandstand sat in the center of the rectangle, not far from Richard Henry Pratt's house, and the area that surrounded it was used for drilling. Around campus there were remnants of the old fort, including a cemetery that included soldiers who had fought in the Civil War. Near this cemetery ran a creek and a second waterway. During winter months, both students and members of the Carlisle community skated on the frozen water.

Given the nature of Carlisle's controversial objective, Pratt knew the school would be examined from every angle. Image wasn't everything, but in his mind it meant a lot. Pratt made sure his school was kept in excellent shape at all times, inside and out, including the grounds Charley passed through on his walk to class. No disorder. Nothing out of place. Paths were cleared or covered in the winter to keep walkers away from the elements. In the summer, flower assortments decorated the lawn. The campus was aesthetically pleasing and constantly improving. Another distinguishing feature was the tall picket fence that surrounded the campus. The fence was erected by Pratt to prevent the unwanted or announced from entering the school grounds—and to keep his students from leaving them.

Perhaps there were times when Charley Bender walked to that fence and wondered what life beyond had in store for him. Once considered by whites a threat and a barrier to progress, by the time Bender was a boy the American Indian population had dwindled; he belonged to a clear minority. So at birth he and other American Indians of the time were destined to make a choice: either live the traditional life or head in the opposite direction.

Carlisle was clear about which was the preferred option, and that was part of the lesson plan as Charley began his daily academic classes. The school claimed to offer numerous subjects, including geography, chemistry, physics, history, and biology, but though Charley Bender was ready to learn, he was not challenged as much in the classroom as he was at every other turn. The reason for this disparity was not hard to discern: many believed American Indians were not capable of high intellect. One person who held such a view happened to carry the title of federal superintendent of Indian schools.

Estelle Reel was the first woman nominated to a position that required U.S. Senate ratification when President McKinley appointed her superintendent of Indian schools in 1898, a post she held for a dozen years. In 1901, Reel presented the "Uniform Course of Study," which educators were supposed to follow. As Bill Crawford pointed out, she believed Indians did not have the same intellect as whites and designed educational programs for an "inferior" race. Reel didn't think it was her job to create curious thinkers. Instead, she wished to develop dependable laborers. She also believed Charley Bender and his fellow American Indians needed physical conditioning to "counteract the influences of unfortunate heredity."

Said Reel: "Allowing for exceptional cases, the Indian child is of lower physical organization than the white child of corresponding age. His forearms are smaller and his fingers and hands less flexible; the very structure of his bones and muscles will not permit so wide a variety of manual movements as are customary among Caucasian children, and his very instincts and modes of thought are adjusted to this imperfect manual development. In like manner his face seems stolid because it is without free expression, and at the same time his mind remains measurably stolid because of the very absence of mechanism for its own expression."

Conversely, Pratt didn't believe Indians were inferior. But he was of the mind that the Indian way of life was no longer worth pursuing. So he promoted the liberal arts, including arts classes, though even these were not always of the freethinking variety. Students, for example, were not allowed to create Native crafts, but were encouraged instead to create Western artwork. (After his retirement as a baseball player Bender made and sold paintings of landscapes. His interest and dexterity in art may have begun at Carlisle.)

Pratt's goal was to impart so-called American values, and he taught Charley Bender about the almighty importance of consumption. Though not

51

afforded private moments, Pratt encouraged his students to have private possessions. "Education consists in creating wants," he said, "and imparting the ability to supply them."

Charley's teachers had been handpicked by Pratt. Everyone who worked at the school was required to be loyal and morally in sync. They were not to use alcohol or tobacco and they were expected to be churchgoers. (Not long after he founded Carlisle, Pratt supposedly gave up tobacco himself so he couldn't be called a hypocrite.) Many of Bender's teachers were Quakers from the Philadelphia area, most of them women, all of them white. They didn't necessarily have prior experience working with American Indians, but they bought into Pratt's program. It's not entirely clear what precise curriculum was followed in Charley's classrooms. The three Rs were taught along with science and art. Verbal ability was perhaps the most emphasized academic pursuit. Especially in the early years of the school, as Genevieve Bell noted, Carlisle relied on the "object" method of instruction—that is, the teacher would show a ruler, ball, or carrot, and the students would speak, write, and read the term almost in unison—made famous by Helen Keller. By the time Charley was a student there, the school required some basic literacy, and so possibly the lessons were increasingly rigorous. Yet the point wasn't necessarily to wrap minds around the most complex ideas of the day. Pratt believed in "acculturation under duress." He wanted Charley and his fellow students to progress academically, but he also intended to send them through a wringer of mental conversion. Rules drilled into students went beyond raising one's hand in class; they were about knowing, for example, that it was wrong to eat in the bedroom.

As Bender sat in class listening to his teachers' lessons, the average age of his fellow students was about fifteen. Some were as young as seven, others in their early twenties. Altogether there were about a thousand students from seventy-five different tribes. According to Bell's research, many students were at a fourth-grade level or below, and, given his prior education, Charley must have found much of the instruction mundane. But the same desire to better himself, the instinctive drive that had pushed him to run away from home to school, may have been what allowed him to take as much from Carlisle as it was able to give. As a Major League baseball player his brain would be given as much credit for his success as his right arm, and undoubtedly he cultivated his intelligence at Carlisle.

Much of what Charley Bender said and thought during his time there is not a matter of record. At some point, though, there must have been some serious introspection. Surviving academic records do not paint a full picture, but anecdotes suggest a bright young man who was eager to learn. He was not demonstrative, but his command of language, whether verbal or written in his neat penmanship, was so sharp that the few words he spoke carried inordinate weight. He may have been seldom challenged in class but he often voluntarily went to the library to check out books to expand his intellectual horizon.

Bender was counted among Carlisle's most astute students by at least one credible source. T. S. Eliot said of Marianne Moore that her work formed "part of the small body of durable poetry written in our time." The would-be literary giant—she would win the Pulitzer Prize and the National Book Award—was a schoolgirl living in Carlisle during Bender's time there. Moore later taught at the Carlisle Indian School for five years. Decades later, memories of Bender remained planted in her mind. "He was older than we were; but we all knew who he was," she said. "He was impassive, inexpressive, very tall and handsome."

In 1960 Moore was staring at Bender's picture when a writer from *Sports Illustrated* asked her to talk about Carlisle athletes of the day. "There was something Grecian about them." Bender, she said, was hard to miss. "Charles Bender! Charles was intellectually impressive."

Perhaps Charley took to books more than other athletes at the school because he didn't feel like he was one of them. Early in his teens, he was not an athletic star, and a future job in pro sports must have seemed as likely as a post in the governor's cabinet. Carlisle had various newspapers, and while students operated them, Richard Henry Pratt, or his proxy, was supposedly the de facto editor. As Linda Witmer pointed out in *The Indian Industrial School*, Pratt often used these newspapers as tools of propaganda—not only to mold the minds of his students, but also to project an image of the school that extended beyond the campus. The papers' content consisted of school news, editorials, and, of course, Pratt's moral flavor. Charley Bender, the kind of pupil Pratt was eager to hold as an example, later contributed an essay to one of these papers, the *Red Man and Helper* (Pratt wasn't subtle), published on February 14, 1902, as part of "Orations of the Graduates." Bender's words, articulately delivered, provide a revealing snapshot of his mindset by this point in his life and the education he had received. He was on the verge of adulthood and near the end of his formal education when he wrote:

> What holds the Indians back? is a question of great importance, and ought to be the subject of serious thought for every true American citizen as well as every Indian youth.
>
> When the whites first landed in America they found a fierce nomadic race of people, divided into many tribes having different languages. By hunting, fishing and meager tilling of the soil, they gained a livelihood; when this failed in one place they moved to another but were continually at war with each other without much cause. These were the people, who, since the landing of the whites, have been for various reasons more or less unfriendly towards civilization.
>
> To each one of a tribe is given land enough from which to obtain a living and have something to lay aside, but partly because they know very little outside of the reservation and chiefly because government support takes away the necessity of labor, they do not learn to use their land to any great advantage. As they cannot sell, many rent their lands to white men for small sums. Thus, instead of being a help, their lands have become a barrier to their progress.
>
> Along with this system of giving money, lands and rations, the good government established schools for the Indian youth, hope thus to elevate the whole race. At these schools they are clothed and fed and life is made very easy. Many go there for the purpose of having a good time rather than of getting an education. But is this a characteristic of the Indian only? In great colleges may not the same things be observed among young men whose parents have made sacrifices that their children may have advantages which they did not enjoy?
>
> This great republic of ours seems to have been built up in a wonderfully short time, but centuries of previous training came to its people through their forefathers, and necessity developed their

latent abilities. The Indian knew small necessity, hence the seemingly slight progress that has been made.

For some years he has lived in comparative peace with the ever-encroaching settlers. It has not been many years since the white man on the frontier had to carry a rifle wherever he went through fear of the then merciless Indians. Is it so today? Any person can go among the Indians and be as secure there as among his own people. Why? Because they understand more clearly what the good people of this country are trying to do for them. Among the Indians scattered over this broad land very few can be found today who cannot speak or understand some English. This shows that while their progress is very slow, they are capable of pushing onward.

Still, while this chain, composed of links of annuity money, rations, and free land holds them back, their strides toward civilization will not lengthen to any great extent; but break this chain that binds them; throw them on their own resources; let them stand as individuals; place them on the same basis as their white brethren, governed by the same law, enjoying the same liberties and in time they will prove their capacity for civilization and become loyal, patriotic citizens of these United States.

Clearly, Charley Bender had presented Richard Henry Pratt's philosophy. He stuck to the company line, either because he had forgotten the traditional American Indian life of the kind his mother was living in White Earth or, most likely, because he was willing to offer the expected views. Did he have a choice? Carlisle was a place where American Indians learned to self-censor and where incorrect behavior was sometimes met with a lashing. Besides, Charley knew he wanted a place in the dominant culture, so he was willing to tell the dominant culture that he accepted, or at least conceded, its version of the narrative.

After class Charley spent his afternoons working. He practiced the vocational trades that the Estelle Reels of the world believed represented the height of his usefulness. No doubt Charley spent hours at one or more of a variety of jobs: he likely learned how to build things, make shoes, bake, paint, and develop other marketable skills. Throughout Carlisle's existence students also were encouraged to learn how to manage an agricultural business, and Charley probably became skilled at growing things. Late in life he was an expert gardener; it may have been at Carlisle that he learned how to raise fruits and vegetables. Vocational and agricultural training were followed by extracurricular activities, such as brass band, drama, and athletics. Pratt also took Charley and fellow students on field trips, usually those of an educational variety. Evenings were also filled with activity—study, sermons, singing, and Pratt's brand of lectures.

"You have to stick to it if you want to make something of yourself," he once wrote in a student newspaper and almost certainly repeated to Charley during evening lectures. "My son, observe the postage stamp. Its usefulness depends upon its ability to stick to one thing 'til it gets there."

At these gatherings Charley and other students sang the school song, which went, in part:

> Out of the darkness behind us
> Into the light before;
> Out from the long separation,
> In by the open door;
> Here in an equal freedom
> Victor and Vanquished meet;
> Here we have learned the lesson—
> Duty may crown defeat.
>
> This was the land of our fathers,
> Centuries long to rove—
> Must we be alien and homeless,
> Here on the soil we love?
> No! for the future beckons
> Out of our old alarms
> Out of the tribal fetters,
> Into the nation's arms!

Civilized people went to church, so on Sundays Charley and his fellow students were required to attend. Christian traditions were also followed during the week.

Pratt made a to-do of holidays. Christmas morning was celebrated with ringing bells, carols, and small gifts. Decorated trees were erected around campus, and in the middle of the day, after church, Charley and his fellow students were treated to a large, festive meal. Students commemorated other holidays as well, including Founders Day and Thanksgiving, which included a traditional supper.

Fall, winter, or spring, whether it was an ordinary Monday or Easter Sunday, Charley Bender's days were filled with class, work, homilies, and military-style drills. They were the kind of days that went by in a flash. The constant drilling was physically draining and often sucked the life out of kids. But coming from a house in northern Minnesota that may also have been chaotic and lacking in personal attention, Charley seemed to thrive in the structure Carlisle provided. Throughout his life, he would follow a busy, regimented lifestyle. He was so active—hunting, fishing, painting, swimming, bowling, and so on—that one wonders where he found the energy. But, then, when you're searching for home it's hard to stay still.

That Bender never became one to sit on a rocking chair and count the ice cubes in his lemonade is perhaps a manifestation of his years at Carlisle. There weren't many leisurely moments at Richard Henry Pratt's school.

"We keep them moving," Pratt said, "and they have no time for homesickness—none for mischief—none for regret."

Charley's room had been inspected. In the distance, "Taps" played. At nine o'clock he placed his head on a pillow.

In nearly four decades of operation the Carlisle Indian School produced just 761 graduates. Charley Bender was one of them. Despite the lack of formal scholarship, he received a quality education for the times. In 1902, few Americans attended school beyond elementary grades. When he left Carlisle, Charley was at about a tenth-grade level, which was more education than most people his age—white, American Indian, or otherwise—received. Perhaps more salient was the training Carlisle gave him. Bender was pushed to learn *something*, even if it wasn't Shakespeare or calculus, nearly every daylight hour.

His years there instilled in him a sense of curiosity and a will to learn.

Charley Bender was a member of the Carlisle Indian Industrial School's Class of 1902. Cumberland County Historical Society, Carlisle PA.

He did not go on to earn advanced degrees, but he seldom met a person who was his intellectual superior. It was common during his playing career for Bender to be referred to as a scholar and a gentleman and, undoubtedly, the mannerisms that prompted such descriptions were formed during his days as a Carlisle cadet.

Bender also learned how to persevere, how to put his head down and move forward in the face of trouble. Of the estimated 10,600 students who attended Carlisle from 1879 to 1918, between 1,000 and 1,500 of them ran away, and perhaps as many as 1,000 died after acquiring any number of communicable diseases. Complete attendance and mortality records are not available, but so many students passed away while attending Carlisle that the school had its own cemetery. Whether one was a straight-A or an educational underachiever, just surviving Carlisle was a feat. And an experience not soon forgotten.

"Carlisle was created by the American government for a specific purpose, in a specific place and operated for less than forty years," Carlisle historian Genevieve Bell said. "It was inhabited by individuals who gave it substance and meaning, who called it home or hello or someplace in between. And whether they chose to be there or not, Carlisle became their community and an extraordinarily important reference point which they would evoke throughout their lives."

By the time he left Carlisle not only had Bender developed personal traits that would serve him throughout his life, he had answered the question: he would enter the dominant white culture with both feet. In reality, it was less a conscious choice than it was a decision by default. He had long been cut off from his family. Even if he wished to reconnect, there were few desirable prospects at White Earth, and given that his father was white he had no natural role in the tribe. He had been in government boarding schools for more than a decade, and after these mind-shaping experiences he decided to chart what he thought was the best possible course.

Which didn't mean the path ahead would be clear.

About six years later, Carlisle sent its best-known graduate a questionnaire. At that point, he was in his mid-twenties, had several Major League seasons under his belt, and reason to believe his best years were to come. He knew that Carlisle had often held him up as a success story, and he wouldn't have had to say much to convince others that he was happy. But some of his answers were telling.

"Wouldn't advise any of the students at Carlisle to become a professional baseball player," he wrote. "It's a hard road to travel. Many temptations along the wayside."

For all the obvious reasons, American Indians, even those with rare baseball talents, struggled to fit into white society. Though Bender apparently had done nearly everything Richard Henry Pratt had asked, he was still faced with no easy quandary: he wanted to join the dominant culture but often that dominant culture saw in him nothing beyond what prejudiced eyes can see. As a Major League Baseball player, he faced unique challenges in that he had to manage the bigoted tension in full view of a public that watched his every move and in front of writers who described his every action.

Bender's essay published in the Carlisle student newspaper was not the last time he told the world what it wanted to hear. As a baseball player he downplayed his racial identity while he was forced to become accustomed to the characterizations in the press. He was regularly described as the "grim Chippewa chief," the "artful aborigine" and "the Carlisled son of the forest." Writers simply didn't feel obligated to treat him as an equal, even after he proved he was a supreme player in the sport they covered for a living.

Amazingly, though, Bender denied the prejudice that had punched him in the nose. In 1910, he told the *Chicago Daily News*, "I adopted [baseball] because I played baseball better than I could do anything, because the life and the game appealed to me and because there was so little of racial prejudice in the game. . . . There has been scarcely a trace of sentiment against me on account of my birth. I have been treated the same as other men."

A lie. Bender made the comments during the prime of his career, while metaphorically standing in a nearly all-white crowd among people who would read his words. Making waves would have only made his life all that more uncomfortable.

Try as he might, Bender could scarcely avoid all forms of confrontation. Clark Griffith, a player who used slurs during bench jockeying, supposedly baited him viciously on May 4, 1906, and Bender was said to lose his cool, threatening the New York player-manager physically. Bender was thrown out of the game, according to the *New York Times*, for arguing with umpires. The *Philadelphia Inquirer* said Bender's ouster came immediately after a pickoff attempt at third base that was not called his way; he had thrown his glove forcefully to the ground in protest. His feelings, the *Inquirer* said, were "probably slightly ruffled by the taunts of the New York coaches." It's been written the incident was racially motivated, and perhaps it was, but interestingly the Highlanders' pitcher that day was none other than Louis Leroy, himself an American Indian.

But such incidents were rare, and when they did occur Bender often used them as motivation to prove people wrong. The day after he was thrown out of the game, Bender, the *Inquirer* said, "begged" Mack to give him the ball again so he could "erase the blot" of the previous day. He not only beat the Highlanders with his arm, he also hit a home run.

He learned to bite his lip and not to protest, which is an easier approach when your actions speak eloquently enough. Besides, when you're trying to find a home among a group of people it's not wise to make those people feel uncomfortable. In the same Carlisle questionnaire, he had been asked if he was married. He didn't just answer the question, he volunteered that she was "German-American." He wanted people to know his wife was white. In fact, most everyone in his adult life would be white, including many of his friends. Bender was said to work behind the scenes to advance the cause of American Indians. As a young Philadelphia Athletic one spring he returned to Carlisle to help coach the baseball team. According to Jeffrey Powers-Beck, Bender may have encouraged Mack to donate uniforms to Indian school baseball teams and used his connections to help American Indian players land tryouts. But instead of becoming a vocal champion, not a viable option anyway, he would take his every athletic and intellectual ability to fashion himself into an understated star in the white world. This was not a surprising decision—it's what Richard Henry Pratt had prepared him to do.

And soon after leaving Carlisle, doors would open to him that would not be open to other American Indians. Because by the time Bender departed he had made a shockingly rapid advancement as a baseball player—helped in no small way by a legendary coach of another sport.

Chapter Seven. Glenn Scobey Warner is the godfather of modern football. Perhaps that's why his well-known nickname, Pop, still is so appropriate. Warner coached for more than four decades and has been credited with numerous innovations—screen plays, single- and double-wing formations, and numbering players' jerseys among them. Some say the seamy lineage of the win-at-all-costs side of the college game can be traced back to him as well. Once Richard Henry Pratt embraced the idea that athletics were a means to instill character he didn't settle for intramural exercises on the lawn. He wanted the best teams in the country. He wanted to win. So Pratt recruited Warner from Cornell University—first to coach the football team and eventually to take over the athletic department. Warner arrived at Carlisle in 1899 and stayed for four years before he returned to Cornell. Eventually, he was lured back to Carlisle. It was during his second stint in western Pennsylvania that he coached Jim Thorpe, one of the greatest athletes of the twentieth century, and developed a national football powerhouse. It was during his initial tenure that Warner crossed paths with a skinny batting practice pitcher. His role is no minor footnote in the life of Charles Bender.

While at Carlisle, Bender played football, basketball, track, and baseball. But he was not an exceptional athlete, at least not right away. In his mid-teens Bender was weak and slow, he said, as rheumatism had whittled his five-foot-eleven frame to about 140 pounds. Bender didn't love football—"I didn't care for the game," he said, "I hated to practice; all the Indian boys hated to practice"—but he hung with the team as a reserve end. Playing with the practice squad he took regular beatings—he recalled later that he even broke a couple of ribs—but that was far better than the alternative.

At Carlisle, even a decade before the glory years of the Thorpe-led teams, being on the football team had its privileges. As Bill Crawford noted, Warner made sure his athletes had clean socks, medical attention, tutoring, and good housing. He was there when they needed a loan or when they found trouble. It's not simply a modern phenomenon; athletes have long received preferential treatment. Warner was coach, manager and, in some cases, agent to his athletes. Putting up with tough practices was a cheap admission fee.

Varsity athletes lived in their own dorm and were afforded the chance to leave campus, sometimes out of uniform, and some of the most well known were able to depart without a chaperon. Townies knew about the athletes and spent time with some of them. There were incidents in which Carlisle athletes were found in bars where locals had knowingly served them booze. It's not known when Charles Bender took his first sip, but it's certainly likely he knew about alcohol's appeal before he entered adulthood.

Perhaps the greatest perk was being allowed to stay away from the "government gravy," as Bender and others referred to the standard student body fare. Football players had their own dining hall and a chef who served them more generous portions. At Pop Warner's training table the football team was served steaks, roast beef, and potpie. Bender ate well and over time he started to fill out.

Given his early talents, it's unknown why Bender was so attracted to sports. Maybe he just had fun and his life needed some of that. Maybe, too, he embraced sports because the school encouraged participation. Carlisle viewed athletics as another way to assimilate students. Pratt initially preferred military drills, marching and band performance, but he became a booster of his school's athletics programs because he came to see that sports emphasized the kind of discipline he espoused. If his athletes became successful, too, there was another upside: teams traveling around the country, with Carlisle's initials stitched into their red and gold uniforms, would advertise his school in ways that could not be conveyed in newspapers or pamphlets.

Pratt also saw that athletics would instill American pastimes. "If it was in my power to bring every Indian into the game of football," he said, "I would do it, and feel that I was giving them an act of the greatest Christian kindness, and elevating them from the hell of their home life and reservation degradation into paradise."

Often, though, athletics at Carlisle offered one avenue in which American Indians could face white peers on a level playing field, and so when Carlisle athletes took the field they played more for Native pride than school pride. "[The Carlisle Athletes] did not manifest a school spirit, but they did have a racial spirit," Warner said. "They seemed to recognize that it was upon the athletic field that the Indians had an even chance . . . and they wanted to show that, given an even chance, they were the equal of their paleface brothers."

Though Carlisle is most often recognized for the success of its football teams, as Jeffrey Powers-Beck said in his examination of the Carlisle baseball program, during Bender's years at the school there was a great deal of enthusiasm for baseball among players and fans. The *Red Man and Helper* in 1901 asked, "Couldn't all school be base ball?" Carlisle fielded multiple teams, and other students often played informal games on school grounds. Baseball was Bender's game, but even so he aspired only to his class team. His first noteworthy achievement, at least as he saw things, was when he made the class team—not the varsity—at Carlisle.

Bender's height made him a natural first baseman, and he often played right field. Only after he pitched in spot relief for the team's regular pitcher was it apparent he could be something more. He began making himself useful by throwing indoor batting practice, and he impressed Warner enough that the coach added him to the team as a reserve. As a sixteen-year-old he was a part-time player, but he had developed to the point where he was allowed to play in the field. In the spring of the equivalent of Bender's junior year members of the team approached Warner and told the coach that the skinny kid deserved a shot.

"Bender was with the smaller youngsters, so he wasn't on our club," Warner said. "But he used to come out and throw batting practice. I hadn't seen him until some of the boys told me I'd better give that boy

Bender a suit because he could sure pitch. I did and he pitched for me for two years."

Despite the talent base and the storied success of the Carlisle football team, surprisingly, the Carlisle baseball team was never especially strong, as it usually lost more than it won. Warner turned Carlisle into an incubator of great athletes, but despite all the time he spent training American Indians, as Powers-Beck said, he may have adopted a "racial theory" about athletics. "Track and field seem more adapted to the Indians than baseball," Warner said.

Warner may have believed his athletes were not as well suited to baseball. In any event, over time he deemphasized the game in favor of football and track and field. Warner, in a 1909 issue of *The Indian Craftsman: A Magazine Not Only About Indians But Mainly By Indians*, wrote: "The success of the Indians has been due to the rough, hardy outdoor life that the players have been inured to since the time they were born. In addition to this purely physical explanation, there is a psychological one; the Indians know that people regard them as an inferior race, unable to compete successfully in any line of endeavor with the white men, and as a result they are imbued with a fighting spirit, when pitted against their white brethren, that carries them a long way toward victory."

Warner was a bright man, but he may have not understood baseball well enough to make assumptions about any person's ability to play the game. Or, more likely, he simply preferred football and track. A multisport coach such as Warner could be successful, even if he wasn't a master strategist, if he could motivate and condition gifted athletes, and such tools translate best in sports where sheer athletic ability is a large part of the equation. Baseball, though, is a skill game, one where speed, strength, and adrenaline take even a great athlete only so far. It doesn't matter if you can steal bases if you haven't learned how to reach first.

At some point Warner clearly became involved in the baseball world, using his connections to help some of his players sign contracts (deals he often personally profited from). But many Carlisle boys hadn't played the game before arriving at the school. They needed ground balls. They needed fungoes. They needed to be taught fundamentals. Sure, they were fast and could throw the ball hard, but they required the level of instruction football players received and, as Powers-Beck said, that may not have always happened. Therefore, they struggled in the field. Often the team's best pitchers, such as Bender, threw good games but didn't receive defensive support. Too few balls in play were turned into outs.

However, Bender didn't believe his coaching at Carlisle hampered his progress. In fact, he said the opposite. Whatever the reasons—maybe because Bender had a rare level of cognitive ability—Warner had an affinity for Bender and wanted to help him succeed. Perhaps Bender's lack of ability on the gridiron, too, prompted Warner to focus less on making him a serviceable end and more on helping Bender throw the ball past hitters.

Warner said Bender was the "brightest boy in school and had the record of drawing more books from the school library than any other student and he was about the youngest of any of Carlisle's graduates. He was also a crack shot with a rifle. He'd go out in the nearby hills for a couple of hours and come back with enough grouse over his shoulder to feed the whole school."

Bender later said Warner was "a natural leader" with "untiring patience." He called Warner a good teacher in all sports, including baseball, and credited the coach for helping him develop. As a Major League pitcher Bender was exceptionally good at changing speeds and he said that came from Warner. "Warner . . . taught me virtually all I knew about pitching," Bender said, meaning up to that time. "He had read a lot and talked with different baseball coaches and showed me how to work a change of pace. The value of a slowball was explained and taught to me by Pop."

Warner also instilled in Bender the confidence that he could do more than win games for Carlisle. When you come from a small town in northern Minnesota without much firsthand knowledge of the game it's no minor thing to have someone hint that you have the ability to turn into the kind of player who will be written about a half-century after your death.

"When I was a slim kid at Carlisle," Bender said, "not ever knowing what my future would be, Warner made me feel that I could become a good pitcher."

Talent without opportunity doesn't amount to much, and Warner also is credited with giving Bender his chance. He allowed the right-hander to pitch to batters on the first team and, Bender said, "I thought I was the biggest guy in school."

The record of Bender's performance in Carlisle games is incomplete. For example, the Carlisle baseball team supposedly played a game against Cornell in the 1901 Pan-American Exposition in Buffalo. But surviving reports do not reveal whether Bender participated (a rudimentary box score indicates he at least did not pitch). What's more, any numbers or pitching lines gleaned from line scores hardly provide meaningful context.

In his first game for Carlisle, Bender relieved Arthur Pratt, one of the team's top pitchers, and was, according to the *Carlisle Daily Herald,* "a little wild at first but kept the visitors' hits well scattered." Soon he became a regular starter, quickly proving himself as a pitcher who could make batters miss; in one game he struck out eight men. "Young Bender pitched the entire game in a very credible manner," the *Daily Herald* wrote. Bender, years later, recalled the game with pride. "There has never been a thrill to match that first victory for Carlisle," he said.

Some athletes blossom in their late teens. As youngsters they were unremarkable, but after puberty they have a growth spurt and suddenly possess a more useful set of physical tools. This seems to have been the case with Charley. He filled out, he shot up, and he used his clever mind to pick things up quickly. In 1901, the year before he graduated, Bender was, according to Powers-Beck's analysis, the third-best pitcher on the staff behind Pratt and Louis Leroy. By the start of the following season, he was the team's captain—and its ace.

Which didn't mean he won many games. As Carlisle's *Evening Sentinel* reported about a game he pitched against Dickinson College, "Bender seemed to have the better of the argument, but his support was not sufficient to enable him to win the day. He seemed to strike out the Dickinson men at will and allowed but two scattered hits."

Warner said Bender battled Eddie Plank of Gettysburg College several times during his Carlisle career, and, supposedly, the two dueled for fifteen innings one afternoon. But such stories may have been revisionist history. It's likely Bender and Plank crossed paths before they played together with the Philadelphia Athletics, but Plank was already in the American League by 1901. They couldn't have faced each other often, if at all.

Whatever the competition, Bender developed quickly. Unlike many young pitchers with live arms, he learned the value of changing speeds effectively, without changing his delivery. He also learned to handle matters beyond questions of how to pitch to good hitters.

In 1901, while Bender and Carlisle faced Harrisburg, Dick Nallin, later a Major League umpire, was sent down to coach first base while Bender was pitching. "To heckle me," Bender said, "Nallin shouted, 'Come on and pitch, you big Injun!' I didn't like the way he said 'Injun' or something. Anyway, I dropped my glove and started for Dick. The first baseman kept us apart."

That may have been Bender's first conflict on a baseball field. It would not be his last. In fact, that summer, he clashed with another man. This particular story the newspapers would write about decades after Charles Bender had thrown his last Major League pitch.

Charley Bender was up to his ears in hay when his boss called out. Man named Swanson wanted a word. It was the summer of 1901, and Bender was working on a farm in Williams Mills in Bucks County, Pennsylvania, as part of the Carlisle outing program.

The outing program was the centerpiece of Richard Henry Pratt's assimilation indoctrination. Students were employed outside of school for part of each day—working for farmers, companies, and tradesmen in outlying counties some distance from Carlisle—or during the summer. Usually, Carlisle helped students secure placement in desirable locations. The rationale: introduce a new paradigm. Pratt placed Carlisle students in white homes as a way to end prejudice—both ways. Students were sent to middle-class families, usually in the northeast, for work-study experience "to learn English and the customs of civilized life."

By being immersed in white culture, American Indians would learn about family life while learning how to make a living. Above all else, outings were intended to increase awareness about how to live in proper— white—society. American Indians of the time, Pratt believed, were suffering from a lack of participation, and participation was more than half the battle. As Linda Witmer noted, Pratt believed the outing program was the "Supreme Americanizer." His mantra: "There is only one way; to civilize the Indian allow him into civilization. To keep him civilized, let him stay."

Outings lasted anywhere from weeks to years. Before participating, students were required to pledge that they would obey their employers and continue the good-life fundamentals taught at Carlisle (attend church, take baths, abstain from tobacco, liquor, gambling). Before he sent Charley and other charges on outings Pratt told them that they were not merely employees but rather they were supposed to become members of the family.

"No feature of the work is more productive of good results than that of temporary homes for our students in good families," Pratt said. "The order and system so necessary in an institution retards rather than develops self-reliance and forethought. . . . The thousand petty emergencies of every-day family life they do not have to meet. Placed in families where they have individual responsibilities, they receive training that no school can give."

The outing program's aims may not have been altogether pure. As Bill Crawford pointed out, outings were an economical way to train students. Supposedly, half of earnings were placed in a trust—an account students received upon leaving the school—and at least part of the other half of the stipend was apparently paid to Carlisle. Outing experiences also were not always successful. Some students landed in abusive situations. Others, suddenly outside Pratt's purview, used the opportunity to engage in activities forbidden on campus.

How did Charley Bender feel about being dropped into a white family, one in which he didn't know a soul, in a strange place? The Educational Home had had a similar program, and he went on six different outings while at Carlisle (at least one per year; always at different sites in Pennsylvania or New Jersey). So Bender went on outings annually for eight or ten years. He never publicly hinted that he suffered. And he didn't feel he was exploited, at least not without receiving benefit in return. Years after he had left Carlisle he said the "best training" he ever received was from "good Quaker folks" during summers he lived the life of a rural Pennsylvania farm boy.

Charley Bender was working for David Hertzler at such a farm when Swanson came calling. During the day Bender toiled on the farm, and in the evening he practiced with the nearby Dillsburg baseball team. Swanson was a representative of the Dillsburg club, and he needed an arm for that week's game. Bender climbed down from the stacks.

"What will you pay?" Bender said.

"What will you take?" Swanson said.

"Five dollars."

"We can't pay it."

Bender turned and climbed back onto the load of hay.

"We'll pay it," Swanson said.

If a man becomes a professional baseball player the day he first receives payment for his services, then Bender ceased being an amateur the following Saturday afternoon when Dillsburg faced Churchtown in a contest for community supremacy.

Money exchanged hands. That was the only aspect of the game that matched any loose definition of the word professional. If the tales told years later are to be believed, and they are impossible to verify, the bases were stones. There was no small amount of hay on the field. The left field "fence" was a cabbage patch not far beyond the shortstop. Not exactly the Polo Grounds. But when you're a farmhand making twenty bucks a month it might as well have been.

From slab to home, though, the game was baseball and Bender overpowered his opponents. Unfortunately, his infielders were not Eddie Collins and Frank Baker. The rare instances in which batters made contact became adventures. Bender's catcher also couldn't keep up as nearly every third strike was dropped. By the ninth inning Dillsburg managed to be losing a game in which its pitcher was nearly untouchable.

The score was 9–5 with the bases full when Bender lost a ball in the cabbage. Yet after Dillsburg lost the game in the tenth the club's owners were furious and stormed off the field. Bender had struck out twenty-one batters and hit a grand slam. Thank you very little.

He was worried about the loss because he thought collection of his paycheck would be dubious. He nipped at the heels of the manager, following him from the field to the boarding house where the team dressed. When the two reached the boarding house the door was slammed on Bender's face.

Charley camped outside the dressing room. Eventually, the manager came out. He had a hatful of coins, mostly pennies and nickels, and handed them to Bender. The collection had been low, he said, so he had only $3.20 to offer.

"I'll give you the $1.80 the next time I see you," he said.

Bender saw that manager again on the eighteenth of never. He returned to Carlisle that fall and resumed his life. Decades later Bender told that story and newspaperman Ed Pollock wrote about it.

"They say this is a small world," Bender said, "but I've been looking for that fellow for [40 years] and haven't found him yet."

In 1942, Pollock shared the anecdote with his *Philadelphia Evening Bulletin* readers. A few days later a package postmarked Dillsburg, Pennsylvania, was delivered to the newspaper office that contained a canvas bag of coins. Each coin was dated before 1901. There were Indian-head pennies; a three-cent piece dated 1864; a two-cent coin minted a year later; and two thin 1875 dimes.

There was also a note: "We have searched our files and found your claim against our club of $1.80 to be correct. After the 1901 season we harvested cabbage and collected enough money to pay you off. However, we had no idea of your whereabouts until recently. The club has decided not to pay any interest as we believe we were overcharged."

When Pollock handed Bender the money Bender laughed. "What a comeback!" he said. "Those boys really came up with a great idea."

He laughed some more after he was handed a letter, which instructed him to sign and return an enclosed receipt. "You know," he said, "it only goes to prove what I have been contending all along—that in this world there are a few honest palefaces."

Bender tucked those coins in a bureau drawer in which he stored emblems and World Series mementos.

After he returned for his final year at the Carlisle Indian School, another problem arose, and this one didn't have a funny ending. According to his official Carlisle school record, in 1902 Bender was "expelled for treachery to the base ball team." Details of the story are unclear; Bender's existing school record does not elaborate, but he did talk about the incident years later. He said that in 1902 he was sent to Dickinson's prep school, but remained the captain of the team at Carlisle. The Carlisle nine had a break of two weeks in the schedule and the Dickinson captain asked Bender to take the trip with his team, saying he had fixed it with the Carlisle authorities.

"You must understand that anything went in those days as far as athletics were concerned," Bender said. "Many of the Dickinson College football players, for example, were going to prep and men were interchanged at will. I took it for granted that everything was OK—and it would have been, if a most unusual situation had not come up." Carlisle and Dickinson were scheduled to meet in a dual track meet and the star sprinter of the Dickinson team also was a pitcher on the baseball club.

"He told the captain, young man named Cannon, that he was sick and could not make the trip," Bender said. "Cannon then approached me. But the Dickinson athlete competed against Carlisle in the track meet and won two first-places. The officials at Carlisle immediately charged me with being a party to the deception. I was brought up on the carpet and ordered out of school."

Whatever the precise transgression, the matter was neither as final as the word "expelled" nor as dire as the word "treachery" implies.

Bender's views of Carlisle were not often reported. The few comments offered suggest he harbored little if any resentment toward the school. "It seems to me," he said years later, "it was almost a crime against [American Indians] to discontinue Carlisle."

Throughout his life, as he was asked about his career, Bender usually deflected credit to others. He was not one to press his finger to his own chest. Pop Warner undoubtedly helped Bender transform from a hard-throwing raw athlete to a pitcher with some semblance of a plan on the mound. Had the Carlisle nine been led by a different man, one with a more substantive baseball background, well, it's hard to say Warner's influence would have been irreplaceable. But the football coach did leave a mark in Bender's brain. At least Bender believed Warner was crucial to his development. A better description than teacher-pupil is that Bender took Warner's minimal coaching and squeezed every ounce out of the sponge.

Which was apropos of Bender. In many ways he was a natural athlete. But the "natural athlete" tag conveys a specific connotation; one thinks of a great athlete who didn't have to practice, a specimen blessed at birth with all necessary ability. Although it's true that Bender became an outstanding athlete, that's not the full explanation. He wasn't hatched as a great pitcher.

Throughout his prime one of his rare gifts was the ability to invent himself, whether that meant developing better control, teaching himself a new pitch, or learning a new hobby without the aid of formal instruction. He learned because he wanted to learn and because he was resourceful enough to figure things out. He was a jack-of-all-trades, and if he was going to do something, he wanted to understand the task and to do it well. "Bender can . . . play three-cushioned billiards well enough to take care of himself and he can stand up after dinner and make a speech or sing a song and get away with it," Christy Mathewson said years later, "[and] he does not need a guardian when he engages in the manly sport of poker."

Joe Astroth was a catcher for the Philadelphia Athletics in the early 1950s when Bender coached the A's pitchers. Astroth said Bender had a philosophy that applied equally to baseball as it did to chores around the house: "When you come up against something new don't be afraid to attempt it. Try to solve it before you call the expert."

After leaving Carlisle, Bender would eventually pitch for one of the legendary managers in the history of baseball and play alongside some of the brightest men in the game. But throughout his life, more than anyone else Charles Bender's finest teacher was Charles Bender.

This unusual level of self-reliance undoubtedly came from years spent at Richard Henry Pratt's school—whether he was in the classroom, in a farmer's field, or on a baseball diamond. Carlisle may have had a provocative mission, but the school taught Bender how to find his own way in the world.

And in the moments before the start of the 1914 World Series there was no doubt he alone steered his ship.

Chapter Eight. As Charles Bender stood, all eyes on him, in the middle of the diamond moments before the game, he must have at some point turned his face toward the visitors' dugout. If not to size up his opponent, then to see what all the commotion was about. As Bender threw his final warmup tosses, the Boston Braves were being whipped into a frenzy by their manager.

George Stallings's breath could wilt plant life. The Boston skipper was educated and dressed like a southern gentleman, wearing a bow tie and fedora. But he was not as smooth around the edges as he appeared. He possessed a creative and crass vocabulary and was said to have had something of a belching problem. Gumption leaked from his ears. Not long after Bender's lunch with Grantland Rice and Oswald Kirksey, with his team sitting in last place in early July, 15 games behind the New York Giants, Stallings made an announcement: "My team is ready now and we'll win the pennant." Pardon?

In many ways the Braves' style of play reflected their manager's disposition: sharp and sassy. The Braves believed will was as much a factor in winning as was pitching and defense. Then again, they needed to believe that. This was not a collection of superstars. With few exceptions, they were has-beens and never-weres. Hank Gowdy had started with the Giants but John McGraw thought so little of the catcher he let him walk.

Inexperienced first baseman Butch Schmidt had been jettisoned by the Highlanders five years earlier. After being obtained from Brooklyn in August, third baseman Red Smith had promptly bolstered the lineup, but he broke his leg days before the Series began. His replacement, Charlie Deal, was waiver bait.

Second baseman Johnny Evers was the elder statesman and the only regular over the age of thirty. The future Hall of Famer had been on his way to the Federal League, but was lured by Boston president Jim Gaffney, who gave him a fat salary and substantial bonuses; Evers reportedly received an enormous sum for an aging middle infielder. But he earned his dough, winning the Chalmers Award as the National League's most valuable player, leading the Braves with his guile as much as with his glove.

Evers had a prominent jaw and spent a lot of time reading the baseball rulebook; it was said he kept it under his pillow. He was so full of electricity he could not wear a watch. Or at least that's what people said. He was called The Crab because of the way in which he scrambled for ground balls and because he wasn't often in a good mood. He may have been wound tight, but he was the team's catalyst and captain.

"Evers would make you want to punch him," Walter James Maranville said, "but he only thought of the team."

Maranville, better known as Rabbit, was Evers's double-play partner. He was also his pupil. In 1954, Marie Bender would sit next to Maranville's wife during the ceremony in which their husbands were inducted into the Hall of Fame. In 1914, Maranville was in his second full season. Small and unattractive, he was eminently useful on the bases, when he reached them, and was a terrific shortstop.

Stallings's team was the first to use widespread platooning. He rotated his outfielders, a motley crew: Possum Whitted and Les Mann in center; journeyman Herbie Moran in right; Joe Connolly and Ted Cather in left. None of them instilled fear in opponents. But the Braves were able to scratch together a lineup that scored the third most runs in the league. Evers was frequently on base and Connolly, though he did not cut an imposing figure, slugged a lot of extra-base hits.

The manager also had three good pitchers in a rare groove. From July 16 on, Bill James went 18-1, Dick Rudolph 17-1, and George Tyler 10-6. A fourth pitcher, George Davis, pitched a no-hitter that season. But

James was a one-year wonder; Rudolph, like Gowdy, had been cut by Mc-Graw; and Tyler's experience before 1914 was three losing seasons. In other words, the Braves consisted of "one .300 hitter, the worst outfield that ever flirted with sudden death, three pitchers and a good working combination around second base." That was the opinion of none other than the Braves' own manager. Before the 1914 World Series few baseball men went out of their way to mount a counter argument.

But Boston made up for its lack of talent by feeding off Stallings, whose dial was always turned up. The team's New York–based owners, who knew about his ability (in 1910, he unexpectedly kept the Highlanders in contention), had appointed him in 1913. From that point on, he never took his foot off the pedal. Even after the Braves won the pennant Stallings pushed his team as earnestly the rest of the year as he did in July.

"I don't want them to get in the habit of losing," he said.

Not only did Stallings threaten to fight Mack, before Game 1 a noisy Philadelphia fan named C. P. Callahan annoyed Stallings so much that Stallings landed a blow. A scuffle ensued and players had to restrain the pair. Once in the dugout Stallings raved up and down the bench, exhorting his players, cursing over and over. No matter how well his team performed, never a smile, never a sign of satisfaction. No, he wasn't just happy to be there.

Stallings pressed his players like a salesman with empty pockets. Evers talked after the first game about the manager's mindset before it: "Up and down the bench he slid and showed his teeth until he had every man on the club fighting with the crazy frenzy they say a soldier shows when he goes into battle and once gets a taste of it."

Once wrote Damon Runyon: "Stallings harried them with verbal goad . . . He spoke rudely of their personalities. He abused their ancestry. Invective fell from his tongue in a searing stream as he crouched there conning the field before him, his strong fingers folding and unfolding against his palms as if grasping the throat of an enemy."

The Athletics, seen as a collection of gentlemen, were used to opponents trying to crawl under their skin. Connie Mack, straight as a bat, was the face of the team and it was not uncommon for players to ride the A's for their comparatively squeaky, proper manners. Bench jockeying was nothing new in 1914, but the Braves took the practice to an art form.

Stallings read newspapers and used any scab of information he could find to rile his players, who spoke to their opponents with colorful adjectives. The Braves ripped Philadelphia outfielder Rube Oldring because he supposedly had deserted his wife. They criticized Eddie Collins for signing with a more lucrative newspaper syndicate. Of course, they disparaged Charles Bender's lineage.

During the Series the *New York American* anonymously quoted a member of the Athletics: "This fellow Stallings was talking the other day about sportsmanship," he said. "Our boys can stand a lot of riding. We are used to it, because everybody knows that Connie's system is to play baseball and win the games with better ball playing. We don't ride anybody, but we don't mind a team getting after us ordinarily. The Giants tried it every year, but there was a limit to even what McGraw would stand for. But there is no limit to what these fellows have pulled off on the field. It's one way to win ball games and it's no alibi for yourself if you lose on that account. . . . [But] if the fans in Boston could be told some of the stuff these fellows have pulled they wouldn't have a friend even in their own home town."

Umpire Bill Dineen would caution the Braves several times for their sportsmanship, but the Braves only kept coming. Before the first pitch, Stallings shouted at his players. "Get in there and beat that big Indian," he said. "You can do it. Wait and pickle that fast one."

There was a reason why Charles Bender was put in such a tense situation. He had started the first game of the 1910, 1911, 1913 Series and, here again, received the start for the 1914 opener because there was a switch inside him that, once flipped, took his game to another level. The larger and louder the crowd, the greater the stakes, the more steely was his spirit.

"I never saw a man who was so sure fire in winning a game," Connie Mack said years later. "He was a wonder."

Matters of race aside, by the start of the 1914 Series Charles Bender suited his era as though outfitted by a fine cosmic tailor. Many baseball men, including Ty Cobb, referred to him as one of the most cerebral pitchers of the day. Bender was "one of the craftiest pitchers ever in baseball," Cobb said years later. This was no minor compliment, since perhaps at no point in baseball history was duplicity at such a premium as in the years that encompassed Bender's career. He was a thinking man playing a thinking man's game.

The Deadball Era, generally regarded as the period between 1901 and 1919, was a distinct time in baseball history—even though the game was anything but static during this two-decade period.

For one thing, the ball, despite the thought the term implies, was not always, in fact, dead. During his first eight years in the Major Leagues, the ball Bender threw pretty much lived up to the name. Because it was made with a soft rubber core, it didn't travel as far or as fast as a modern, cork-centered ball hit with the same force. But during the second decade of the era, Ben Shibe, the man who signed Bender's paychecks, patented a more tightly wound cork-centered ball. Every so often since there has been debate about whether the ball has been livened or deadened. But Bender and the other Major League pitchers threw a ball that at least closely resembles the one used ever since by nearly every father who has played catch with his son.

This new ball was created to reduce costs, but also because a livelier ball would lead to more scoring—and baseball needed more scoring. In 1908, after a decade and a half of the same pitching distance and essentially the same rules, offense was losing to defense. The Major League batting average was a paltry .239 and in 1909 (.244) it was scarcely better. After the cork-centered ball became official in 1911 the game went from black-and-white to color. Suddenly there were more extra-base hits, more hits of all types (the aggregate average was .266) and run scoring increased dramatically. In fact, there was a greater leap in scoring between 1910 and 1911 than there would be between 1919 and 1920, the transition year often associated with the end of the "dead ball." Here's how lively matters got in the Deadball Era: In 1911 Joe Jackson hit .408 and *didn't* win the batting title.

Composition, however, is not the only noteworthy characteristic about the ball in play during Bender's career. Use was another factor. Although, according to research by Robert Schaefer, it's a myth that only one ball, no matter its condition, was used per game, balls were left in play long enough to at times—after being batted, scraped, and soiled all afternoon—become disfigured.

Since a doctored or abused ball can be made to break sharply, Deadball Era batters had a distinctive approach to their jobs. As Schaefer said, instead of swinging from their heels, even great hitters such as Honus Wagner and Napoleon Lajoie choked up, either with their hands together or inches apart, and they tried to slap balls through holes in the infield with short-arced, compact strokes. Such swings were so ingrained as being the proper way to bat that even after the lively ball was thrown into play hitting strategy remained essentially unchanged (until Babe Ruth came along, swung from his heels, and revolutionized the game).

The emphasis was on situational hitting, hitting to specific areas of the field, and bunting for hits. The rarity of long blasts, by definition, meant that one-run tactics—sacrifice bunts (even a star like Cobb was called upon to give himself up), stolen bases, the hit-and-run and the bunt-and-run—were used during Bender's career like a fireman uses a hose. Bender had to contend with plays such as double steals and advancement of two bases on a single sacrifice with regularity. This type of baseball came to be called the "inside game" or "scientific baseball."

The choke-and-poke style allowed fielders to creep in. Infields were drawn in during game situations that would surprise the modern fan, and outfielders played so shallow they factored in the play more often.

Because rallies were less frequent, teams were aggressive—perhaps overly so—base stealers; even slow players and pitchers were called upon to run. Bender stole 20 bases in his career, a large total for a pitcher in later eras. This breakneck philosophy resulted in such low stolen-base percentages that by running so often teams may have hurt more than helped themselves. But fans didn't go to the park during the Deadball Era to see 500-foot home runs. Instead, they sat on their seat edges anticipating plays such as the double suicide squeeze, and the Philadelphia Athletics were among the play's best practitioners. Here's how it worked: With runners on second and third, a bunt was placed in the direction of the second baseman, hard enough to evade the pitcher's reach. With the first baseman charging for the bunt (which would, if done right, go past him) and the second baseman sliding to cover first, the ball would hit an "empty" area as the runner on second rounded third and headed home.

If offenses during the era were employing extreme small ball, they were helped by certain realities. Bender, and the fielders behind him, relied on small gloves of poor craftsmanship while trying to field defaced balls skipping on patchy playing surfaces. So fielding averages were not especially high. In his fifteen-year career, Bender allowed 287 unearned runs while often pitching in front of one of the best infields of the era. By contrast, another Hall of Famer with comparable numbers, Robin Roberts, who pitched three more seasons than Bender during a career that stretched from the late 1940s to the mid-1960s, allowed almost 100 fewer unearned runs.

The men who played during the Deadball Era helped change the perception of professional baseball. Sure, there were dolts in the game, roughs who would threaten umpires, and men (see: Cobb, Ty) who would kick second base closer to third to make a steal easier. But the vulgarity and violence of the 1890s, which kept some fans from the ticket booth, made way for a surprising number of cultured men and authentic characters. These classy, articulate players, men such as Christy Mathewson, Eddie Collins, and Bender, undoubtedly made baseball more attractive to the mainstream.

Whatever their academic records, players of this time had baseball smarts and were given more freedom to use their noodles. They implemented strategy without permission from the bench. Pitchers and catchers, for example, called their own games. Batters and base runners, rather than base coaches, flashed their own subtle signs to put a play on. Managers didn't micromanage. Real men knew when to bunt.

Charles Bender's intelligence was especially useful in the game played during the Deadball Era. Of course, there were pitchers with more impressive pedigrees. By 1914, Walter Johnson was in the midst of a career that allowed men of the era to say with a straight face that they stood before the greatest pitcher of all time. Mathewson had just completed his last outstanding season. The Big Train and Matty were at the 1914 World Series. There to see Bender, the Deadball Era's great clutch pitcher, pitch.

He would begin his work on this day, October 9, 1914, at five minutes past two, when Herbert Moran dug his feet in the batter's box. That's when Bender kicked his leg in the direction of the dome outside Shibe Park and hurled the ball across the heart of the plate. Moran left the bat on his shoulder—the first strike of the World Series. The Boston right fielder fouled off the next two pitches and then popped another foul, one that fell into first baseman Stuffy McInnis's glove. One down.

Johnny Evers was welcomed with boos and hisses from the Philly faithful. He swung at the first pitch and gave the catcallers reason to clap—an infield fly to Collins.

Joe Connolly, the No. 3 hitter, allowed a called strike, then fouled one off. Bender's next pitch curved around Connolly's bat.

The switch was on.

Chapter Nine. Indeed, as he walked off the mound after the top half of the first inning, Charles Bender seemed to befit his time and place. In the day, the word *money* was a common attributive noun. The term was used in various sports and industries but was only applied to a certain kind of performer. A money player, or pitcher, is one who excels when pressure is greatest. In baseball Bender was the example. "I consider Bender," Connie Mack said, "the greatest money pitcher the game has ever known."

Mack's opinion was not unique. By 1914, Bender had earned a reputation for clutch ability, and though that reputation was created during the postseason, he also raised his game in important moments other than those that unfolded during the World Series.

Perhaps the best example was Bender's performance during the 1907 American League pennant race. One of the tightest chases in history, throughout that summer the Philadelphia Athletics, Chicago White Sox, Cleveland Naps, and Detroit Tigers played hopscotch, and during July and August, with the Athletics on his back, Bender took control of the game.

On July 4, he threw a two-hitter to beat the New York Highlanders. On July 8, he stopped the defending American League champion White Sox. Four days later Bender struck out eight St. Louis Browns. On July 18 he

"I consider Bender the greatest money pitcher the game has ever known," Connie Mack said. National Baseball Hall of Fame Library, Cooperstown NY.

shut out Cleveland. He made it back-to-back shutouts a week later, defeating Chicago. Over twelve days, from July 30 to August 10, he started, completed, and won five games, including two against offense-heavy Detroit, the second of which was a 1–0 victory over "Wild" Bill Donovan, who pitched for a team that on most days provided terrific run support.

Later in August the Athletics traveled to Cleveland for a four-game series. Bender won the first game, beating future Hall of Famer Addie Joss while striking out seven. He won despite five errors in the field behind him. He also saved the last game of the series, coming in for two hitless innings of a two-run contest.

It was a remarkable stretch of pitching. In the span of little more than six weeks he had thrown 92 innings and started 10 games, and won them all. He allowed a total of 10 runs, earned or otherwise, and never more than 2 in a game. Opponents made only 56 hits while they struck out 43 times. In fact, Bender struck out more than four batters for each one he walked. He wasn't just winning games; he was dominating the best teams in the league. Eight of his wins came against clubs that had been ahead of Philadelphia before the run began. In those 8 games he allowed 8 runs.

Entering play on July 8, the Athletics had been in fourth place, 7½ games out. On August 20, the day after Bender slammed the door on the Naps, the A's were a game and a half up. And Bender's best game of the streak had yet to be pitched.

On August 21, he was baffling the White Sox in Chicago, as through seven innings the Sox had managed just two hits. The eighth was more of the same. Bender whiffed Lee Tannehill, Billy Sullivan, and Frank Smith on eleven pitches. They were Bender's sixth, seventh, and eighth strikeouts of the game. He was so good on this day that as he walked to the Philadelphia dugout at the end of the seventh White Sox fans clapped.

When Bender stepped to the plate in the ninth inning the game was scoreless. The Chicago fans offered Indian cries and a band in the stands began to play what the *Philadelphia Inquirer* called a "ghost dance from Hiawatha." With Bris Lord standing on second and two out Bender smacked a solid single to center field. Lord raced around third and tried to score the go-ahead run, but was nailed at the plate on a throw from Fielder Jones.

In the ninth, the White Sox doubled their hit total with a pair of singles and pushed across the winning run. It's one example of why a pitcher's win-loss record is a flawed way to measure his performance. "If any pitcher ever deserved to win it was certainly Bender today," the *Inquirer* said.

To sum up, as sabermetrician Chris Jaffe has noted, from June 24 to August 21, Bender started a dozen games, the A's won all but one of them, and the opponents scored just 13 runs.

After his winning streak and the ensuing 1–0 loss at Chicago, Bender became gradually less effective, and the A's barely eked out a 7-6 win in his last start on September 14. Though they had 17 games to go, Bender did not start again, indicating that either he had arm problems or was sick. Following Bender's last start the Athletics were in first place by 2½ games over the White Sox. Without him they fell out of first, a game and a half behind the Tigers.

Another factor amplifies Bender's performance. As Jaffe said, the team Bender pitched for was overachieving, as the Athletics' run differential was far less than what it should have been for a contending club. In other words, Bender peaked against tough competition on a team that was playing over its head. His performance—as well as the manner in which the A's stumbled once he was relegated to the sidelines—may have enhanced Bender's big-game credentials in Mack's mind.

"I really think we should have won that year," Mack said. "We were several games ahead in mid-September and closing at home, while Detroit had to make an eastern trip, so things were all in our favor. However, I was having a lot of trouble with my pitching. Coombs injured his arm early, but what hurt us most was that Bender's arm went absolutely lame at a time when we needed him most."

During the 1914 World Series and throughout his prime, Bender was depended upon by no less of a baseball man than Connie Mack. But the early narrative of Bender's life was fragile; few details pointed toward a life of such renown. The thread that stretched from his infancy to the place he then occupied was long and thin and winding. However, few rise to the top without a break. That Bender's life took a sharp, fortuitous turn not long after he celebrated his eighteenth birthday, well, there were human beings who deserved one less.

In early June 1902, a few months after he graduated from Carlisle, Bender
was handed a contract by John McCulloch, manager of the Harrisburg
Athletic Club, a semipro team in the Cumberland Valley Association, for
the balance of the 1902 season. This was not an especially unusual signing. Carlisle played games against area teams, and several of the school's
better players played in the league. Pop Warner often had a hand in such
transactions, and he took a cut of the signing bonuses paid to many of
his athletes. The salary paid to Bender was good, about $150 per month.
Some sources say the figure was less, about $125, but in any event the
money was well more than he had seen in his life. "It looked like a fortune," he said years later, "and I grabbed it."

At the time Bender was a student at Dickinson College's prep school.
Bender is often credited with having attended college; he did not. Dickinson's records on Bender are limited, for two reasons: First, he attended
the prep school, which would later be known as Conway Hall, as a high
school sophomore for about one semester. Second, the college's administration building burned in 1904, and records prior to that time, even
for more established students, are spotty.

When Bender signed McCulloch's contract he did so as Charles Albert,
leaving off his proper surname. Bender's plan was to play the season and
then return to Dickinson for further schooling. If he received money for
baseball he would not retain his amateur status and using Charles Albert,
technically, was not a lie. During the summer of 1902 everyone in Harrisburg called him Albert and for years many others did as well.

"I just used the first and middle name of my right name," Bender said.
"But Mr. Mack remembers that under the surname of Albert he got my
contract for $100 and he has called me Albert ever since."

Bender made his debut with HAC, as the team was called, two days after he signed the contract pitching against a team from Chester, and,
simply put, he was not impressive. He didn't receive much help from
his fielders, which would be a theme during the season, but he was battered around the yard. He allowed two home runs, sixteen hits, and
seven runs in a loss.

"Albert, the Indian twirler, was in good form," the *Harrisburg Telegraph*
said, "but he could not stop the Chester sluggers, who simply hit the ball

at will." Perhaps he just needed to acclimate himself, because that outing would ultimately prove to be an aberration.

There are times when a man has so much athleticism that on physical ability alone he can master a league. This doesn't happen often in the majors, where the talent margin is minute. But it happens in semipro circuits, where the gap can be substantial. Sometimes, a single team's roster will simultaneously include players who are at the baseline of their careers and others who have reached the high point of their athletic lives.

In 1902, Charles Albert often competed with and against men who wouldn't see a Major League game without a ticket. He, on the other hand, was climbing toward stardom. He thrived because he was a supreme athlete and because for the first time in his life he was able to fasten his sharp mind to a subject that gripped him.

Although he hadn't had many at bats at any level, he quickly emerged as the team's top hitter and regularly batted third in the HAC lineup. He often made extra-base hits, including a home run and a double in his second game. In his third game he made three hits against the Harrisburg Giants, the city's black team.

When he wasn't pitching Albert played in the field, usually at first base or in right field, and he also spent time at second base and center field. His subsequent outings on the mound went better, too. For example, when he came on in relief against the Maryland Athletic Club he struck out eight, including one inning in which he fanned the side on ten pitches. "The Maryland hitters could do nothing with him," the *Telegraph* said.

Throughout his life, even after his playing career had ended, Bender was always slim. But by 1902 he had begun to show that money hadn't been wasted on Pop Warner's steaks. Tall and solid, closer to the 185 pounds he was said to weigh as a member of the Philadelphia Athletics (he may have weighed five or ten pounds more than that), not only was Bender athletic, he looked the part, filling out his gray HAC uniform.

He looked like a player beyond his years and almost immediately was given a chance to prove it. Bender had been on the team ten days when it was announced that the Chicago Cubs would visit Harrisburg for an exhibition game against HAC. In other words, having pitched scant innings anywhere other than Carlisle, none of them on an established minor league team, Bender suddenly would face living, breathing Major League hitters.

It wasn't as if he had advanced to a point where he deserved to receive a chance to face the kind of competition that can change the direction of a career. There were pitchers who toiled far longer, pitchers with more impressive résumés, pitchers who never received the chance that hopped into Bender's lap. He was at the right place at the right time and when presented with a rare opportunity he lifted himself to a higher level than perhaps even he thought possible.

If a twenty-first-century incarnation of the Cubs were to stop into a town such as Harrisburg and play a club team it would be nearly as shocking as if Babe Ruth returned from the grave and hit a homer. In 1902 the event was not so unusual, which is different than saying it was common. Newspapers noted that this would be the first time a National League team visited Harrisburg. "A large crowd will no doubt attend to see what the HAC can do against the [National League] team," the *Telegraph* said, "but more will attend to see Chicago—because it is Chicago."

McCulloch was Bender's manager for all of ten days. Four days before the Cubs game, McCulloch resigned and was replaced by Cal Snoddy. Snoddy apparently didn't have a drastically different opinion of Bender than did McCulloch, and days before the game he announced that Bender would be on the mound against the National Leaguers. In other words, the formalities had been dispensed with. Let's see what you can do, kid.

On June 17, 1902, with Philadelphia Athletics manager Connie Mack sitting in the stands on a personal scouting trip, Bender shut out the Cubs. Well, at least that's the story that's been handed down through the years by writers who didn't appreciate facts getting in the way of a good story. But the story's still good, even when the facts are taken into consideration.

The Harrisburg Athletic Club, formed in 1901, had some four hundred members, including many who became prominent leaders in city politics and business. The club plotted handsome grounds on Hargest (City) Island, the original name, an island in the middle of the Susquehanna River across from the Harrisburg city center. In order to reach Island Park to face the Chicago Cubs Bender and his teammates likely had walked across the Walnut Street Bridge to the ballpark. By the time the

Cubs took the Island Park field the stands were packed and, the newspaper noted, there were many more ladies in attendance than usual.

One might suppose that in a meaningless exhibition game Cubs manager Frank Selee would play a collection of names that wouldn't ever find a place in the *Baseball Register*, that Bender would face a lineup with no great shakes. But this was 1902. Teams did not have deep rosters or thick directories of available players on which to call. Indeed, Bender did not face a nine that would ever be compared to the 1927 Yankees, but a hundred years later some names Bender faced that day are well known by baseball fans.

Joe Tinker, in the first year of his Hall of Fame career, played shortstop. Several other Cubs regulars were in the lineup. Johnny Kling batted fifth. Kling carved out a fine Major League career and was one of the better catchers of the first decade of the twentieth century—a defensive standout who could hit, too. Germany Schaefer played third base. Jim St. Vrain pitched for the Cubs. He was hardly a Major League ace, but in 1902 he threw ninety-five innings of 2.08 ERA baseball and, no doubt, he was big-league caliber. This was hardly a Carlisle intrasquad game.

As for Connie Mack, he was in Chicago, not Harrisburg, that day as his team was facing the White Sox. And Bender didn't shut out the Cubs. He didn't even win the game. There was a shutout that day—*by* the Cubs, not *of* the Cubs. But Bender was good. He was very good.

"Chicago Was Held Down" was the headline in the next morning's *Telegraph*, which did not provide much in the way of play by play. Bender allowed three runs, but at least two of them were unearned, in a complete-game effort. Only six hits, including two doubles, were made off him. Chicago scored in the third and fourth. In the fifth inning Bender retired the side on seven pitches and for the game only seven Chicago hitters reached base.

In the final five innings—during which, in theory, he would be most susceptible to fatigue and the increased difficulty of pitching to hitters who were seeing him for the second, third and fourth times—Bender was at his best.

"Even the leaguers could not hit the Indian twirler," the *Telegraph* said, "for Albert was in good form and had the National League sluggers at his mercy." He was eighteen years old and he had just negotiated his way through a big-league lineup.

"Albert's work held the visitors down." That was the newspaper talking. Soon others would start to talk, too.

The story follows that after Bender's fine performance against the Cubs, the Philadelphia Athletics immediately signed him. Not true. Though his performance caused a stir, and though clearly his showing against the Cubs was a turning point in his baseball career, Bender remained with the HAC for the rest of the summer.

Two days after his performance against Chicago, Bender had a three-hit game while playing first base. On June 23, he pitched against the Cuban Ex-Giants, a talented black team, and was impressive, striking out eight and walking one.

"The visitors tried to find Albert's curves," the *Telegraph* said, "but he kept them guessing and several of the dusky sluggers simply fanned the wind." Harrisburg lost the game, 4–3, and the paper reported that the Giants played "dirty." In one incident the Giants second baseman tried to block Bender off the base but instead only wound up with a sore leg.

Bender's control was good for a teenager playing in the highest league of his life. Typically, he would walk a batter or two while striking out five or more.

On the last day of June, Bender had a banner day against Shamokin. He pitched a shutout, struck out eight, walked two, and allowed as many hits (four) as he made himself, including a double and a triple. Three days later, against a team of college players, he threw another four-hitter, this time allowing a run and three walks.

He was starting to be noticed for his "headwork," as the newspaper called it, and Harrisburg was drawing bigger crowds, said to be in excess of two thousand. "Albert uses his head to a great advantage," the newspaper said. "The Indian, as usual, was in the game at all stages. He is a wonder and he earns all of his salary."

In mid-July HAC again faced Maryland and Bender was sensational. He allowed five hits and struck out nine against three walks in a 5–2 victory. "That Indian wants to play the game all by himself," the paper said. "He is what the big leaguers call a 'find.'"

A few days later Bender was charged with three errors, but probably deserved only two. Nonetheless it was an off day. He didn't pitch especially well, and a team from Atlantic City beat Harrisburg. The paper lamented, "even Albert had three errors yesterday." The next day Bender made two hits and stole two bases and played a flawless center field, but that wasn't the big Bender story.

The paper the following morning ran the words "Albert Will Stay Here" in larger type than was used for any baseball development all season, Cubs coverage included. Apparently, Bender had flirted with the idea of jumping to another semipro team, one in York, because he felt he had been "badly treated." Fans in the right-field bleachers had heckled him; they didn't want him to forget his poor performance. Bender told the newspaper that the best players make errors and no one makes them intentionally.

"A player has as much feeling as any of the spectators and hisses and jeers when errors are made are uncalled for," he said. It's not known whether the jeers were racially motivated, but it wouldn't have been out of the ordinary for an American Indian to face such hostility, as Bender would soon enough realize.

Manager Snoddy assured Bender he would be treated fairly from then on and Bender remained. A day later he pitched against Jesse Frysinger's strong Wilmington Athletic Association. Near the end of July, Bender was "invincible" in a win over Montgomery, striking out seven and walking one. He allowed just four hits.

A note in early August said Bender led the team in hitting, but no numbers were used to support the statement. On August 4, Bender turned a rare trick. He threw nine no-hit innings and still lost the game. Harrisburg was beaten in the tenth, 2–1, when a runner who reached on an error scored on the Philadelphia Giants' only hit of the game. Bender walked six batters, but it was a fine performance.

His walk totals rose as the summer wore on. Of course they did. Snoddy was throwing Bender several times a week. If he didn't start the game on the mound, Bender often finished it there. Innings pitched totals are not available, but Bender must have thrown a season's worth that summer. "Albert," the *Telegraph* said, "can always be depended upon to pull Harrisburg out of a hole."

Despite the increased workload, he was still striking out his fair share, including fifteen batters over consecutive starts one week in late August and early September, and twelve in a mid-September win over Penn Park.

"Penn Park's heavy hitters were at his mercy," the newspaper said. "Albert's great headwork when his opponents had men on base was the subject of much favorable comment." Two days later he struck out nine Roxborough hitters.

Shortly thereafter the newspaper reported that Bender's performance had received attention in important quarters: "Albert will be missed next season. Connie Mack has the knack of finding good pitchers. Albert will be all right."

Tales about Bender's signing—that Mack personally scouted him and that he was plucked immediately after handling the Cubs—obscured the precise details of his discovery. For all its coverage of Charles Albert's exploits that summer, local newspapers failed to shed much light on the particulars of Bender's first big-league contract.

Bender always said that Frysinger, the Wilmington manager, served as Mack's proxy. Frysinger liked Bender's presence, the way he went about his business on the mound, and the results he had against top-flight hitters. At some point in the summer Frysinger called Albert aside and asked him a question: "How would you like to pitch for Connie Mack in Philadelphia?"

"I was so excited I didn't even ask the terms," Bender said. "I just signed. Later I read the figures—$300 per month—and thought I had taken my first step to becoming a millionaire."

Mack recalled the story years later: "I also paid the manager of the Harrisburg club $100. I've forgotten the man's name, but should remember it, because that was one of the greatest bargains in baseball."

At the end of the season, the *Telegraph* commented that 1902 had been "one of the most successful [baseball] seasons in the history of this city." Charles Albert was a primary reason for the platitudes, and he was depicted in several newspaper cartoons with captions that referred to him simply as "the Indian." One had him juggling an impossible number of baseballs.

"Albert, the Indian wonder, goes into a game with his whole heart and every move he makes shows that he is in the contest to win," the *Telegraph* said. "His pitching placed him at the head of successful twirlers and under the care of Connie Mack next season he should become still more famous. His actions when pitching are quite humorous at times and a number of local artists have made various sketches of this wonderful twirler."

In the latter months of 1902, Bender had to decide, just as he had six years before, whether to stay in the east. He had graduated from Carlisle, played baseball with the Harrisburg Athletic Club, and "made good," in the common parlance. But although he had to have been excited about the prospect of starting a big-league career, he had little money and had to, in his words, "scratch to make ends meet."

Bender didn't have a natural home in the area nor did he have any common source of financial support. He may have contemplated a return to White Earth, where he'd have a place to stay, could perhaps find a job, and bide time until spring. But Charley Bender's self-reliance—he showed at age twelve that he was capable of charting his own path, even if it meant leaving behind his family and culture—was such that he may not have seriously considered the option. Bender was confident and independent. He had to be. Instead of heading to his mother's house, in the fall the eighteen-year-old returned to the city of Carlisle.

"I went back to Dickinson in the fall and started practice with the football team," he said. "After one week, the dean called me to his office and gave me the bad news. He told me that the athletic director of Carlisle had called and said they would sever all relations with Dickinson if I was allowed to play. That meant the end of my schooling."

Bender went into town, bought a double-barreled shotgun, some shells, some clothes and went hunting at Williams Grove. He deserved a holiday. After all, it's not easy work going from a spare pitcher on a less-than-extraordinary prep school team to big league-signed in a span of two years.

"It was the finest vacation I ever had," he said. "I walked seven miles a day to go shooting, either at the North or South Mountain. In December, I went into a jewelry store to learn clock making.

"Then the day of all days came, when I set off for Jacksonville, and the Athletics' training camp."

Chapter Ten. Charles Bender had one of the great age-nineteen seasons in Major League history. He won 17 games, completed 29, and tossed two shutouts. He threw 270 innings of 3.07 ERA ball, which was about league average that season, and he ranked tenth in the American League in strikeouts per nine innings. Whatever way it's quantified, Bender had an outstanding rookie campaign. However, 1903 wasn't a year about numbers. It was a year about stories.

That March the Philadelphia Athletics held spring training in Jacksonville, Florida. The team hopped on a Merchants and Miners ship out of New York and headed south. Bender had not been on a boat that big—"it looked like a ferry boat to me," he said years later—and he frequently found himself confused and disconnected from the rest of the team.

"I was at sea, both literally and figuratively," he said, "from the first day."

At one point, while he was looking for teammates, Bender stopped on the stairs and gazed across the water. He hadn't before been afforded such a view of the ocean and he decided to breathe it all in. As he stood still, his profile outlined by the horizon, outfielder Socks Seybold spied him and yelled, "You lost again, Chief?" Over the years Bender and others told that story, sometimes with a different teammate than Seybold calling out, to explain how he was tagged with the nickname. The partic-

95

When he broke into the big leagues, Charles Bender was
a shy, well-mannered young man who chose his words
carefully. Courtesy of Fred Wardecker.

ulars of the story have validity, though it's naïve to think Bender wouldn't have acquired the name regardless of whether he ever surveyed a large body of water.

"It was a rough voyage, that first trip," Bender said. "If it hadn't been for [first baseman] Harry Davis, who took me in tow, told me what to do and looked after me like a father, I think I might have died—or at least have been quite seasick. [Davis] was so good to me. I almost learned to worship him. I took his advice on anything and everything." (Years later, Davis would be there for Bender when he found himself in another tight spot.)

During that first year of his career, and for years after, Bender was noticeably reserved. On the road, he remained near the hotel, often by himself, immersed in a book. When he was with teammates he sat, unemotional, listening to the small talk and clubhouse banter. He was said to dress well. When reporters talked to him, every word was parsed in Bender's mind before delivered aloud with a low, gentle voice. At times the pause between question and answer was embarrassingly long. Bender stood with determination in his eyes. Though he used what one writer called "immaculate English" his responses were terse, and reporters, used to bumptious ballplayers, were taken aback.

Bender was likely concerned about his image. How could he not be self-conscious? It's a logical reaction for any sensitive, unheralded rookie thrown into a clubhouse filled with household names. Given that this sensitive unheralded rookie happened to be an American Indian trying to dispel a set of stereotypes that were so pervasive they might as well have been written on the outfield wall, it's not hard to understand why he chose his words carefully. He would have enough doubters, without making more with loose lips.

So his words were always couched so as to not offend. He would make vanilla statements such as, "I was enthusiastic about the game from the moment I saw it played. I resolved to be a pitcher—since then I have tried to be a good one. What success I have had I owe to Manager Mack and my teammates."

Even if his mouth remained closed, Bender's first spring training had to have opened his eyes wider than he thought possible. Six months earlier he was pitching in the Cumberland Valley Association. Eighteen months before that he wasn't even considered the top pitcher at his prep school. He was an American Indian alone in the dominant culture, starting his career, trying to find his place, traveling with a big league team. Not just any big league team, either. The Philadelphia Athletics were the reigning American League champions. The roster was full of talent—and deep in characters.

In Jacksonville the Athletics bunked at The Casino, so called because the year before it had been one. The place was indicative of the plebeian accommodations offered big leaguers in the early years of the American League. Teams didn't stay in swanky digs. The gambling hall-turned-hostel had no beds, so cots were installed in a big barnlike structure. Players slept five or six to a room, a word that in this case must be used loosely. Partitions were erected, and at that there were still only four rooms in the joint. The players' "private baths" were pitchers and washbowls.

The Athletics ate meals nearby at Wolfe's Café. It was there that Osee Schrecongost—teammates and the press called the catcher Schreck—is said to have pulled his famous steak trick. In those days it was not necessarily an honor for an establishment to host a group of the best ballplayers on earth. It was an inconvenience. Whenever an Athletic ordered a steak, Wolfe would go back to the kitchen and yell, "One baseball steak." Soon the sound of a wooden mallet could be heard as Wolfe's cook mashed the meat. The players got the hint: "baseball steaks" were delivered to the more unsavory customers.

A baseball steak was placed on Schreck's plate that, for whatever good beating was administered by the cook, remained an aerobic exercise to swallow. At one point the catcher stood up and nailed the steak to the wall.

"It created quite a commotion," Bender said. "Wolfe was awfully sore, and for a while it looked as though we would lose our eating place, but Connie [Mack] finally talked the proprietor into letting us stay."

George Edward Waddell was another man who had to have made Bender scratch his head. The man they called Rube—some nicknames don't require elaboration—was a walking carnival. Gawky and standing over six feet, Waddell had a hasty fastball and a quick-cutting curve. He chased women as well as fire engines. In fact, Waddell may have been mentally retarded. But he often led the league in strikeouts.

The stories about Waddell are legion. In fact, there are so many absurd tales—with so few of them tied to first-hand reporting—it's impossible to know where truth ends and myth begins. Several of the most oft told were chronicled in after-the-fact newspaper and magazine articles, including those in *The Sporting News*, and many have found their way into books. Prominent sportswriter Frederick G. Lieb wrote about several of the anecdotes in his biography of Connie Mack.

For example, after the Athletics acquired Waddell, Mack had to hire detectives to escort him to Philadelphia since Waddell couldn't be trusted to board a train alone. After a strong bullpen Waddell would pour ice water on his arm. "I've got so much speed today," he would say, "I'll burn the catcher's glove if I don't let up a bit." As Waddell trotted to the box fans called out "Hey Rube!" and he acknowledged them with deep bows. Apocryphal or not, an inordinate number of the most dramatic stories took place—or at least were reported to have taken place by Lieb and others—during Bender's first spring in the big leagues.

In Jacksonville, Waddell tried his hand at alligator wrestling. He also fell hard for a north Florida brunette. As the yarn goes, one day after a workout he went to meet his date at a café they frequented but instead found her sitting at a table with another beau. When the angry Waddell barged over, she turned him away. Waddell was so heartbroken he said he no longer wished to live.

Waddell supposedly ran down to the old Clyde Line dock with Schreck following after him. Without pausing the 195-plus-pounder dove face first into the water. Only there wasn't much of it. Waddell's alleged suicide attempt came at low tide. Instead of the usual ten feet of water at the dock, there was about a foot. So Waddell plunged into the muck almost to his shoulders. He nearly choked before Schreck and a few dockhands, grabbing him by the feet, pulled him out. "He didn't threaten to commit suicide by drowning for some time," Bender said. "Waddell could swim like a fish—in water, but not in mud."

Another story has it that Rube disappeared for two days. Mack was standing outside of his hotel with Danny Murphy when they heard a band coming down the street.

"It's the minstrel show that's in town," Murphy said. "Let's watch the parade."

As the band approached, there was Rube, leading it, tossing his baton into the air. "Hello, Connie," Waddell said, without breaking stride.

Waddell was so difficult to control, it has been written, that one year Mack hired a bodyguard for him—a burly former constable. The constable lasted about two weeks. Bender and Harry Davis were sitting in front of the Euclid Hotel in Cleveland one night at about eleven o'clock when a cab drew up and Waddell stepped out. Rube reached into the cab, pulled out the constable, tossed him over his shoulder and carried him into the hotel.

"Gettin' in a bit early, aren't you, Rube?" Davis said.

"Gettin' in, hell," Rube said. "As soon as I put down this drunk, I'm startin' out for the evening." After Mack heard that story the constable was relieved.

Schreck and Waddell weren't just battery mates, they were drinking buddies and roommates. During those days, players slept two in a bed on the road. At one point, or so goes the tale, Schreck whined to Mack: "The Rube eats crackers in bed. I don't like to sleep dunked in cracker dust."

"I'll speak to Rube about it," Mack said.

Said Schreck, "I want you to put it in his contract that he can't eat crackers in bed."

The Athletics trained at Phoenix Park that spring and changed in the attic of a two-story house near the park. Their lockers were nails in the wall. The only shower bath was a hot sulfur spring that ran through a pipe and onto the players' heads. In the years to come teams would make radical improvements to training facilities, but given where Bender came from and the opportunity at hand he didn't complain.

Instead, he started putting his mind to work. He spent much of that first trip watching pitchers such as Waddell and Eddie Plank, learning their tricks and adopting their approaches.

Plank, named Gettysburg Eddie because of his birthplace, was perhaps the best left-hander of the era. He shut out more teams than any lefty before or since with a sweeping, crossfire delivery. Like Bender, Plank didn't pitch in the minors before reaching the big leagues. He was thin but he could throw hard. As Jan Finkel pointed out in *Deadball Stars of the American League*, Plank fidgeted frequently before delivering each pitch.

He adjusted his cap, his shirt, his sleeve. He often asked for a new ball. He might tighten his pants. Check for wind patterns. Then he was ready to pitch. "As if that was not enough," Finkel wrote, "from the seventh inning on, he would . . . talk to himself, and the ball, out loud: 'Nine to go, eight to go' . . . and so on" until he made the twenty-seventh out. In other words, Plank could be maddening. But when you're as good as Eddie Plank, people put up with you.

Whereas Bender gained a reputation for pitching well in big games, Plank's performance in the clutch was often overlooked because he usually pitched just poorly enough to lose. He had a 2-5 record in the World Series despite a 1.32 ERA.

Plank, who went from a prep school at Gettysburg College to the A's in 1901, once said, "There are only so many pitches in this old arm, and I don't believe in wasting them throwing to first base." Quiet and practical, Plank and Bender had similarities, and they developed the kind of bond that forms among people who work together a long time. Plank was a member of every A's team Bender played on.

That spring Bender also began studying big-league hitters, trying to develop ideas of how to pitch to them. Mack gave Bender his first tryout in an exhibition game against the Philadelphia Phillies, allowing him to pitch the whole game. Bender impressed, beating Tully Sparks. By the time the season opened he was a Major Leaguer.

Talking about his team's prospects before the season, Mack said, "Our only weakness is in the box. The loss of [Bert] Husting was a blow. But I think I will be able to get together a good staff. Albert Bender, the Indian, who pitched for Harrisburg this year . . . should help us."

Bender always labeled as his biggest thrill the time he won his first Major League game in his initial outing during the tail end of a Patriots' Day double-header, April 20, 1903, at Boston. Plank started the game for Philadelphia, but the future Hall of Famer couldn't get anyone out. As Plank was battered around Connie Mack sent Bender to the bullpen.

"I think I'll soon be needing you," he said.

Though relieved of the pressure of a tight game—the Athletics were trailing 6-0 when Bender toed his first Major League rubber—he was frightened in the way rookies usually are. In addition to all the typical reasons to be nervous, Bender was pitching against Denton True Young, a pitcher so accomplished that years later a prestigious trophy was named after him using his more common nickname, Cy.

"Golly, I was scared—my first Major League game," Bender said, "and against Cy Young. Oh my!"

Though his control was not superb, Bender didn't pitch scared. He held Boston to one additional run and the Athletics rallied to a 10–7 victory.

"I was good and wild and good and fast, so they didn't feel like stepping up to the plate," Bender said. "I was throwing sidearm, underhand, and every sort of way, as any other rookie would."

The lone run against Bender was a home run by Buck Freeman, a rocket that, if the stories are to be believed, nearly scraped the edge of the moon it was hit so far. One description had the blast sailing over a block of houses beyond the fence, landing in the second story window of a house. "Bucky Freeman, a great hitter in those days . . . was Boston's right fielder," Bender said. "I got two strikes on him in the eighth inning, then tried an underhand curve, high and inside, and he sent it high and far away."

Bender pitched six innings and struck out one. He went 1-for-3 at the plate and made an error in the field. His line wasn't perfect, but he was still eighteen (he would soon turn nineteen) and had just beaten one of the greatest pitchers in baseball history. A better start must have been unimaginable.

"That night," he said, "I felt like I was walking on air."

Mack met Bender in the dugout after the game. "Nice going, Albert," he said.

Bender would hear his manager utter that simple declaration frequently during the next dozen years. (It's been said Mack never called Bender "Chief." Although Mack may not have used the pejorative to Bender's face, he did use it while talking about Bender in the press.)

For his performance, Bender earned a tryout in the rotation and seven days later was handed his first American League starting assignment: pitching opposite the wily Clark Griffith, pitcher-manager of New York. No problem, skip. Bender threw a four-hit shutout.

The 1903 season was memorable to Bender as much for what occurred off the field. That season he established two of the most important relationships of his life. During Philadelphia's first swing through Detroit, he found his life partner when he met a young woman named Marie Clement. Marie was thin, pretty, feminine, and she went to Tigers games with her girlfriends. After meeting Bender she suddenly had reason to no longer root for the home team. They married on October 3, 1904, in Detroit in a small ceremony before two witnesses.

On their honeymoon, Bender took his bride to the lakes and fields of the Midwest, where they hunted quail and went duck shooting. Along the way they went on an overnight trip to Cleveland, where Charles bought his bride a complete hunting outfit, and then west to Devil's Lake. Not exactly Niagara Falls in terms of romance, but the trip was typical Charles Bender.

"He taught me how to shoot, hunt and fish, and many years later he taught me how to play golf," Marie said. "I went with him on most of his hunting and fishing trips. I loved it."

Early in their marriage, Charles and Marie lived on Hanover Street in Carlisle. A Carlisle newspaper reported that Charles gave Marie an allowance to buy furniture, china, and linens. Marie used to wear her hair fluffy, but Charles didn't like that. He also didn't like rustling silk. He bought Marie soft silks because he didn't like her wearing clothes he said he could hear two blocks away.

Bender did not like to take his work home with him. When he walked in the door he tried to put baseball behind him, but throughout Bender's career Marie, who was often described as "charming" by those who met her, went to most home games and tried to be an active participant in her husband's career. She scoured newspapers for baseball news, kept several scrapbooks, and when she attended double-headers she'd pack a lunch.

Inevitably, Charles's private battles would force them to deal with matters of an especially emotional variety, the kind of trauma that either tears a marriage apart or solidifies the bond in unbreakable ways. Because people who live together rarely write letters to one another, and given that outsiders aren't permitted to truly understand a marriage, it's impossible to provide a nuanced portrait of the Benders' private life. By all accounts, including from those who saw the couple together in their later years, Charles and Marie were very much in love. They remained together the rest of their days.

During the 1903 season, Bender also came to know a man who would be like the father figure he never had growing up. The architect of modern baseball's first dynasty was a tall stick of subtle contradiction. Kind and strict, tolerant and firm, he was a mama's boy, a gentleman, and a relentless competitor. Born Cornelius McGillicuddy, Connie Mack managed the Philadelphia Athletics for a half century, winning 968 more games than any other manager in history. And yet he lost more than he won. The Tall Tactician. The Wise Old Owl. No matter what he was called Mack became so indelibly linked to the A's that soon after the team joined the American League the newspapermen began referring to them as the Mackmen.

Standing about six-two and scarecrow thin, Mack wore a three-piece business suit, a starched collar, necktie, and a black derby or straw skimmer—a costume he sported even in the heat of summer. He was a superb judge of talent, but perhaps his greatest skill was his ability to deal with each player individually and with respect. Mack did not need to yell to coax his players into following his directives. Instead, he merely revealed his penetrating Irish blue eyes. Besides, when you're comfortable in your own skin you don't often feel the need to berate other people.

"Mack understood the need to handle each man as an individual," Norman Macht, Connie Mack biographer, said. "He demonstrated his confidence in them by giving them the responsibility of creating ways to win. . . . He focused on his objectives, told his men what he wanted to accomplish, and suggested ways they might achieve them. He then left it to them to carry out the mission. He didn't do all their thinking for them."

Mack didn't signal his players' every move or call pitches from the bench. The A's were allowed to arrange their infield defensive alignment and they flashed their own signs when they judged the right time for the hit-and-run, the steal, the double steal. Mack, using a scorecard on which he kept score with a pencil, famously waved the card to deploy his outfielders. He knew his pitchers' strengths and opposing hitters' tendencies, and put them together to position the outfield. Before games Mack would gather his team to discuss strategy, but during games he essentially left them alone. He was so discrete—he entered the dugout before the game and rarely left—that fans didn't know what he looked like. It was said during his career that every Catholic priest was an unofficial scout for Connie Mack. He dressed like a deacon and acted like one, too.

"In all the years I've known Connie Mack," said Clark Griffith, whose playing and managerial careers often found him on opposite sides of the diamond from Mack, "I've never known him to do a mean thing."

Mack's righteousness did not endear him to all, but most of his players respected him and were loyal to him. Several of Mack's core players, including Bender, returned to work for him after they retired as players.

"He really respected his fellow man," Rube Bressler, an A's pitcher, said in *The Glory of Their Times*. "If you made a mistake, Connie never bawled you out on the bench, or in front of anybody else. He'd get you alone a few days later, and then he'd say something like, 'Don't you think it would have been better if you'd made the play this way?' And you knew damn well it would have been better. . . . In my opinion, Connie Mack did more for baseball than any other living human being—by the example he set, his attitude, the way he handled himself and his players . . . He was a true gentleman, in every sense of the word."

Though Mack employed Charles Albert Bender, Macht said it wouldn't be accurate to ascribe sociological aspects to the manager's actions. He was not as overtly racist as many others, but he was a product of his time and place, nothing atypical, and he could not be classified as a pioneer in race relations. He saw in Bender a pitcher of promise, not a chance to further a cause. But Bender was fortunate to break into the big leagues with Connie Mack's team. "I'm proud to work for such a man," Bender said.

Speaking years after Bender left the Athletics, Marie was quoted as saying about Mack that he was "the grandest man who ever lived." Mack, she said, "has been a true friend and has taken care of us on all occasions, always looking out for our best interests."

In 1903, Charles Bender became acclimated to life in the big leagues, and that also meant settling into his first home ballpark. If the place looked as though it had been thrown together in a hurry that's only because it had been.

The Athletics' initial park was located on a rectangular lot on Philadelphia's north side. After Connie Mack arrived in Philadelphia in 1900 following his award of the franchise by American League President Ban

The first team Bender (head poking over shoulders) played on included one of baseball's all-time characters, Rube Waddell (arm around teammate).

National Baseball Hall of Fame Library, Cooperstown NY.

Johnson, not only did he have to find money and players, he also had to find a place for his team to play. Mack walked the city's streets, inspecting vacant lots, finally settling on one that was bordered by Twenty-ninth Street, Columbia Avenue, Thirtieth Street, and Oxford Street. He signed a ten-year lease and had just five weeks to construct a single-deck wooden grandstand.

Columbia Park was built at a cost of about $35,000. According to research by Rich Westcott, its original capacity was ninety-five hundred with "covered, wooden grandstands extending on either side of the field from home plate to first and third bases," and admittance was a quarter. A wire screen ran along the top of the grandstand roof. This was either a strange form of decoration or, more likely, a makeshift way to retain foul balls. Bleachers stretched from the grandstands down both lines and there was another thin section spread across left field. The cubbyhole that served as a press box was located in the usual spot behind home plate. A twenty-some-foot high wire fence extended from the bleachers in right field to those in center. Not only were there no luxury boxes, there weren't any dugouts. Bender and his teammates sat on benches at the side of the field. The Athletics dressed in a small common clubhouse under the stands. Visiting teams didn't enjoy such luxury; they changed in and out of their uniforms at a hotel. In other words, aside from the four-bases diamond in the middle of the field, the modern fan would not recognize much about the place as a big-league park.

Columbia was located in the so-called Brewerytown section of the city. During games, the aroma of brewing beer from nearby breweries often soaked the air. The smell was unmistakable to fans and was pleasing to the nose of more than one player on the field. While the team played at Columbia, manager Mack and many Philadelphia players, including Bender, lived in adjacent neighborhoods and were able to walk to the park.

Emil Beck lived in the neighborhood as a youth. "Rube Waddell, Chief Bender and a lot of the others lived in the area," Beck told Westcott years later. "You could often see Connie Mack and some of the players walking through the neighborhood. We used to chase after them as they walked to the ballpark.

"It cost a quarter to see a game. You had to pass through big steel turnstiles to get into the park. There weren't many vendors in there, but you could get a hot dog and a soda.

"The crowd was pretty refined. Everybody rooted for the Athletics. It was a good park for watching a game."

In the fall of 1903, after Bender had successfully broken into the big leagues, Mack called him into his office and handed him three hundred dollars—enough money for Bender to make a trip back to northern Minnesota to reunite with his family.

"It was a very fine thing to do," Bender said, "for I know the club did not make much money."

Bender would develop better control than he exhibited in 1903, but that he walked just 2.17 batters per nine innings was impressive for the youngest player in the American League. Since 1893, when the current pitching distance was established, he is one of only nine pitchers in history to have walked fewer than 2.2 batters per nine innings at age twenty or younger and, according to Chris Jaffe, he's one of six twentieth-century pitchers to throw 200 innings in a season as a nineteen-year-old. But the year was more remarkable for the memories he piled up than for the batters his whiffed.

Charles Albert Bender had beaten Cy Young as an unheralded rookie on his way to a season that could not have been more improbable. His team didn't win the pennant but it finished a strong second. He was already pitching on the same staff as two future Hall of Famers, including one of the game's all-time characters. He returned home the conquering hero, established himself as a professional, and took his first giant leap in the dominant culture. He learned about life in the big leagues, settled into his first Major League park, and became acquainted with a man for whom he would be employed for many fulfilling years, a man he would eventually consider his lifelong friend. And in Marie, Bender had met the woman who would be at his side for nearly every meaningful moment of the next half century—for every championship start and for every epithet from the stands. She would be there for the full arc of life's triumphs and trivialities, and she would be bedside the moment Bender took his last breath.

Not a bad year.

Nice going, Albert.

Chapter Eleven. A baseball fan who knows only one thing about the 1905 World Series likely knows that during that Series New York Giants pitcher Christy Mathewson achieved the otherworldly: three shutouts in six days. Although that never-to-be equaled performance (no pitcher is likely to *start* three games in six days ever again, let alone throw three complete games, let alone three shutouts) cemented Mathewson's mythic status in the pantheon of pitchers, the Series also served, albeit more subtly, as Charles Albert Bender's coming out party.

Few, however, could have expected his arrival. By mid-summer 1905, following his breakthrough season in 1903 and an illness-plagued 1904, Charles Bender had become an established Major League pitcher. But given his early track record—he was 9-9 while pitching for a team good enough to win the American League and had gone 36-34 with an ERA at about league average during his first two-plus seasons—and his fragile health history few could have imagined that he would soon flower.

Over the previous winter Bender allowed his hair to grow uncharacteristically long, and his arm grew increasingly strong. Connie Mack was so impressed by Bender's work during spring workouts he tabbed him to start the opener against Boston.

"Mr. Bender has no vermiform appendix to worry him this season, as witness his work in the exhibition series," Mack said. "The Indian was never better at any stage of his career."

On Opening Day, in front of a crowd that included guests Ban Johnson, baseball godfather Henry Chadwick, and John Weaver, mayor of Philadelphia, Bender beat Boston and Cy Young 3–2.

However, that start was more anomaly than bellwether. During the first several months of the 1905 season, Bender was erratic, and at one point the *Philadelphia North American* called him "virtually useless." The newspaper said "Bender seems to be off the reservation this season" and "the opposing team does a ghost dance every time Charles pitches." In short, his control was poor. Bender hit a lot of batters and he walked even more. He pitched adequately in relief but usually struggled in starting assignments. Rube Waddell carried the staff and Bender was a serviceable bit player, certainly not a star.

But something would soon click. In 1905, Bender broke from the crowd of pedestrian pitchers. As the summer progressed, and as the games became more crucial, he shook off a series of ailments and became a dependable pitcher. He went 9-2 down the stretch and showed his first true flash of brilliance. On September 4, he threw a two-hit, seven-strikeout shutout against Washington and two weeks later shut out New York. "There is not much in a name when the Indian is feeling right," the *North American* said, "and he was right today."

Despite Bender's emergence, the Athletics were still in a tight pennant race. They had earned a comfortable lead by Labor Day but the margin almost vanished as Chicago went on a tear, winning nine of eleven. The A's led by percentage points on September 28, when they came home from the road for three games with the White Sox, a series that was perhaps the most anticipated baseball event in Philadelphia history to that time.

Cozy Columbia Park was jammed for the three games, and ropes were stretched around the outfield. Homeowners on Twenty-ninth Street sold "tickets" at two bits a head for space on their rooftops. Eddie Plank won the first game 3–2, and on September 29, Bender prevailed in the second. He struck out five and allowed just one run as the Athletics played Nick Altrock, Ed Walsh, and Piano Mover Smith to a tune of extra-base hits. The final was 11–1.

"Bender rose to the situation, and scalped Chicago in the second game of the championship series yesterday," the *North American* said. "The Indian's speed baffled the visitors. . . . His hurling was at once plausible and scientific, being entirely too deep for the Sox.

"Bender sailed along like a duck in a puddle until the fourth. George Davis was an easy out, [Nixey] Callahan ticked off a bundle of fouls and then beat a cheesy grounder to [Lave] Cross. [Jiggs] Donaohue doubled and [Danny] Green flied to [Harry] Davis. [Ed] McFarland was intentionally walked. . . . The crafty Indian passed the bad paleface, got [Lee] Tannehill in the box and struck him out. Whereat a mighty shout went up. That was Bender's best stunt."

Chicago won the final game of the series but left Columbia Park a game behind with only a week to go. "That was the vital game for us," Mack said of Bender's effort.

That Bender turned a corner was due in part to his improving control. Whereas before he had a tendency to become wild, suddenly he pulled himself together and generally was able to put the ball where he wanted it. That was never more evident than entering play on October 5, as the Athletics held a two-game lead on Chicago with four games to play, and Philadelphia had a scheduled double-header at Washington.

Bender started the first game and scattered six hits, shutting out the Senators 8–0. He was never sharper as he struck out seven against a single walk. It was a fine performance, but Bender wasn't through for the day.

After Washington forged a 3–0 lead in the third inning of the second game Mack called on Bender for an encore. It was not uncommon in the Deadball Era for managers to push their starting pitchers, to ask them to make multiple starts in a short span of time. But almost immediately upon entry in the league Bender was said to have low stamina. He needed several days of rest between starts, or so went logic espoused in the press (logic not discouraged by Mack), and persistent ailments did nothing to dissuade that line of thinking. However, in the rare instances in which Mack asked Bender to pitch without customary rest he often flourished.

With Philadelphia on the brink of a World Series berth Bender wanted the ball, and after Mack handed it to him the right-hander promptly struck out six of nine Washington batters. He held the Senators in check much of the rest of the afternoon, and the eventual 9–7 victory all but clinched the championship. It was an incredible one-day performance. Bender pitched fifteen innings, won two games, and struck out fourteen Senators. What's more, he was the hitting hero. At the plate he made five hits in six official at bats, including two triples and a two-run double in the fourth inning of the second game that pushed Philadelphia ahead. On the day he drove in seven runs.

"Charles Albert ached to take another crack at the enemy," Philadelphia sportswriter Charles Dryden said. "His chance came in the third. . . . Squaring his long, flat feet at the plate, Charlie blazed away and a triple bumped the distant fence. Monte scored and Charles Albert plunged into third base like a bundle of old clothes."

After the performance the press began to pay more attention to him.

"Bender proved the man of the hour by . . . such batting as seldom falls even the greatest slugger," *Sporting Life* said.

"This was for sure a red-letter day in the career of our noble red man," Dryden said. "He played the cowboys, the Indians, the stage coach, the bullets, Buffalo Bill, Custer's last stand and the whole shooting match. Hooray for Charles Albert!"

And, after the Athletics clinched the pennant, the *North American* said Bender "is the talk of the town and deserves to be."

He preferred to remain out of the spotlight but that became increasingly difficult as tokens of esteem were thrown his way. One man recognized him on the street and promptly purchased a twenty-five-cent cigar and handed it to him as a throng gathered around. Another person gave him a couple of puppies.

Bender managed to escape public adulation the morning after his both-ends effort when he took a lift to the top of the Washington Monument. He wanted to appreciate a "calm and comprehensive view," one paper said, "of the great city which he held under his brown thumb the day before." Whether or not he recognized the multilayered metaphor, Bender enjoyed the view from the top.

But he was not done rising.

Ironically, Bender's role in the 1905 World Series was influenced before his hot September stretch. On September 8, the A's were on the train at the railroad station in Providence, Rhode Island. They had been playing in Boston, but Mack had given one of his pitchers, Andy Coakley, permission to visit his family in Providence, and Coakley rejoined the club as the train rolled into the station.

At the time, it was proper that skimmers, popular summer hats, were not worn after Labor Day. When spotted after the holiday ballplayers enjoyed smashing them, and while the A's were in Providence, Rube Waddell was playing that game. "The Rube has declared war on straw hats," Gene Mack, Connie's brother, whispered to Coakley. "Better watch yours."

In those days players carried their own luggage. As Fred Lieb told the story Coakley placed his skimmer under his coat, but Waddell, according to details that varied depending on who was telling them, eyed Coakley as he walked to a Pullman and ran after him. Coakley raised his bat for protection and a spiked shoe scraped Waddell's chin. "That made Rube mad and more determined to smash Coakley's hat," Lieb wrote, "and in the scuffle Waddell tripped over a bat and fell heavily on his shoulder. That night he slept by an open window, and the next morning he couldn't raise his arm above his shoulder. Though Waddell tried to come back, his shoulder remained tender for the balance of the season.

Mack blamed Waddell's arm stiffness not on the wrestling match so much as on Waddell's sitting in shirtsleeves by an open window during the train ride. Whatever the reason, Waddell had a bum shoulder and, despite efforts to return, was not able to help the A's in September and would not be available to pitch in the World Series. Rumors circulated that gamblers had gotten to Waddell, but there's little evidence to support the suspicion. The first rumor circulated in early September when there was a reasonable chance the A's wouldn't even reach the postseason.

"Anyone who knew Waddell knew how silly and ridiculous such rumors were," Mack said. "Money meant little to the Rube. He loved to play ball and to win, and he always was loyal to me."

Had Waddell been available for the 1905 World Series, it's almost certain Mack's rotation would have been different, with Rube the cinch Game 1 starter. Would Bender still have pitched in the Series? Probably. Though he had only the fourth best record on the staff, behind Waddell, Plank, and Coakley, he was in too much of a groove to leave on the bench.

The 1905 Series was the first one officially set in place as a postseason contest, and the event captured the national imagination, pitting the country's two largest and liveliest cities. So intense was the build up, so high the anticipation by fans throughout a baseball-crazed country, that legendary writer Ring Lardner dubbed the event the "World Serious."

After childish spats prevented a 1904 World Series, the two leagues were more or less at peace. The American and National leagues were considered about even; their representatives in the Series were not. The New York Giants had the best team in baseball, winners of 105 games in the regular season. They came from the biggest city and drew the most attention wherever they went. This was in no small part because of their manager, a man who did not require an introduction in Philly.

John McGraw, who would go on to win 2,763 games, second-most in history, called the 1905 team the best he managed. The Giants were runaway winners in the National League, a powerhouse. Mike Donlin, a smooth outfielder, drove the offense; he was among the top five in the league in batting average (.356), on-base percentage, and slugging, and he stole 33 bases. Third baseman Art Devlin tied for the league lead in steals with 59. Catcher Roger Bresnahan, a budding star, hit .302. At first base was Dan McGann, who had 42 extra-base hits and stole 22 bases. Sam Mertes, another outfielder, drove in 108 runs. Billy Gilbert was at second and Bill Dahlen at short. The Giants roster was filled with some of the best names in the game.

McGraw's well-rounded offense scored 44 more runs than any other team in the league. His pitching staff was not as deep, but it didn't need to be. The Giants had Christy Mathewson, the most popular player in the game and baseball's best pitcher. At twenty-four, Matty was heading toward the apex of his career. He had gone 31-9 with 32 complete games and 8 shutouts. He pitched 338⅔ innings and won 8 more games than any other pitcher, and his 1.28 ERA led the league.

Matty had excellent control, as he allowed fewer than two walks per nine innings. He led the league in strikeouts and already had pitched two no-hitters. No other pitcher was in his class, and joined with twenty-two-game winner Red Ames and Joe McGinnity, who won twenty-one and threw 320⅓ innings of 2.87 ERA baseball, headliner Mathewson had more than capable backups. New York gave up the second-fewest runs in the league.

On paper, the A's were inferior, but they were consistent winners throughout the season, never finding themselves in a long losing skid, and they produced more runs than any other team in the junior circuit. First baseman Harry Davis led the league in doubles, home runs, runs batted in, and runs scored. Outfielders Topsy Hartsel led the league in walks and on-base percentage, and Danny Hoffman was tops in stolen bases.

Philadelphia had great pitching, but without the services of Waddell, who went 27-10 with a 1.48 ERA, one of the few men on the planet to rival the mighty Matty was frustratingly on the shelf. With Waddell, the Athletics' rotation would have matched up favorably in every start of the Series. Eddie Plank won 24 games, Coakley went 18-8 with a 1.84 ERA, and Bender had the hot hand. Without Waddell, the margin of error would be small.

In those days a coin flip decided home field. Garry Herrmann, National Commission chairman, tossed up a half-dollar, and Philadelphia owner Ben Shibe successfully predicted "heads." The schedule alternated games between Philadelphia and New York. In a clubhouse talk to his players, Mack tabbed Plank in the opener and then turned to Bender: "You'll go in New York, Albert."

Before Game 1 at Columbia Park, when A's captain Lave Cross and McGraw met with the umpires to present lineup cards, Cross gave McGraw a package containing a small white elephant statue. The gag was not lost on McGraw. In 1902, sportswriters had surrounded him after he jumped from the American League's Baltimore Orioles to the National League's New York Giants. The Baltimore club had dissolved at the time the American League was created. The writers fired questions at McGraw, no fan of the young league and its president, Ban Johnson.

"What do you think of the Philadelphia A's?" one writer asked.

"White elephants!" McGraw said. "[Philadelphia owner] Mr. B. F. Shibe has a white elephant on his hands."

The press wrote about white elephants as if covering a circus, and cartoonists drew them in the newspaper as if it was a daily requirement. Mack just laughed. He put white elephants on the team's blue warmup sweaters, had one flying from the center-field flagpole, used one as a paper-weight and hung white elephants in his office.

"Boys," he told his team, "we accept McGraw's appellation. We will name our Philadelphia A's the White Elephants." The franchise Shibe and Mack formed in 1901 decades later moved to Kansas City and eventually landed in Oakland. A century later, a White Elephant remained stitched into the team's uniforms.

"Inasmuch as these were the days when the Republican Party was winning elections with the elephant," Mack said in his autobiography, "I was thankful that John McGraw's quick wit had not called us donkeys." (Mack was so closely associated with the elephant, according to one apocryphal tale, that after his team won a World Series, his players presented him with a two-ton elephant, which walked through the streets to Mack's house and ate from his lawn.)

Before the 1905 World Series, as the crowd roared with laughter, McGraw placed the elephant on his head, bowed, and danced an Irish jig. When McGraw sent his team onto the field his charges were wearing new uniforms—all black with a white NY insignia, white belts, and socks. This move made an impression. New York looked professional.

By contrast, the A's looked lackluster. If nothing else, they certainly weren't lively at the plate. In the first game, Matty dominated, allowing only four hits in a 3–0 shutout. He struck out six and didn't allow a single walk.

When the A's traveling party pulled out of Broad Street on the way to New York before Game 2, a loyal fanatic, late to the going-away party, dashed out to the gate with three bundles of flowers for Bender. He was already in the parlor car, so pitcher Weldon Henley grabbed the roses and took them to Bender, who passed them among the ladies on board.

In New York he would receive brickbats, not bouquets.

The second game marked the first time a modern World Series was played in New York. There was a large, boisterous crowd and at one point before the game a mob poured onto the field. It was a hostile environment for any pitcher, especially one with a different shade of skin. But Bender was levelheaded, described by the *New York Times* as "the much favored brave."

Bresnahan led off the game for the Giants with a double to left and the Giants knocked on the door early. But right fielder George Browne popped up trying to sacrifice Bresnahan to third. Bender then coaxed a pop up out of Donlin and struck out McGann to end the threat. "When Bresnahan, the first paleface to tackle him, poled out a double Charles never blinked," the *North American* said. "He went right on pitching while Roger stood glued to the bag until the side died out."

Bender struck out Mertes to begin the second. Dahlen then walked and promptly stole second base. Bender walked Devlin and the Giants had another excellent chance to score, but the two runners attempted a double steal and the lead runner, Dahlen, was cut down at third by A's catcher Osee Schrecongost. When second baseman Billy Gilbert grounded out to short the inning was over.

The A's scored an unearned run in the third when Schreck reached on a McGann error and later came around to score—after a "neat bunt," a sacrifice in front of the plate, by Bender—on a Bris Lord single to left.

Bender then found a groove. He sent the Giants down in order in the third, faced the minimum in the fourth—after Donlin, who had singled to right, was caught trying to steal second—and retired all six batters he faced in the fifth and sixth innings.

Donlin doubled to lead off the seventh, but Bender came back to strike out McGann, retire Mertes on a fly ball to center, and Dahlen on a pop out to the catcher in foul territory. After the ball sank into Schreck's mitt for the third out, the *North American* noted, the catcher "made an ugly face at the people." At that point Bender had retired fifteen of the previous seventeen batters and the A's were feeling as though they were back in the Series.

"A riot of sound broke out in the seventh following Donlin's two-bagger among the grass-pressers in right," the paper said. "The roar continued when Bender struck out McGann, making it three straight for Handsome Dan."

The A's scored twice in the eighth. A Hartsel double was the big blow, scoring one run and setting up a second.

New York threatened in each of the final two innings. Devlin singled to center to lead off the eighth and Gilbert followed with a fly out. Sammy Strang came off the bench to pinch hit for McGinnity, and Bender sent him back to the dugout on three strikes. But Bresnahan reached on an error by Philadelphia shortstop Monte Cross and there were two runners on when Browne grounded out to second, failing to keep the threat alive.

The ninth was similar—another A's error, this one by Danny Murphy, allowed Donlin to reach base to start the inning. Bender walked McGann but got Mertes to pop to short. Each of the final two batters, first Dahlen, then Devlin, grounded out to Murphy. "The surpassing part of Bender's performance," *Sporting Life* said, "was his remarkable work when it seemed that New York must score."

Bender had matched Matty's 3–0, four-hit shutout with one of his own. He had allowed three walks, but struck out nine, a high total in the Deadball Era.

"So tight was Bender in his pitching habits that the Giants were all but useless," the *North American* said. "His leathery darts shot past their hearts and under their noses until even the partisan New York crowd cheered the Indian. He was boss of the encampment at every stage of the way. . . . The Indian continued his great pace. He coaxed out slow bounders and pop flies and induced the best sluggers to hit at his foolers."

The *Philadelphia Public Ledger* also piled on the praise. "Great is Bender," the paper said. "Mighty his arm, cunning his skill, inspiring his name."

Two days later most members of the A's and several Giants players attended Philadelphia's Chestnut Street Theater for a show. Each Athletic was recognized as he entered the theater. First came young Philadelphia backup infielder Jack Knight, with a lady friend, and Bender followed modestly behind. A newspaper noted that, "the great Indian pitcher tried to hide behind the curtain while the crowd cheered him." Lave Cross and his wife occupied the front stage box on the right with Eddie Plank. Lord was in the box with Knight and Bender, who received as much applause as did Joseph Cawthorn, star of *In Tammany Hall.*

On the other side of the house were Hartsel, Cross, Murphy, and Davis and his wife. After the second act, Bender was handed a large bunch of American Beauty roses, and the crowd called for a speech. He bowed and remained silent. He had achieved notoriety, but he wasn't yet ready to embrace it. The *North American* notes that Bender was cheered again when the papoose chorus—a chain of children in Indian costumes—came tripping on the stage.

The Series was tied 1–1 and spirits were high in the Quaker City. But, alas, the Game 2 runs were the only ones the Athletics would score in the Series.

Mathewson started with two days' rest at Columbia Park in Game 3 and pitched another four-hit shutout, this time winning 9–0 as the Philadelphia defense fell apart behind Coakley. The next day, McGinnity tossed a 1–0 shutout against Plank, who was brilliant. A fumbled grounder, an infield out and a single produced the only run.

The Series started on October 9 and ended October 14, when McGraw—despite being ahead 3–1 in games and with an off day the following day—sent Mathewson to the mound on one day's rest to face the second hottest pitcher going, Bender. It was a terrific day for baseball and, as reported in the *New York Times*, the crowd was impatient, waiting to celebrate.

"Clinch it today," they called out to McGraw.

"That's what you'll get," he said.

McGraw sneered at Bender. "It'll be off the warpath for you today, Chief," he said.

"I'm sorry, old Pitch-Em-Heap," Mike Donlin added, "but here's where you go back to the reservation."

Bender kept his cool. "It's uncertain," he said, "but I did it once, and I am going to do my best to do it again."

The day of the game the *North American* provided reason for optimism: "But there is still hope! Mr. Bender may pitch Matty to an indefinite shutout, for both are long on that kind of slinging." Bender was good—he allowed only five hits, one fewer than Matty—but not quite that good.

When Bender took the mound the crowd in the Polo Grounds was unrelenting. "Back to the tepee for yours," hooted a rooter. "Giants grab heap much wampum," yelled another, mocking an Indian yell. Bender looked on unresponsive. But as the taunts drew to a crescendo, he stood for a moment and looked around at the scene. Perhaps he was reminded of how fantastic it all was, how if he had dreamed of this moment as a child someone would have thought him delusional. The newspapermen didn't ask what he thought about at that moment, but he thought of something. And that something made him smile.

If nothing else, the grin should have told the audience that on this day he would be indifferent to their calls. Time and again during the game, Bender was yelled at, in an effort to rattle him, but the noise might well have been directed at a brick wall. Bender remained focused on his task. Eventually, he was so effective that the jeers turned into cheers. Yes, there were times when even the New Yorkers applauded Bender's performance.

But there was only so much one man could do. New York made its runs in the fifth and the eighth. In the fifth, Mertes walked and Dahlen followed suit. With two on base the crowd roared for Devlin to drive the ball. McGraw had other ideas, ordering Devlin to bunt, sacrificing the runners to second and third. The crowd grew louder as pointed insults were directed at Bender. But if he was bothered, he didn't show it. Gilbert made a sacrifice fly and Bender escaped with only one run scoring. In the eighth, Matty scored on an infield out after he had walked and moved to third on a double. Bender was never rattled and refused to be knocked out of the box. He wouldn't allow the crowd to have the satisfaction of seeing him depart before the final out.

The runs were enough, however. As Fred Lieb noted, before the Series a Philadelphia newspaper had put up a gong west of City Hall at Fifteenth and Market streets. They were to ring the gong once for Athletic doubles, twice for triples and three times for home runs. The gong was about as useful as the Easter Bunny on Christmas. The Athletics made five doubles, no triples and no homers for the five games. Collectively, the A's hit .162.

The game took an hour and a half, and after Mathewson whipped the A's the police were unable to stop fans from flooding the field. Matty, who in his three starts struck out eighteen batters, allowed just fourteen hits and one walk—*only one man reached as far as third against him*—in twenty-seven innings. Hats, canes, and umbrellas were tossed about as Matty was mobbed on his way to the Giants' center-field clubhouse.

As Connie Mack watched that scene he must have wondered what might have been. The landscape of baseball history is littered with intriguing what-ifs; Mack and Matty were involved in one of them.

There had been a time when the Philadelphia manager had a young

Mathewson under contract. In September 1900, after the Giants sent him to Norfolk because he wasn't living up to his promise, Mack offered Mathewson a $1,200 deal with a small advance, which he signed. But not so fast, Matty, the Giants said. After news of the transaction spread, Giants officials summoned Mathewson to New York, where they mentioned that the new circuit was not a stable form of employment. Not only was the league unlikely to survive the length of Mathewson's career, the team said, if he didn't sign with New York he risked being blackballed from the National League. The tactic worked; Mathewson didn't keep his word to the A's and instead signed with New York. Mack considered legal action but never followed through. Matty may have later become the national poster boy for goodness, but in Philadelphia they didn't forget his broken promise, and Philly fans let him know it when he came to town. (Incidentally, a year later, Mack signed another future Hall of Famer, Vic Willis, to a $3,500 contract, and this time offered a sizeable advance, hoping to make the offer stick. But a similar scenario played out; Boston matched Mack's offer and Willis stayed put.)

Imagine, as Mack biographer Norman Macht has suggested, a pitching staff of Mathewson, Plank, Waddell, Bender, and Willis (and later Jack Coombs) . . . The A's might have won the first eight or ten American League pennants. Leaving Willis out of this revisionist history, had Mack and Matty been paired not only might the A's have won even more pennants, considering the copycat nature of baseball, perhaps church going would have been considered a requisite for championship play. (And given the speed with which baseball tends to change possibly yet today the Philadelphia press would be admonishing the Phillies to attend mass en masse on Sundays.)

What might have been didn't change what was. The 1905 World Series was the signature opus of Christy Mathewson, the All-American idol. The Colossus. The Christian Gentleman. The man lionized by so many for being the game's seemingly squeaky clean superstar. "Christy Mathewson," Grantland Rice once said, "is the only man I ever met who in spirit and inspiration was greater than his game."

Against the light of Matty's star, Charles Bender's performance was obscured. But the Series was a milepost in his career. He had turned a corner. He had seen up close a model for how he would develop his game, with control and class, in the years to come. And he had pitched in base-ball's greatest exhibition and acquitted himself well, allowing two runs and nine hits in seventeen innings of work against the greatest team in the land.

"If I'd started the Chief against Matty in the opener," Mack said years later, "they'd still be at it."

It was performances like that one that made it a non-decision for Con-nie Mack to hand Bender a fresh ball before games like the opener of the 1914 World Series. And after his first inning, Mack had seemed right to brush off Bender's mention of illness.

Chapter Twelve. Conventional wisdom was that George Stallings would start Bill James opposite Bender in Game 1, but the Boston manager tried to keep everyone guessing, including his own staff. The night before the game Stallings called Dick Rudolph aside and told the pitcher he likely wouldn't pitch unless the A's were running up the score. "Rudolph," Stallings said later, "went to bed that night with no anxiety on his mind." Right before the game, Stallings told Rudolph to warm up alongside James and George Tyler. The manager wanted Rudolph to prepare for the game still unawares. After the warmup, Stallings told Rudolph that he threw the ball so well that he should start. Stallings's plan all along.

Rudolph, a five-nine-and-a-half 160-pounder, was savvy if not strong. He also was focused even when he had reason not to be. His pregnant wife was said to go into labor during the game, a fact that wouldn't concern him enough to affect his performance.

When Eddie Murphy, the A's right-fielder, led off with a single to center and one out later Eddie Collins walked, Philadelphia looked ready to assert itself as expected. But Rudolph, who *Sporting Life* said was "visibly nervous," escaped when Frank Baker hit into a double play.

In these early innings Rudolph's approach was to waste pitches, trying to make the A's chase. When the A's caught on, he began filling the strike zone with fastballs, curves, and change-ups. Or at least that's the strategy as reported in newspapers after the game. In fact, Rudolph's pitch selection may have been altogether less complicated than that.

History remembers them as the Miracle Braves. Possibly, however, their sudden success was not divine creation, but rather a radical result of a wild pitch thrown by a minor league pitcher named Russ Ford one nondescript afternoon in Atlanta six years earlier.

On a rainy spring morning, Ford later recalled, he threw a ball that got away from the catcher and sailed into a wooden grandstand upright. On the subsequent pitch Ford noticed the ball dived in unintended ways. He had discovered that if you put a small scratch on a baseball you could make it do unnatural things. An otherwise unheralded pitcher, Ford reached the majors in 1910 with the New York Highlanders and went 26-6 in his first year. He began intentionally doctoring the ball using emery paper, and disguised his pitches as spitballs. He followed his 1910 season with a 22-11 mark. The next year he slumped and developed a sore arm that wouldn't go away. In 1912 he lost an AL-high 21 games. But, even after leaving the American League, he may have inadvertently altered a pennant race.

George Stallings—same guy—managed Ford in New York, and the manager may have learned what his pitcher was doing to fool hitters. Ford was not one to make wild accusations, but he did believe the emery ball played a role in Boston's success. "I've a strong hunch that George Stallings, as manager of the Boston Braves in 1914, got [the emery ball] for Dick Rudolph, George Tyler, and Bill James," Ford told *The Sporting News* in 1935.

Decades later it would be impossible to prove Ford's claims, but from May 15 to October 1, Boston won 91 games and lost just 44. That's a stretch of success that drastically belied the talent on the roster—and the run was fueled by a cadre of pitchers who had the summer of their lives. James won 37 games in his *career* and 26 of those victories came in 1914. James and Rudolph both threw more than 330 innings and their names were at or near the top of most pitching metrics.

By 1914 the emery ball was not a secret. Ford concealed his weapon for as long as possible with thousands focused on his every move, but eventually others used the pitch. Run scoring in the American League was low during the 1914 season, and perhaps the emery ball had something to do with that. The pitch was clearly difficult to hit, so much so that the following year American League president Ban Johnson banned its use. But that action came after the 1914 World Series.

If Rudolph wasn't throwing emery balls he was likely throwing spitballs, which were en vogue during the Deadball Era. Introduced around the turn of the century, pitchers freely applied an assortment of substances such as tobacco juice and licorice juice. Among other tactics, some used slippery elm to produce more saliva. Bender tried to throw a spitball but summarily abandoned the pitch. Above all else, he was a believer in control and throwing the wet one was like driving on an icy hill. The pitch demanded its thrower withdraw his powers of control.

"It must have been 1906 that I opened the season at the old Columbia Park," Bender said. "We played the Red Sox, and I came into the ninth with a lead, and I got the first two fellows out. But the next three all doubled, and then I walked two to load the bases. I went to three-and-two on the next batter before he fouled off a couple of pitches. But the next one I threw hard, low and over the outside corner. The umpire called it a strike and we won. I never threw the spitball after that. Oh, I faked it through the rest of the season, and I suppose some of the batters thought I was throwing it. But I never did. No pitcher's any good unless he knows where he's throwing the ball."

Bender understood his craft. A pitcher must throw the ball through the strike zone, but in such a way that the batter cannot make good contact. In order to reach baseball's top tier of performance, a pitcher must have pistol-like accuracy; a mistake of a few inches can mean the game. It's a physical action, but pitching is also a mental exercise. The history of baseball includes tales of physical specimens who could throw a ball through a barn but too often missed the broad side of it. Command is more than half the battle. Bender's greatest attribute was his control, and his control was the product of an intelligent mind at work.

In the twelve seasons Bender pitched for the Philadelphia Athletics leading up to the 1914 World Series, five times he ranked in the top seven in the American League in fewest walks allowed per nine innings. Four times he ranked in the top five and in 1912 he led the league. But walk rates only tell part of the story. A pitcher can throw the ball over the plate all day long, never walk a batter, and still not hold down a job. Bender studied opponents and devised an assortment of pitches to disrupt hitters' timing. He would throw breaking balls and change-ups when behind in the count, when batters were expecting fastballs. Even more rare, he would alter his delivery to present a different picture to the batter.

Bender's peers and opponents often talked about his ability to think his way through a game. His intelligence was exemplified in his understanding of one subtlety of his profession: pitching is a Zen activity. Bender was smart enough not to think too much.

He didn't break into the American League with exceptional command, but he figured out that control was an important element—many of his contemporaries believed speed was the thing—and he set about to develop it.

"I was as wild as they come in my first year with Connie Mack," he said. "What a workout I gave the catcher."

Bender did not receive much formal coaching before reaching the Major Leagues. In those days young players didn't attend instructional schools, but by the time they reached the big leagues most had received at least a modicum of coaching. Bender's apprenticeship was extremely short, even for the times. It showed. "When I tried to pitch to the batters, that is outguess them or pitch to their weakness, I never knew whether the ball was going to be caught by the catcher or the first baseman," he said. "And if I did get it near the plate it usually was in the middle and was good for long base hits." Athletics captain Harry Davis was the first to tell Bender the only way to get control is "to work for it."

"It was three or four years before I really was able to throw a ball where I wanted to," Bender said, "but from then on I knew the value of control, and practiced continually."

Even at the major league level there weren't pitching coaches. But he was fortunate to play alongside savvy baseball men and to work with outstanding receivers. Osee Schrecongost also taught him about control. The catcher would hold up his glove hand and have Bender pitch not at the mitt but to a certain spot in the mitt. "Every day, Schreck would line [Plank, Waddell, and me] up together, give each one of us a ball and hold his mitt at different spots," Bender said.

But the trick was not learned in any one exercise. Bender practiced constantly, ran until his "tongue hung out," and threw the ball almost every day. At the time, far less was known about pitcher preservation, and he did not save his arm for his starts. Because his work produced results Bender developed a theory that the ability to throw the ball over the plate was a function of work.

He also began to preach at the altar of control. "A pitcher who can put the ball where he wants to," he said, "can win with anything."

Billy Evans became a Bender fan while umpiring many of his starts. Evans was not the most reliable source in baseball, but he wasn't short on superlatives when discussing Bender, as he did in the *New York Times*.

"In all my career as an umpire I have worked back of few steadier pitchers than Bender," Evans said. "If ever a pitcher used his control to the utmost advantage it was Bender. If a batter had a weakness, and most of them have, Bender played up to it all the time."

Evans queried pitchers about what tools were most important for success. Most said speed or a wicked curve. Others cited an off-speed pitch. "Bender's reply to my question impressed me forcibly," Evans said.

"Of course, control is an acquired possession, as is the curve and the change of pace, while speed is a gift of nature," Evans said, quoting Bender, though likely not verbatim. "Speed, therefore, is about the only part of a pitcher's makeup that cannot be developed. Speed without control, however, avails nothing. Speed with control alone will make a great pitcher."

Added Evans: "I know of one batter in the American League who is lucky to make a foul when Mack's star is on the rubber, yet against the average twirler he is regarded as a good hitter. This certain player has one great weakness. It seems practically impossible for him to hit a certain kind of ball. Seldom does Bender ever pitch him anything different. I have seen Bender fan that certain player so often that it is always a relief to see him approach the plate on a warm day. You are positive there is going to be considerable air disturbance."

Evans told the story of a game in which Bender pitched against the Senators at Philadelphia. "The way he was warming up," Evans said, "it didn't seem possible for any club to do much with his offerings." But Washington batted out five hits and by the time the first inning ended Bender was dripping with perspiration.

"I was umpiring the bases that day," Evans said, "And I realized I never saw him show more stuff, yet never saw him hit much harder. As the inning ended Bender turned to me and said: 'Have I got anything on the ball, Bill?'"

"To me it looks as if you had a world of speed and a great curve, but evidently your stuff don't look that way to the Washington boys."

Bender smiled. "I'll have to slip them something different next inning."

Instead of coming back with speed, in the second Bender's fast one was such a decided contrast that Washington's timing was thrown off. "Incidentally," Evans said, "he would slip [in] his slowball and his fadeaway, with a result that the side was retired in order. During the rest of the game Bender pitched like a man with a sore arm, yet Washington made only one hit in the last eight innings."

Perhaps Charles Bender worked so hard on his control because it was one of the few things in life he alone could influence. When he was throwing the ball over the plate nothing, not even the most vehement forms of prejudice, could get in the way. He also practiced control because, even if control compromises velocity, it's an intelligent way to pitch.

"Control is the greatest requisite," he said. "Without control you are like a ship without a rudder. No matter how much power you have, you are unable to get results."

The second inning of the first game of the 1914 World Series marked a rare instance in which Bender's control failed him. He started the inning by walking center fielder Possum Whitted. Butch Schmidt, the first baseman, took a strike then flied to left. Then into the batter's box stepped Hank Gowdy.

Gowdy was an unexceptional catcher, the sixth hitter in Stallings's lineup, and not an offensive force. But there were a lot of eyes on Gowdy, including all female pairs in Shibe Park. Before the Series newspapers published a story that Gowdy's sweetheart had promised to marry him only if the Braves won the world title.

"If you haven't got a pennant," went the ultimatum, "you needn't come around."

A funny story, but a false one.

"Don't let them kid you," he told *Baseball Magazine*. "There's nothing to it. A friend of mine thought he'd have some fun with me, so he sent that fairy story around. Why, the girl is my cousin."

But in this Series Gowdy would perform as though inspired by love. With the count full Bender grooved a pitch that Gowdy whacked to the left-field wall for a double that scored Whitted. Rabbit Maranville followed with a single to center, plating Gowdy. Bender ended the inning only with help from Charlie Deal when the Boston replacement third baseman grounded to shortstop Jack Barry, who flipped the ball to Eddie Collins to start a double play.

The Athletics also broke through in their half of the second. Stuffy McInnis walked on four pitches. Amos Strunk took two balls and a strike then shot a liner to right for a single. However, Moran muffed the ball and McInnis came all the way around to score, as Strunk took third. The A's were in position to rally with one in and one on with none out.

Then Dick Rudolph made better pitches. He got Barry to chase an outside curve for strike three. Wally Schang then grounded to Evers at second, who threw home to cut off the run. There was a close play at the plate, but umpire Bill Dineen called Strunk out.

The next batter was Bender, who rubbed Louis Van Zelst's back and strode to the plate. Van Zelst, when he was seven years old, had fallen off a truck and became hunchbacked. Years later he had met Connie Mack and Mack liked the young man so much Van Zelst became the team's batboy and mascot. Rubbing a hunchback for luck was part of baseball tradition, and Van Zelst did not fail the A's. A favorite of fans and players, he "brought" the A's four pennants in the five years he was on the job.

Bender's wish was to extend the inning. He was a good hitting pitcher. For example, in 1906 he hit three homers, including two in the same game, to rank eighth in the American League. Because Bender was such a good athlete, over the years Mack used him in the field once in a while and as a pinch hitter on occasion. Against Rudolph, however, Bender managed only a roller that Maranville handled. Inning over.

But the Athletics had cut the Braves lead in half, which helped the crowd forget the stunning sight in the top of the inning, when Bender did not appear to be in control.

A wild Bender. That was inconceivable, given past performance—including one afternoon in particular: the day Charles Bender was almost perfect.

Chapter Thirteen. Jack Graney almost spoiled the occasion before it was one. The 1910 season was off to a fine start on May 12. Charles Bender had won his first four decisions, and the Philadelphia Athletics were leading the American League when Graney, Cleveland's left-handed leadoff hitter, slammed a liner off Bender into center that the *Cleveland Plain Dealer* later called a "savage drive." Rube Oldring sprinted in and plucked the ball off his shoe tops. Had the ball not been caught Graney may have been standing on second or third and this game likely would have been tossed onto the heap of other nondescript games that even baseball historians don't ruminate over. Instead, Graney trotted back to the visiting dugout at Shibe Park, and Bender began flirting with history.

He moved to the game's second hitter and Art Kruger bounced to third. Terry Turner followed Kruger and bounced to short. Three-up, three-down.

Bender had no more trouble in the second. He retired Napoleon Lajoie, one of the finest hitters of his or any other generation, George Stovall, and Ted Easterly in order. The Athletics scored in the bottom of the second, when shortstop Jack Barry drove home Danny Murphy, who had doubled with one out and advanced to third on an error.

Bender fanned his counterpart, Fred Link, to end the third. Another 1-2-3 inning.

He was clearly on his game, but there was more to Bender's sharpness than the ordinary sort of groove every talented pitcher intermittently discovers. Bender was dealing Cleveland hitters a pitch they weren't used to seeing.

The pitching gods didn't send a flash of light. At least not one Bender ever shared in surviving printed materials. It doesn't appear anyone ever taught him the pitch currently referred to as the slider. Like a lot of baseball inventions—in fact, like the origin of the game itself—there probably wasn't a single brainchild. The pitch evolved over time. As long as human beings have been throwing objects, they've been trying to make those objects do clever things as they sailed through the air.

What is known is that there isn't a record of a Major Leaguer throwing the pitch before Bender, and Bender definitely threw the pitch. According to prominent baseball historian Bill James, Bender is the first pitcher who clearly and unarguably threw a modern slider. Though that's different than saying unequivocally that he alone is responsible for the pitch's creation.

If Bender didn't invent the slider at least it can be said he largely came to throw it of his own volition. And wouldn't it be scrumptious irony if a man named Bender invented a pitch that could be accurately called by his surname?

Graney opened the fourth by again making Oldring exercise, this time less vigorously. Kruger then lifted a ball that Topsy Hartsel grabbed in left field. There were two down when Turner dug in for the second time. A shortstop, Turner didn't have any power, and he really didn't make a lot of singles, either. He would go on to hit .230 in 1910, leaving one to wonder why Naps manager Deacon McGuire wrote Turner's name in the third spot of the batting order. One of Turner's few redeeming qualities as a hitter was his eye. He wasn't afraid to take a walk, and after Bender's full-count fastball sailed into the dirt and umpire Bill Dineen called a fourth ball Turner was pleased to trot to first.

Actually, Turner may have been too giddy. With Lajoie at the plate he immediately bolted for second. The thought, of course, was that a steal would provide the great Lajoie—he was so good the team used his name as its name—with an opportunity to drive in Turner from second and tie the score. Instead, Turner took the bat out of Lajoie's hands. Philadelphia catcher Ira Thomas threw a peg to Eddie Collins at second. The play wasn't close.

The Athletics added to their lead in the bottom of the fourth. Frank Baker led off with an infield single. He advanced to second on an error and to third on a Harry Davis sacrifice. Murphy hit a screamer past Cleveland third baseman Bill Bradley, scoring Baker, making it 2–0.

In the fifth, Lajoie grounded to Barry. Bender struck out Stovall and Easterly. As one hyperbolic Philadelphia newspaper account said the next morning, Naps hitters "fell like prep school batters before the projectiles that the Indian shot to the plate."

At the time, Bender didn't even have a name for the pitch. He just knew how to throw it. Very well. As the authors of *The Neyer/James Guide to Pitchers* pointed out in that era anything and everything that broke was called a curve. The pitch referred to in the twenty-first century as the slider was first called a nickel curve. It wasn't called a slider until the 1930s. In fact, the pitch has had many names over the years: sailer, slide piece, slide ball. James said the derivation of the pitch's name is fairly clear. George Blaeholder called it a "slide ball," which was shortened to "slider" in the same way that in the late twentieth century the "cut fastball" became the "cutter" or "split-fingered fastball" became "the splitter."

Apparently, George Uhle, who began his career with Cleveland in 1919, at one point claimed to have invented the pitch. According to *The Neyer/James Guide to Pitchers*, other possible inventors include Blaeholder, Cy Young, Pete Alexander, Johnny Allen, and Red Ruffing. Elmer Stricklett, known foremost as a spitballer, may have brought the pitch to the Major Leagues. There will likely never be a single accepted originator. One claim Bender has to the slider's creation is the fact he taught Bucky Walters the pitch. "Chief Bender showed me how to throw [the slider] in 1935—and he said it was old then," Walters told *The Sporting News* in 1955.

When a man throws a no-hitter he's often both very good and very fortunate. The game isn't fair. Scorching line drives often find mitts and dribblers sometimes are hit so perfectly weak as to evade even the best infield defense. On a given pitch a fielder might stand six inches to his right or a foot to his left, and that adjustment may place him in a position either to barely make the play or just miss doing so. Charles Bender's no-hitter is not riddled with instances in which he was especially blessed with breaks. But in the sixth inning he did receive the kind of defensive gem that made his effort an ounce easier.

Bris Lord, a once and future Athletic, opened the inning with a long fly ball off Bender that Danny Murphy risked his sanity to catch. The ball had drifted foul by the time it hit the right fielder's leather, but Murphy was racing so hard his momentum carried him beyond the playing field. He had to vault himself into the paying customers to avoid a head-on with a cement wall, a battle that usually favors the wall.

Had Murphy not made the play Bender may very well have retired Lord anyway. Possibly, the play made no difference in the result of the game. Perhaps, though, the extra pitches expended on Lord would have made a later at bat more toilsome. Or maybe Lord himself would have made better use of Bender's next offering. Speculation is not a board game, but it's just as fun.

In order to throw his unnamed slider, Bender gripped the ball like a four-seam fastball. During the delivery he rolled his wrist slightly, which made his middle finger slide toward the outside of the ball. This quick flick of the wrist, often called "cutting the ball," created diagonal spin.

He threw the ball so that it moved from the center of the plate and broke toward the inside corner for a left-handed hitter and outside for a right-handed hitter, usually with a drop. The pitch moved just enough to make it tough on the hitter to get good wood on the ball. Bender had a crooked index finger on his right hand from a broken bone, and sometimes he pitched with a small splint. But that wasn't the important finger.

"The middle finger is the 'key' finger to a pitcher," Bender said. "It is the one with which a pitcher grips the ball and so long as it is in good condition a hurler should be able to pitch good ball."

It's not known whether his slightly disfigured finger had any effect on his nickel curve. More likely, he gained effectiveness from the length of his fingers, which allowed him to whip the ball with the force of a stronger man.

Philadelphia tallied single runs in the sixth and seventh to make the score 4–0, but it was becoming apparent that no more runs would be needed. This was a Thursday afternoon and the crowd was small. After Murphy's valiant grab the picture was starting to fill in for fans and players alike. By the seventh inning each out received more applause, each inning's end treated with more noticeable relief. People began to realize they might be seeing something rare. Bender's control was superb. As the *Philadelphia North American* said in the days that followed: "Inning after inning he made the Cleveland batsmen dizzy with his smokeballs."

As the game progressed, every move Bender made was watched and reacted to. Philadelphia fans were knowledgeable and demonstrative on ordinary days. They certainly didn't hold back in the midst of a no-no. Every time a Nap went down the cheers intensified.

Bender said later he didn't realize he had a no-hitter going until he returned to the bench in the seventh. That's when one Athletic player said something to him. It is a cardinal sin to even mention the word while a pitcher has the potential to join the club of men who've sent a team home without a knock. One player learned that lesson at that moment as another, not recorded for posterity, shouted, "Shut up—you'll break the spell."

Lajoie, the cleanup hitter, led off the eighth. This was his third crack, perhaps the best chance Cleveland would have to tarnish Bender's line. Lajoie fouled off the first offering, and then Bender delivered two balls— one inside, one out. Lajoie next cut at a ball over the plate and drilled it toward right field. Was it struck well enough? Long enough? Danny Murphy didn't have to move far to make the catch.

The tension swelled. Stovall grounded to Baker and the third baseman handled one of the toughest plays of the day. Baker then caught a foul pop up from Easterly. Almost there.

In a sentence, a slider is a fastball with some lateral and downward movement. In a few more sentences, a slider is thrown at a higher velocity than a standard curveball, and so the break is shorter and sharper than that of a garden-variety curve because the pitch has a shorter time in which to act. Whereas a standard deflection of a fastball is up-and-down, when a right-handed pitcher such as Bender throws a slider the spin axis is such that the deflection is nearly left-to-right. In other words, if a batter has sharp eyes he can pick up the slider because the spin of the laces creates a red dot.

If a batter doesn't eye the red dot, a slider is easily confused with a fastball because it's thrown nearly as hard and travels nearly as fast. If you've seen enough sliders to know to look for the red dot, and have good enough vision to find it, hitting them is perhaps easier than hitting a pitch that moves more. That's the rub. The Naps hadn't seen many pitches of the kind Bender was breaking off.

As Cleveland hitters stepped out of their dugout to face Bender they passed Cy Young and Addie Joss, two pitchers on the Naps' staff who had thrown no-hitters. While at the plate they stood in front of Dineen, himself a player-turned-umpire who had tossed a no-hitter in 1905. That the trick was being turned on them was no easy feat. This was not the powerful Detroit Tigers lineup, but it was a good-hitting team. The *North American* later published an editorial about Bender's effort, calling him a "credit to baseball," and saying, "To hold such mighty hitters as Lajoie, Stovall, Turner and Easterly powerless . . . is nothing short of phenomenal."

In the ninth inning, Hartsel hauled in Lord's fly to left. Bender struck out Bradley. Down to his twenty-seventh out, McGuire sent Elmer Flick to pinch-hit for Link. Philadelphia fans knew Flick well as he had stints with both the Phillies and the Athletics early in his career. McGuire wasn't calling on Honus Wagner, but Flick had a good stick. His average was a shade over or under .300 each season between 1902 and 1907. He won the 1905 batting title and later was voted into the Hall of Fame. Though a dubious choice for Cooperstown, he was certainly competent.

Bender quickly fell behind and three pitches later Flick took a healthy cut, but didn't get enough lumber on the ball. Instead of pushing one past the infield, he popped the ball back. Thomas danced gingerly underneath as Bender tried to will the baseball into the catcher's mitt.

Once Thomas secured the ball Bender did something he rarely did: yelled. It was less a cry of jubilation than it was a plea to Thomas. Bender rushed toward his catcher and grabbed the ball, tucked it into his pocket and, as fans piled onto the field, he dashed to the clubhouse.

Bender was not a one-trick pony. He was a pitcher's pitcher. He fooled around with different pitches and developed command of several. As a result he had an impressive arsenal at his disposal. He eventually threw a submarine fadeaway—a pitch that moved like the screwball, away from a left-handed hitter—and an occasional change-up, which in Bender's day was referred to as a slowball. Teammate Bob Shawkey believed Bender's knack for fooling hitters was largely a facet of this ability to change speeds.

"The Chief had a great curveball, but I'd say his greatest success came on the change-up he threw off his fastball," Shawkey said. "They'd swing at his motion, and that ball would come floating up there. It was beautiful to watch."

In 1911, Bender talked about his repertoire with *Baseball Magazine.* "I use fast curves, pitched overhand and sidearm, fastballs, high and inside, and an underhand fadeaway pitch with the hand almost down to the level of the knees," he said. "They are my most successful deliveries, though a twisting slow one mixed up with them helps at times."

Bender's best pitch, however, may have been his fastball. Teammate Eddie Collins said that neither Walter Johnson nor Amos Rusie "had any more speed when [Bender] was at his best." While it is unlikely he threw *that* hard, Bender's speed made an impression. "[Bender] makes the baseball look like a pea," New York Giants leadoff hitter Josh Devore said. "Who can hit a pea when it goes by at the speed of light?"

Jack Lapp, one of several Athletics catchers who caught Bender over the years, said the pitcher "threw a ball that was so light it felt almost like a tennis ball."

Bender's vast assortment of offerings may have also included, of all pitches, a knuckleball. In *The Story of Bobby Shantz,* Shantz said that Bender, his pitching coach, taught him how to throw one. Perhaps the knuckler was another way in which Bender confused hitters.

Reporters rushed to Bender after the game. "It was the men behind me that helped to do it," he said. "Both Oldring and Murphy made wonderful catches. . . . It was just an ordinary championship game to me. I tried to win it, of course, and when in the seventh inning I realized that Cleveland had not made a hit, I determined to get something I have never obtained before."

Bender responded to questioners with self-effacing answers. Whether or not he wanted to, he knew his place was not to brag.

"What do I owe my pitching ability to? None other than Connie Mack," he said. "Fans think that I am an old-timer, but they are wrong. I am a youngster and hope to win many more games for Connie Mack."

The game lasted an hour and thirty-six minutes as Bender faced the minimum twenty-seven batters in the 4–0 win. He retired the Naps 1-2-3 in eight of nine innings. It was the second no-hitter in Athletics history, the first in Shibe Park, and the thirteenth in American League history. It's hardly a stretch to say that he had just pitched the greatest game in Philadelphia since the Athletics joined the American League in 1901.

During his first eight years in the Major Leagues, Bender had continued to hone his craft. Though his win-loss record fluctuated over that span, his ERA dropped every year, to a career-best 1.58 in 1910. That year he also won a career-high twenty-three victories against only five defeats, which gave him the league's top winning percentage. Having been plagued by various illnesses during several of his initial seasons, Bender was in the best condition of his career, and his reputation as an intelligent pitcher was growing.

"Brains played as much a part in the master triumph of Bender's as mere strength of the arm," the *North American* said. He is "a student as much as he is a pitcher."

Years later he was asked about his nearly perfect game. "I almost had heart failure before it was over," he said. "Didn't think I could get away with it until two were out in the ninth. Then I almost missed it. . . . Well, Flick got two strikes and then popped up a little foul behind the plate. . . . Thomas was the catcher and he went for the ball. It bounced right out of his glove and over his head. But Ira lunged around and grabbed it again—and held it. Whew."

Thomas also recalled the game years later. "I thought that Indian would scalp me that day," he said. "Until then I never knew how mad an Indian could get. Usually the Chief just smiled his way through the tight spots— the smile that wrecked a batter's confidence—and pitched curves that broke their backs."

Chapter Fourteen. Bender followed his no-hitter with a four-hit shutout of Chicago to win his first six decisions. With the no-name pitch in his hip pocket, he threw a one-hitter in mid-June and started 1910 with a 10-1 record as he and the Philadelphia Athletics soared to the top of the baseball world with few people doubting their legitimacy. Even Connie Mack, a man who displayed bravado about as often as a member of the clergy curses in church, was fired up early.

"We have played three games so far this season and lost two of them," he said, "yet I will say that I have the strongest and most resourceful team that I ever shaped for a pennant fight, and I don't except the Athletics of 1902 and 1905, which won American League pennants. . . . I won't mince words one bit: nothing on earth can keep the Athletics out of the pennant running this season except wholesale accidents and the collapse of my pitchers."

Usually, the Athletics were at least in the mix. By 1910, in addition to Mack's two previous league championship teams, the A's finished second in 1903, 1907, and 1909. In fact, they may have missed winning the 1909 flag only because of late-season injuries that were more difficult to shoulder after the team's lethargic play in the early months of the schedule. They finished 3½ games behind Detroit and, based on the number of runs they scored and prevented, may have underachieved by a fatal

During the 1910 World Series Bender was "the big noise in baseball in Chicago." Chicago Historical Society. SDN-058734.

margin. A slow start would not be a problem in 1910. Mack knew there was something special about this team.

"I know it's not my habit to be so optimistic at the brink of a six-months pennant campaign," he said, "but I can't exaggerate the strength of the team that I have this year. Just watch our smoke."

Mack liked to use Bender in games that were likely to draw a large crowd, and so he had started the home opener, pitched a shutout, and went 2-for-4 as the Athletics beat New York 6–0. "Chief Bender, nourishing an arm sublime," the *North American* said the next day, "was always interfering with the best laid plans of [manager George] Stallings and the Highlanders."

At the end of June, Bender was 12-2 after beating Boston. "Bender is shooting poisoned darts at the palefaces this season," the *North American* said.

But in July he missed two weeks because of "an illness" that was not explained in the press. By this time the Athletics were starting to run away from the league—they already held a seven-game lead by July 13—and so no minor malady was seen as potentially crippling, especially since Philadelphia had other pitchers capable of eating innings in Bender's absence. In fact, as good as Bender was in 1910, it would be hard to argue that he was even the most valuable pitcher on his own staff.

John Wesley Coombs, nicknamed Colby Jack in a nod to his alma mater, had the year of his life. Coombs entered the 1910 season a lifetime 35-35 pitcher and by the end of the summer nearly doubled his career win total. Using a refined sinker and excellent control, Coombs threw 353 innings of 1.30 ERA baseball that season. He led the American League in wins with thirty-one, including thirteen shutouts; even in the Deadball Era, it was a remarkable year.

At one point, Coombs pitched five times in eleven days and won all five games. He threw 16 shutout innings in a single game and during one stretch went 53 straight innings without yielding a run. Coombs anchored a staff that easily led the league in fewest runs allowed. Cy Morgan went 18-12 with a 1.55 ERA, and Eddie Plank, even in an off year, posted a 2.01 ERA with sixteen wins. At various times, Bender was ill, Plank was off his game, and Harry Krause injured, but Coombs stabilized the rotation, and Philadelphia had a staggering team ERA of 1.79.

There was no area of the game in which the 1910 Philadelphia Athletics were inadequate. Their pitching staff was augmented by excellent team defense. They also had one of the top lineups in the American League. By this time, Eddie Collins, a player Mack called "a marvel," had established himself as a star. Who was the greatest player in the land? Ty Cobb. But when baseball men debated the question Eddie Collins's name was always in the conversation.

The slick-fielding, sharp-minded second baseman arrived in Philadelphia in 1906. He had played football at Columbia University and, in an effort to preserve his amateur status, initially played under the name Ed Sullivan. Turns out, he was a big show. Collins settled in as a regular at second base in 1908 and was eventually nicknamed "Cocky" because, well, he was. But he had the physical ability to reinforce his confidence. He stood close to the plate, seldom chased bad pitches, and hit to all parts of the field. In Collins, Bender played with one of the most accomplished all-around ballplayers ever to play the game. "Collins sustained a remarkable level of performance for a remarkably long time," Bill James once wrote. "He was past thirty when the lively ball era began, yet he adapted to it and continued to be one of the best players in baseball every year . . . his was the most valuable career that any second baseman ever had."

Collins had an exceptional career, batting .333 over twenty-five seasons. There were few areas of the game in which he did not excel. A left-handed hitter, he made 3,315 hits and stole 741 bases. He was also an exceptional fielder, a fine bunter (no knock in those days), an excellent base runner, and had hit-and-run quality bat control. Perceptive and determined, he helped his mates whether on the field or in the dugout. He was the premier player in Mack's "$100,000 Infield," with Jack Barry at shortstop, Stuffy McInnis at first base, and Frank Baker at third, a quartet that had terrific individual skills and cohesiveness. The A's were close on and off the field, and many relationships would continue into retirement. Over time Bender and Collins became close friends and, years later, when Collins was hired as manager of the Chicago White Sox, he hired Bender to coach his pitchers.

When Bender returned to the A's on July 23 he pitched his first game in fifteen days, and there was no easing his way back into the rotation, no pitch count. A man ready to pitch in the Deadball Era was ready to pitch all day, if circumstances warranted such an effort. Bender went fifteen innings, allowing seven hits and one run. He retired Cleveland in order eleven times in a single outing. When he was beaten four days later, it was his first loss since mid-June.

During the second week of August, Bender tossed a six-hitter to push his record to 17-3 and augmented the Athletics' margin in the American League. By that point Philadelphia had an 11-game lead in the loss column over the Boston Red Sox. On August 24, Bender won his twentieth game, the first time he had passed that benchmark, and again Cleveland was the victim at Shibe Park. He allowed six hits, one run, and struck out a whopping twelve batters while walking just two.

"Chief Bender is truly a wonder," the *North American* said. "He has been winning so often this season that the crowd takes a victory as a matter of course. His work was superb."

In his next start, four days later, Bender struck out eleven, walked one and allowed three hits in a 5–1 victory over the St. Louis Browns. Only four runners reached base. He had notched twenty-three strikeouts in two games, a total not often recorded in the day.

"All the other Browns fell as soon as Bender saw the whites of their eyes," the *North American* said.

Bender had taken his performance near its peak, and plaudits from the press were plentiful. "During several of the seven seasons he has pitched for the Athletics, he has been troubled with serious illness that kept him out of the game for long periods," the newspaper said. "His health has been better this year than ever before, with a result that he has exceeded all past efforts, good as they have been. . . . In condition there is no better pitcher in the world than the Indian."

The 1910 Philadelphia Athletics were the first American League team to top the 100-win plateau. Collins batted .324 with 81 stolen bases, and Baker, emerging as a standout, hit .283 with 74 RBI. The pair led an offense that scored 674 runs, five fewer than Detroit, and hit .266, tops in the league. Philadelphia's winning percentage was .680, the highest in the league's ten-year history. The A's also drew the most fans.

They started slowly but took the league lead in the first week of May, and built a commanding margin by June. By the time the season ended they won the AL by 14½ games. As early as September 2, already sitting on an eleven-game lead, Mack began preparing for a meeting with the Chicago Cubs in the World Series.

Before the 1910 Fall Classic a Chicago sportswriter wrote: "Bender was built for the Cubs [to hit] in the World Series." Charles Bender read newspapers and was fully aware of the people who doubted his ability, whether the criticism was of the usual ilk—sportswriters needing to fill column inches with provocative words to sell newspapers—or those who genuinely believed there was a ceiling on what a man without white skin could achieve. That doesn't mean, of course, Bender listened. He didn't become visibly agitated by the story, at least not publicly. Instead, he cut the pieces out, tucked it into his wallet, and used it to fuel one of the most impressive performances of his career.

Two quasi-controversies bubbled to the surface in the days before the first game. The creative and apparently disparate schedule makers of the American and National leagues decided to end their respective seasons a full week apart. The AL concluded on October 8, the NL on October 15. This fact was known for months, of course, but in the week before the Monday, October 17, Series opener Philadelphia newspapermen were aghast that the local nine had to sit around and accumulate rust while the opponent could continue to remain fresh, playing Major League games. "The idiocy shown in arranging the National League schedule" was the *North American's* phrasing.

Perhaps the most competitive moment of the Series was the coin toss to decide home-field advantage. Charles Webb Murphy, owner of the Cubs, said the flip—in which he was present, representing his team opposite Philadelphia owner Ben Shibe—was unethical. "It was agreed fully before the toss was made that if the coin rolled off the table the toss was to be unfair and another should be made . . . the coin fell to the table and rolled off onto the floor," Murphy said. "[American League] President [Ban] Johnson followed the coin half way across the room and bent over it as it settled to the floor. He then announced, 'It's heads. Uncle Ben, you win.'"

Whether played in Philadelphia, Chicago, or on some other continent, the games were likely going to turn on pitching. Connie Mack had a rotation that set up well for a short series: Bender, Coombs, and Plank.

Mack has "one of the greatest pitching staffs it has been the fortune of a major league club to own," the *North American* said.

"Bender is an ideal pitcher, backing up great speed and good curves with brains. The Indian's very manner in the box is one of overwhelming mastery. . . . In the most critical situation he is as cool and well poised as a man smoking his evening cigar in a rocking chair."

Among Philadelphia fans, the paper said, there was speculation about two points—the outfield alignment and the catching department. Davis, Collins, Barry, and Baker were locks to man the infield in every game of the Series. But it was possible Mack would make a shift in the outfield. Murphy, in right, and Oldring, in center, were fixtures, but Oldring had broken his leg in August, his place taken by twenty-one-year-old Amos Strunk. Bris Lord was the most likely choice in left.

Then again, the Athletics' opponent had its own injury to deal with.

As difficult as it may be for the reader to fathom, there was a time when the Chicago Cubs were consistent, reliable, and so good they were jinx-proof. Led by manager and first baseman Frank Chance, the Cubs won three straight National League championships—in 1906, 1907, and 1908— and consecutive World Series in the latter two years. By winning yet another pennant in 1910 the team put a capstone on a run of historically noteworthy proportions. As Bill James has pointed out, between 1905 and 1910 the Cubs won an astounding 622 games. That is the record for most wins by any team in a six-year period. By a large margin.

The 1910 edition was essentially the same team that had piled up all those victories. At 104-50, the Cubs cruised to the National League flag, beating John McGraw's New York Giants by 13 games. They didn't fall out of first place at any point from May on.

The formula was familiar. These were Franklin Adams's Tinker-to-Evers-to-Chance Cubs, and they played sensational infield defense, anchored by first baseman Chance, the "Peerless Leader," and shortstop Joe Tinker, the same Joe Tinker Bender faced in Harrisburg eight years before and who by now was a celebrity in the streets of Chicago. And no National League team scored as often. The Cubs led the league in runs per game by slugging the ball around the yard. Center fielder Solly Hofman hit .325 and stole 29 bases. Right fielder Frank "Wildfire" Schulte hit 10 home runs, which tied him for the league lead, and hit .301 with

22 steals. In 1911 Schulte would become the first NL MVP when he led the league in homers, triples, and RBI.

The Cubs were also outstanding at run prevention. Mordecai Peter Centennial Brown, a man with more names than a crew of sailors, was the staff ace. They called him Miner. They also called him Three Finger. When he was a boy, Brown was playing on his uncle's farm when his right hand became caught in a feed chopper. His index finger was amputated above the second knuckle, and two other fingers were impaired permanently. Weeks later, while playing with a rabbit in a tub, he fell and broke several bones in the same hand and those bones healed unnaturally. Tragic accidents? No doubt. Such disabilities also allowed him to throw a ball with the kind of movement that—if coupled with the fortitude and skill Brown otherwise possessed—ensured enshrinement in a museum in upstate New York.

Brown won 25 games in 1910, pitched 295⅓ innings, and had an ERA of 1.86, the sixth time in seven seasons he posted a sub-2.00 ERA. During that span he won 145 games, and his line in the history books tells a story of one of the most effective pitchers of the Deadball Era. Amazingly, though, in 1910 Brown didn't even lead his own team in ERA. King Cole became an unexpected contributor in his first full season, going 20-4 with a 1.80 mark. Cole pitched almost sixty fewer innings than did Brown, but he had the kind of season that allowed the Cubs to claim a top of the rotation that could match with that of the A's.

However, the Cubs would be without star second baseman Johnny Evers, who broke his fibula sliding into the plate in early October. "Johnny may never play again, and if he does, he will never be the fast man that he was," catcher Johnny Kling said. "The bone in his foot looks like it is powdered."

The A's would learn four years later that Evers's fate was different than Kling's premonition, but the second baseman's absence would make Chicago less formidable in 1910. Even so, the Cubs were the favorites, at least according to odds-makers.

Famed baseball writers from all over the country, including Hugh Fullerton and Grantland Rice, were on hand for Game 1. Ring Lardner was there, too. A couple even came all the way from Cuba. Several Major League players, including Addie Joss of Cleveland and Bill Donovan and Ty Cobb of Detroit, were there to "cover" the Series as well by watching games and working with ghostwriters.

Philadelphia was wild with anticipation. It had been five years since the A's had won the pennant and, after second-place finishes in 1907 and 1909, A's fans were buzzing. Shibe Park was packed, and youngsters scaled walls in an effort to find a vantage point. Reserved seat prices were fixed at $1 to $3. Of course, those prices were face value. Some $1 seats went for as much as $4.

Before the first game Connie Mack wouldn't say one word in regard to his plans for the battle with the Cubs. "It has always been my practice to announce my battery for the next game to the morning papers, but I am not going to do this in the series with Chicago," Mack said. "Too much hinges on the result of the games, and no person will know the identity of my pitcher and catcher, as well as the rest of the lineup, until the teams are sent in action by the umpires."

But newspapers were free to speculate, and so they did. "Everybody guesses," the *North American* said, "that Bender will be the pitcher used in the opening game."

Privately, Mack called Bender aside. "I am turning this situation over to you, Albert," he said. "I think you can take care of them."

The day was perfect—one of those ideal afternoons for baseball, a day where one would have had to check the calendar to see whether it was, in fact, October and not May. Sun soaked the backs of players as they went through their pregame routines and, as the Athletics took batting practice, there were almost as many photographers on the field as players. Manager Chance went to the A's bench and chatted with Mack. Moments later Chance and Davis were photographed together shaking hands. In front of the Mackmen bench, Louis Van Zelst, the A's hunchback mascot, and Ted Davis, son of the A's captain, played catch. When the Cubs came onto the field they were applauded.

Not that Philadelphia fans were nonpartisan. "Delirium," one newspaper said, had been gathering force for a month, "ever since it became apparent the A's would play for the world title." The fervor climaxed in the moments before the game. As fans stirred in their seats the rest of the city stood still. City Hall, for one, was vacant, and the demand for tickets had exceeded the supply.

Bender went to the mound at 1:59 p.m., but he stood there for thirteen minutes before he threw the game's first pitch. He waited. There was an earnest conference between the four umpires, captain Harry Davis and manager Chance, as the men wrangled over the "moving picture man's" on-field vantage point.

The scene was starkly different from the setting of the Series five years earlier at Columbia Park. Baseball had grown into a bigger spectacle, and the venue, Shibe Park, was to Columbia Park what the Taj Mahal was to a row house in Brewerytown. By now, too, Philly fans had warmed to Bender, and when the right-hander came out to warm up, he had been hailed with shouts from the crowd.

In turn, he gave the faithful something to hoot about. For eight innings he mystified the mighty Cubs.

Jimmy Sheckard, the leadoff batter, fouled Bender's first pitch and Bender tried the corner and missed on the next two. Before he could hurl the ball again, an umpire stopped the game because the moving picture man had roamed behind the plate and the umpire ordered the man off the field. Two pitches later Bender restored order by whiffing Sheckard.

Then Schulte lashed a fastball over Jack Barry's head and into left field. The Cubs' strategy was to test A's catcher Ira Thomas every chance they could, and Schulte bolted for second on the next pitch. Bender's offering was high, not an easy pitch to handle, but Thomas snagged the ball and sent a beam to Collins at second. A beautiful throw. That was perhaps the turning point in the game. Entering the Series it was believed the Cubs could run on the A's backstops. But there would be no rampant running of the bases on this day.

Meanwhile, the A's walked over Cubs starter Orval Overall, who had success in the 1907 and 1908 World Series, but was chased in three innings by Philadelphia. The A's scored three runs and made six hits, and Baker was the offensive star of the game. The third baseman went 3-for-4 with two doubles that may have been triples if not for the overflow crowd in the outfield.

Baker's first hit, in the second inning, was a smash to left that would have rolled a long way. In the eighth he again whaled the ball on a line to the wall in right center, a foot from the top of the fence. The first two times up Chance shifted his outfielders to play for the pull hitter. But Baker went the other way, first for a double down the line, next for a base hit in the third. Bender chipped in a big hit—one that "almost lopped off Zimmerman's right hand with a slasher in the second," is how the drive was described by the *North American*—that plated Murphy for the game's second, and what would prove to be the winning, run.

Baker also acquitted himself in the field as he flawlessly handled five chances at third, none of them easy plays. Barry made a sensational play in the seventh, when he smothered Sheckard's high bouncer and nipped him at first. Bender struck out Schulte, and Baker cut off a hit by making a crowd-pleasing play on Solly Hofman's well-struck ball.

Bender had faced twenty-four Cubs in the first eight frames and twenty-four Cubs were retired. (Twice a player reached first—Frank Schulte in both instances—and each time Thomas gunned him down trying to steal second.) He may have had his second World Series shutout if not for two errors in the ninth. Joe Tinker was the first man to bat in the inning, and he popped a short foul. Thomas got under the ball but didn't squeeze it. With another chance, Tinker singled to center and went to second when Strunk, Oldring's replacement, fumbled the ball. Kling singled, scoring Tinker with the only Cub run of the day. Wipe out either error and it's possible Bender would have exceeded his 1905 performance with a one- or two-hit shutout.

As it was he allowed only three hits—all singles—struck out eight and, despite falling behind several hitters, walked two. The Cubs managed to bat only two fly balls into the outfield. Baker made the last putout at third but tossed the ball to Bender on the way to the bench. The final: A's 4, Cubs 1.

Bender's performance drew raves; he was commended even before he won the game. When he came to bat in the fifth, he received a rousing reception, just after he had fanned two Cubs hitters. After the game, the *North American* said "Bender's name was on every tongue" and the Cubs had been "dispatched by this bronzed necromancer of the knoll."

"I don't believe I ever saw better pitching than Bender did today," American League president Ban Johnson said.

"So well was the right arm of the Indian stored with fathomless curves," scribe James Isaminger wrote.

"It was Bender's day, Bender's game, Bender's glory," the *Philadelphia Press* said. "He put a chain and muzzle on the mighty Cub and tied him to a hitching post."

The *Press* also delved into Bender's backstory: "As he tells the story this prejudice, instead of embittering, hardened him, made him oblivious to the crowds, aroused in him a cool, calculating determination to win in spite of the jeers and cheers. Out of his brave, competent, sensitive soul he has evolved patience, indifference to outward circumstances and the ability to concentrate mind and muscle to their utmost endeavors."

Eddie Collins's column was published in various newspapers: "Bender was absent from our club on the last trip to the west. [He] scouted the Cubs playing in the east. As a result Hofman and Zimmerman were baffled completely by Chief's curves. To Bender alone goes the credit for the stonewall defense. He commanded, directed and instructed his seven assistants in the field while Ira Thomas behind the bat was ever alert for any oversight on the Chief's part.

"If for instance Bender chose to pitch on the outside to a man like Chance, the infield and outfield both knew it and shifted accordingly. . . . As a result, practically all the chances handled by our infield were easy ones. The secret of Bender's success was fundamentally control, the ability to put his curve or fastball where he and [Thomas] diagnosed the weakness of his opponent. . . . Chief relied on his curveball as frequently as his fast one. He outguessed the batter time and time again.

"But it's nothing new for Bender. He is what might be termed a versatile pitcher, always doing the unexpected."

Cobb, or his ghostwriter, also wrote about Bender's "wonderful" work in the *Press* the next day: "Bender's feat can be recorded as one of the greatest games ever known in a big series."

The performance, Cobb continued, "not only illustrates the remarkable nerve, speed and control which the Indian twirler exhibited, but it also shows that the Athletics played jam-up ball. But for two unfortunate and possibly excusable errors in the ninth inning I think the Chief would have not only scored a shutout, but would have finished the game with a record which would have made the baseball statisticians search their books to discover when it had been equaled."

In the 1910 World Series Philadelphia pitchers threw a total of 45⅔ innings and—because of Eddie Plank's sore arm—only two A's threw pitches. Bender was very good and Jack Coombs was even better.

In Game 2, Coombs beat Three Finger Brown, who was touched up for thirteen hits and nine runs, including six runs and three doubles in the seventh, before being pulled. With only one day's rest, Coombs notched another win in Game 3. The A's scored eight runs in the first three innings, bouncing starter Ed Reulbach and reliever Harry McIntire. Murphy's three-run homer in the third became a source of controversy when Chance insisted it should have been declared a ground-rule double. His argument led only to his ejection, the first time a player had been tossed from a World Series game. Coombs also had three hits.

Bender had a chance to seal a sweep in Game 4 as he was scheduled to pitch opposite young King Cole. Before the game the *North American* noted that, "Bender is the big noise in baseball in Chicago. A flock of adoring kids are at his heels every time he leaves the door of the hotel."

The Mackmen made 10 hits off Cole in eight innings but could score only three runs. Bender had an excellent opportunity to break the game open in the sixth, when he came to the plate with the bases loaded, but he was able only to push a can of corn to the outfield for the third out. He pulled out of minor jams in the first and fourth innings and allowed single runs in each inning, then held the Cubs in check for four innings as the A's took a one-run lead, 3–2, into the ninth.

With the count even at a ball and a strike, Schulte doubled to right and Hofman sacrificed him over. Chance then drove one to center that Strunk misjudged; he came in when he should have gone out. The misjudgment resulted in a triple, with Schulte scoring the tying run. Barry forced the game into extra innings with an acrobatic catch against the wall near third base.

With one out and a runner on second in the tenth, Brown, on in relief of Cole, hit a ball to Barry, who made a clean stop and a rapid throw to first. Sheckard then singled to center and the Mackmen's chance at the first World Series sweep was over. Bender pitched well, allowing nine hits in 9⅔ innings while striking out six and walking two. But the nine hits included two doubles and a triple, and every one of the three extra-base drives figured in the scoring.

Brown and Coombs again matched up in Game 5 and both pitchers went the distance. Brown allowed only four hits through seven innings and kept the game close at 2–1. But the floodgates opened in the eighth when Philadelphia scored five runs and Coombs earned his third World Series win in six days.

"It's all over," the *Philadelphia Inquirer* said. "The Athletics are champions of the world, and there is not a flaw to the title."

Coombs or Bender pitched every inning, allowing only 14 earned runs. The pair also went a combined 7-for-19 at the plate, a .368 clip. Offense was perhaps the biggest story of the Series as the A's compiled an astounding .316 team batting average. Collins hit .429 with four stolen bases and Baker hit .409 with six runs.

"I believe," Mack said, "we would win the pennant in any league with the team we have now. . . . too much credit cannot be given Coombs and Bender, our catchers and the other men, especially the infield, for the showing they have made in this series."

The team celebrated the city's first championship with an impromptu party in the lobby of the La Salle hotel. During a noisy reception several players addressed the elbow-to-elbow crowds. "World Champions" banners were hoisted as fans shouted themselves hoarse.

Bender and his wife, Marie, were standing in a corner of the room. Soon the Athletics would board the team train and head back to Philly. Before the train's starting time, several of Bender's relatives and friends from the Midwest, folks who had traveled to watch the Series, appeared to wish him goodbye. And a band of American Indians was there to provide, as newspapers noted, "lusty war whoops" on Bender's behalf. But at the moment, the couple was taking it all in. Meanwhile, Jack Kingston, a vaudeville actor and a Philly fan who traveled to Chicago to witness the historic triumph, led a chorus of "Philadelphia for Mine," a song he wrote on the spur of the moment that was a take off from "California for Mine."

The group sang with jubilant voices:

Philadelphia, you for me, and of you I'll boast
There's no ball team I can see like Mack's who upset the dope;
You can have your Chicago Cubs, Pittsburg may be fine
But the slugging White Elephant, you for me—Philadelphia for mine.

A newspaper reporter approached and asked Marie her view of the events that, no matter whatever else happened, would mean her husband would forever be called a world champion.

"The Athletics won because they were the best team," she said. "I guess the big Chief and Coombs surprised some of the wise persons in Chicago. I am so happy I can't talk."

In 1910, Charles Bender had found glory. Fame followed closely behind. When the train pulled into town thousands waited to greet the champs, many holding copies of the *Philadelphia Evening Times*, which had just hit the streets with the big news.

Following the triumph *Sporting Life* declared that "Bender does not suffer from race prejudice." Without irony, the popular national publication offered proof of the claim: "The Athletics hold him in the highest personal esteem and welcome him to their family gatherings, as well as their base ball coteries. The Indian, according to all who know him, is a fine character—the sort of noble red man that Cooper painted in his novels—clean-minded, sympathetic, proud of his race and their traditions, and yet a good American citizen."

No doubt, Bender had started to receive enthusiastic applause throughout the baseball world—and nowhere was the ovation louder than in Philly.

Chapter Fifteen. The fans that cheered for Charles Bender at the 1914 World Series lived in a city sectioned by lines of ethnicity. Germans, Italians, and Irish—there were large numbers of each—lived in distinct neighborhoods among family and friends who shared common interests and beliefs. More than most major cities during this time, when immigrants were still streaming across the shore, Philadelphia was a WASPy town. American Indians, especially those less well known than Bender, were paid lower wages than whites, and they struggled even more because of the influx of immigrants, who often received jobs they sought. Many whites looked down their noses at Indians. Newspaper classified ads could be found, for example, that openly required that applicants be "Protestant" and "white." No, the city did not always embrace those of other races and ethnicities; the rivers of racism ran through the City of Brotherly Love. But by the 1914 World Series, Bender, whose salary was good, though not likely as high as it should have been when compared with his peers, was in a different category in the minds of many who had seen his finest efforts on behalf of the hometown team. Crowds became excited whenever Bender shuffled, head down, gentle as a breeze, to the center of the diamond.

Many of these fans spent their days working on the railroad, in banks, or at factories. They made engines, steamships, and boilers; nuts, bolts, and rivets; horseshoes and nails. Philadelphia at this time was a world leader in textile production. Workers manufactured woolens, hosiery, and counties of carpet. They made and served some of the most delicious ice cream found anywhere. At one point during Bender's first decade in the city the local chamber of commerce claimed that Philadelphia was the "Workshop of the World."

Bender's career played out in a city that was in full bloom. Between 1901 and 1915 the Philadelphia population exploded. During Bender's early years in Philly the city was the largest in the country in terms of geography. As chronicled in *Philadelphia: A 300-Year History*, by 1904, 129 square miles contained some 300,000 families, many of them living in good homes within walking distance of work or school. At the start of the 1914 World Series, the city had already outgrown itself and had become an early example of urban sprawl. The gridirons of row homes, the railroads, factories, freight yards, and warehouses—often springing up without planning—created congestion and pollution. A city of steam and smoke had replaced William Penn's green country town. The noise made by the internal-combustion engine was a noticeable part of the city's soundtrack. The year Bender first played in a World Series, 1905, there would be fewer than five hundred automobiles registered in the city. By 1918, there were more than a hundred thousand. As Bender and the A's climbed to the top of the baseball world, Philadelphia joined other major cities in constructing buildings that scraped the sky.

The day had passed when the country looked to Philadelphia as a leader in intellect, arts, and letters. "Philadelphia's diminishing role in the cultural leadership of the nation offered further confirmation of a loss of vitality," wrote the authors of *Philadelphia: A 300-Year History*. "The source of many of America's most illustrious writers, artists, and actors in the nineteenth century, the city could claim few such in the early twentieth century." But the city had become a middle-class haven, employing thousands of skilled workers who had good jobs. Many had money in their pockets to spend in Market Street department stores and access to transportation that would take them to ballgames.

The government conducted under Penn's statue at City Hall—then the tallest point in Philadelphia—was accused (with reason) of fraud and mismanagement. The educational system was overcrowded and underfunded. The city was conservative. Cautious. Drab. Philadelphia was a place of conformity, a place where blood counted as much as achievement. Famous journalist Lincoln Steffens proclaimed the city was "corrupt and contented," and in 1906 novelist Henry James wrote in *The American Scene* that Philly was "settled and confirmed and content." Not long after, *Harper's Magazine* said that the one "unforgivable" thing in Philadelphia is "to be new, to be different from what has been."

One way citizens expressed themselves was by joining a service club. Charles Bender, searching for his home amid this city, was among them. When he was twenty-seven years old, he had petitioned a local Masonic lodge, the Robert Lamberton, Lodge No. 487, and was raised on April 4, 1911. Being raised meant Bender had finished the requirments of the master's degree and was considered a Master Mason. Bender's membership would be suspended for five years in the late 1930s and early 1940s, likely because he did not pay his dues, but he was more or less a Mason for forty years.

It's not clear to what extent being a Mason influenced Bender's life, as it wasn't a topic covered in the press. Given the constant reminders that he was distinct from his white friends, he likely used his membership as a way to feel connected, to be counted among those in mainstream society. Freemasons of the time were described as a band of equals joined together in a belief in a supreme being, though Masonry itself does not profess a specific religion. Not surprisingly, Bender's views on God were not written about by sportswriters. But it's likely, given the nature of his boarding school education, that he considered himself a believer and possibly a Christian.

Freemasonry has been described as liberal and democratic, but Freemasons have not been affiliated with party politics. In fact, political discussion was banned at lodges. A Mason at the time was typically religiously tolerant and loyal to the government. A Mason appreciated win-win compromise. The idea was that men who held different views could meet and enjoy each other's company, no matter the hot-button issues of the day. (Though, ironically, Masonry of the time enforced racial segregation.)

Being a Mason was not especially rare during Bender's lifetime. By the 1930s, there were more than two million Freemasons in America, and in Bender's early adulthood a number of public figures were said to be Masons, including presidents McKinley, Roosevelt and Taft. Teddy Roosevelt, in fact, made statements about the organization and, in 1898, wrote that, "I enjoy going to some little lodge where I meet the plain hard-working people on the basis of genuine equality. . . . It is the equality of moral men."

The Masons were one of many service organizations in the city during Bender's life and baseball career. Philadelphians, after all, found identity in the clubs they belonged to, the families they were born or married into, the societies with which they affiliated themselves, and the teams they rooted for.

Philadelphians worked hard and played hard, and baseball helped relieve them of the monotony of industrial work. The city had been a big baseball town for decades, but Philadelphia hadn't seen anything resembling the run these Athletics were on. During the 1914 World Series the city was the capital of the baseball world. Owners, players, managers, fans—nearly every prominent dignitary in the game was on hand. Credentials had been issued to more than a hundred writers from around the country. The press box, on the upper pavilion and directly behind home plate, was packed.

Those in the crowd didn't come to sit on their hands. In fact, at various times during the game there was almost as much action in the stands as on the field. At one point in the first half of the game everyone watched a kid who had scaled the outfield wall and once there disobeyed three policemen before sliding down the Twenty-first Street side of the park. A woman who sat on the roof of a Somerset Street house had a small bulldog with her. In the middle of the game the dog fell off the roof and onto the head of a fan seated on the roof of the porch below. The fan yelled as the dog toppled his derby hat. The dog was not harmed and was carried to the woman, the *North American* said, "who was on the verge of tears."

Those who couldn't get tickets, or a place across the street, followed the game on a scoreboard at Convention Hall. Games would be reproduced at the Forrest Theater with an electric scoreboard. Fans also called the North American Information Bureau. From morning till midnight people rang to find out what was happening in the game. Calls came from all over the country. One man called who couldn't speak English, but, fortunately, an Italian interpreter was found.

Philadelphia hearts were with Charles Bender, and after he glided in to start the third inning, they rooted him on. Boston pitcher Dick Rudolph led off and chopped one back to the box. Bender fumbled with the ball but recovered in time. Bender then again went 3-0 to a hitter, but again battled back, striking out Moran. Evers sent an easy fly to Oldring. One. Two. Three.

Whew.

As he headed toward the A's dugout, closer to the cheering crowds, Charles Bender was used to the acceptance he had been offered by so many Philadelphians. And by then he had proven he was no longer the silent kid in the back of the clubhouse.

Chapter Sixteen. During the sixth game of the 1911 World Series the ball was hit back to the mound four times, and after he gathered it in each time Bender threw to the appropriate base—but not in the usual manner. Instead, as he fired to first or second he flicked his wrist. Tenants of the press box were puzzled to notice that Athletics infielders were visibly upset with Bender during the course of the game, and after the Series Grantland Rice asked about the commotion on the field.

"What were [they] hollering about?"

"I was throwing them curveballs on assists at first and second," Bender said, smiling. "I had a lot of chances in that game."

"Curveballs?"

"Sure. They are young fellows and I just wanted them to know this was just another ball game. I got a big laugh when [they] were handling those curves. I'd like to tell you what they called me, but I'm afraid no paper would print it."

Connie Mack was told that story. "That's the way Bender always worked," he said. "A $5 million ballgame was the same to the Chief as one for $5, so far as tension was concerned. But the bigger the stake, the better Bender always was."

The 1911 Series was perhaps the first one that could be considered an international spectacle. The games were reported across the globe via trans-Pacific cable, and that year *Everybody's* magazine tabbed the World Series as "the very quintessence and consummation of the most perfect thing in America." Despite the heightened scrutiny, several tales from that World Series were oft repeated but seldom verified.

Forty years later Ty Cobb, who covered the games for a newspaper syndicate, swore that during that Series Bender performed the "greatest bit of brainwork I ever saw in a ballgame." As the story goes, Bender was facing John "Chief" Meyers, the New York Giants' fastball-loving catcher, during an especially tight situation. Bender quickly got ahead of Meyers, a .332 hitter during the 1911 regular season, with two off-speed pitches on the outside corner. Then Bender stepped off the mound, turned his back to Meyers, and waved to each outfielder, shifting them, one by one, to the right. Bender's arms exaggerated his intentions. Everyone in the park was supposed to understand that yet another curve would be placed outside, that if the New York catcher wanted to drive the ball the right-handed hitter would have to go the other way. As Meyers stood at the plate, waiting, Bender reared back and zipped a straight one down the middle. Meyers didn't have time to take the bat off his shoulder.

The story may be accurate but the historical record doesn't permit certainty, and there are reasons to believe Cobb's memory may not have served him any better than the memory serves other mortals. Meyers struck out only one time while Bender was pitching in that Series, and he didn't strike out at all against Bender in 1913, the only other occasion they faced one another in World Series play. The lone Bender-of-Meyers strikeout came during the seventh inning of Game 6, a five-run game at that point with one runner on. Newspaper accounts reveal that Bender, in fact, did wave to his outfielders. "As he threw on the outside to left-handed batters he motioned his outfielders to left field," the *Cleveland Plain Dealer* said. "Now he would call them in—now he would wave them to the right."

But at least one newspaper said Bender threw Meyers three "slowballs" and several papers didn't feel the at bat was worth passing mention. Cobb's own column the next day didn't reveal anything definitive, either.

What is clear is that by the end of the 1911 World Series Charles Bender was thoroughly enjoying himself. Whether events occurred as Cobb remembered them, the Meyers play would not have been out of character.

John "Chief" Meyers and Charles "Chief" Bender met in the 1911
World Series. Bender, Meyers said, was "one of the nicest people
you'd ever meet." Chicago Historical Society. SDN-057463.

How many times did Bender throw breaking balls to infielders during big games? Seems unlikely, but Bender loved to pitch in front of big crowds, in big games, and when presented an opportunity to demonstrate that he wasn't disturbed by pressure he reveled in the chance.

There may have been another reason behind Bender's bluster. Perhaps he cut loose expressly because he knew better than most how easily life could pitch curveballs in unexpected places. Newspapers scarcely mentioned the fact, but Bender pitched in the 1911 World Series with a heavy heart.

John and Charles Bender were two sides of the same coin. Whereas Charles adjusted, tried to fit in, brother John carried inner turmoil. Charles was usually noticeably pleasant; John was temperamental. Despite the fact that John was born six years earlier than Charles they looked a lot alike. John also attended Carlisle, from 1896 to 1900, but was expelled for reasons that are unclear. Like his brother he had an aptitude and affinity for baseball, but he didn't develop at Carlisle to the point where he earned a spot on the varsity squad.

John Bender had made a few minor league stops by the time he reached Columbia, South Carolina, in the Sally League in 1908, where he got into an altercation with his manager, Winn Clark, while aboard a ship taking the team from Jacksonville to Charleston. Bender slashed the Columbia Comers manager with a knife and was subsequently blacklisted by the National Commission for more than two years. After the ban was lifted he immediately signed with the Charleston team. John Bender's layoff did not enhance his abilities—he was slow and had a soft bat—and he was released. He drifted north of the border to Edmonton of the Western Canadian League, where he played a competent outfield during the 1911 season and became a popular player.

But on the morning of September 25 he entered the Lewis Bros. Café and was about to order breakfast when, without saying a word, he dropped dead at 9:15 a.m. Local newspapers said he had heart disease. John Bender had married a Charleston girl while playing for Augusta in 1907, and at the time of his death he owned a café in Charleston. He was buried in that city. (It has been written that John Bender died while on the mound in the middle of a game. For one thing, he was an outfielder and unlikely to be standing on the mound. For another, the 1911 Western Canadian League season ended more than three weeks before his death.)

Four days after John Bender died in his early thirties Anna Bender passed away in her late twenties. Anna was born two years after Charles and, like her brother, was extremely bright. It's often the case that children born to similar circumstances react differently to the world. Most members of the Bender family had exceptional drive while a few others struggled to move their feet. Anna Bender was compelled to make herself useful within the dominant culture, and she used education as the vehicle. She attended the Pipestone Boarding School in Minnesota for three years and then went to Hampton Normal and Agricultural Institute in Virginia, where she became the first female Ojibwe graduate.

In 1903, she worked as a housemaid for a family of eight in Hanover, Massachusetts, as part of Hampton's work-placement program. Her sister, Elizabeth Bender, worked a half mile away, and so they spent time together. Because of Hanover's proximity to Boston, Anna and Elizabeth timed a visit for when the Philadelphia Athletics would play at Boston, and they attended a game. A note in the newspaper mentioned that their big-league brother escorted them about town.

Anna was an outstanding student. According to Paulette Fairbanks Molin's research, after graduating from Hampton in 1906 she continued her studies at the Haskell Institute in Lawrence, Kansas. She completed Haskell's business course in 1908 and soon after found a clerk-typist position at an American Indian boarding school in Chemawa, Oregon. She married Reuben Sanders, a boy's industrial teacher, in 1910.

By the time Anna was twenty-six she was established. She had a home, a career, and a partner with whom to share what was expected to be a satisfying life. But the couple would be married for barely a year. The *Chemawa American* reported in an October 6, 1911, article that "Death, the great leveler, claimed Mrs. Anna Bender-Sanders" on September 29. A few days before her death Anna had surgery to remove a tumor. She had previously undergone two operations for appendicitis, the second one performed because of a complication from the first.

In 1891 three young siblings, John, Charley, and Anna Bender, had boarded a train in northern Minnesota headed for a boarding school on the other side of the country. By the start of the 1911 World Series only one of them was still alive.

Charles Bender didn't mourn his siblings' death in public, so it's unclear how much pain he felt or how he coped with that pain. Maybe he drank. Maybe he emptied a barrel of shells in the woods. Or played thirty-six holes every day. What seems likely is that such tragedy intensified feelings already stewing inside him. Bender was a Sargasso Sea. He often appeared the model of calmness, but all around there were powerful currents. And the flotsam would eventually rise to the surface.

But no one in attendance at the 1911 World Series would notice anything wrong with the Philadelphia Athletics' unflinching Game 1 starter. In fact, he looked as comfortable as he ever had been. When the Athletics boarded the train for New York a big crowd gathered to send them off. Bender, the *Philadelphia North American* said, was "serene" and "unperturbed."

Before the 1911 season prominent Chicago sportswriter Hugh Fullerton had written that Bender would not be able to sustain his success because he was long in the tooth. He had been in the league for nine years, but he was still just twenty-seven. In advance of the Series Philly scribe James Isaminger corrected this notion. "Bender is still in his prime," he said.

"Chief Bender, who has never been pressed at any time this season, is in excellent condition for the games. Like last season Bender will probably be Mack's choice for the opening game . . .

"Bender is one of the greatest one-game pitchers in America. He is not an iron man, but when a team needs a certain game, and needs it badly, there is no more reliable pitcher in America than Bender."

Asked about his Game 1 starter, Connie Mack would only say that both teams would have a pitcher on the mound. In fact, before the start of the game Mack had Jack Coombs, Eddie Plank, and Bender warm up. But the newspapermen didn't need Mack's on-the-record blessing in order to figure things out.

"Bender is truly one of the wonderful pitchers of the decade," Isaminger said. "The grinning Indian has all the cunning of his race." In addition to talent, the reason Bender, a "trickster," was the obvious choice was because the howling mob of New Yorkers could not touch him.

"He is, like all Indians," Isaminger said, "as fidgety as a granite block."

The 1905 New York Giants were a juggernaut, but the club's success was not sustained. By the time New York returned to the World Series in 1911 several faces had changed and the team had become younger. Fred Merkle was the first baseman. Larry Doyle at second and Art Fletcher at short formed the double-play combination. Third baseman Art Devlin, one of the few holdovers from 1905, rounded out one of the most capable infields in all of baseball. Meyers was the more than capable receiver, and all three outfielders—Red Murray, Fred Snodgrass, and Josh Devore—could hit.

It was a fine lineup, and McGraw ensured that it was an aggressive one. The Giants stole an astounding 347 bases, still a record and likely forever a record. Five players swiped 38-plus each and Devore led with 61. Basically if you couldn't run you couldn't play for McGraw in 1911. Two other players, Fletcher, a reserve player, and Buck Herzog, who joined the team in a July trade, stole 42 bags between the two of them. The starting outfielders stole 160 bases on their own, and only one of the three played in as many as 150 games.

The Giants ran past teams in the National League, winning the pennant by 7½ games, and some would wonder later whether the team was run into the ground. By the end of the 1911 World Series the Giants looked tired. But when they walked onto the field for Game 1 no one was wondering about fatigue. Fans were too busy looking at the team's fatigues. Once again, as he had done in 1905, McGraw outfitted his charges in black broadcloth uniforms. But this time they did not contain magic.

"We went out on the field first, all dressed in black, and we sat on the bench waiting for the Athletics to walk past us to get to the visiting team's bench," Meyers said. "We all had a shot off in one hand and a file in the other, and we were all busily sharpening our spikes."

The 1911 Series was noteworthy in some quarters because the game's two greatest American Indian players were squaring off against each other. Before the first game Bender and Meyers, a Cahuilla Indian born in the San Jacinto mountains of southern California, were photographed talking to each other.

"I knew [Charley] quite well," Meyers said. "One of the nicest people you'd ever meet."

Naturally, McGraw gave the mighty Mathewson the starting assignment. By 1911 Matty was thirty, and while no doubt still a terrific pitcher—he won 26 games and had an ERA a shade under 2.00—he was no longer infallible. He lost 13 games in 1911 and allowed nearly a hit per inning.

In the second inning the A's accomplished a feat they couldn't manage in three games during the 1905 World Series: they pushed across a run against Matty. Frank Baker began the frame with a single to right, took second on a groundout by Danny Murphy, and third on a passed ball. Baker scored on a single by Harry Davis, the longtime Athletic who came off the bench to fill in for an injured Stuffy McInnis.

The Giants tied it in the fourth. Snodgrass led off and walked. He moved to second on Murray's groundout to second. After Bender struck out Merkle, Herzog rolled a ball to Collins, an easy chance the usually steady Eddie could not handle, and Snodgrass came around to score. Bender then struck out Fletcher to end the inning. But the unearned run would prove costly.

With one out in the bottom of the seventh, Meyers knocked a double to left and scored on a two-out double by Devore. The Athletics managed six hits off Mathewson, one more than the Giants made off Bender, but New York held on for a 2–1 victory. Bender had been masterful, allowing the lone earned run while striking out 11 against four walks.

"The immense crowd alone was enough to unnerve most any one," Charles Dooin, manager of the Phillies, wrote in a column the next morning. "It was the largest crowd that I or any one else ever saw, and most of the time was wildly hilarious." If the crowd wasn't cheering the Giants, they were jeering Bender and the Athletics. Dooin noted Bender often smiled and "never lost good humor at any time during defeat."

The *New York Herald*, in an ode to Matty, said, "You tore the scalp lock off the Chief." Indeed, the box scores read that Bender lost the game and Mathewson won it. But Bender was not out-pitched by Mathewson. He would later say he never had better stuff. And, because of the A's powerful lineup, he would have a chance to prove it before the Series was over.

Philadelphia Athletics third baseman Frank Baker was a thin farm boy whose left-handed stroke was among the most powerful of the Deadball Era. But such distinction requires elaboration. Baker never hit more than 12 home runs in a season, but few others of the time did, either. Baker led or tied for the league lead in homers four consecutive seasons (1911–14). From 1909, when he became a regular and belted the first home run in Shibe Park history, to 1914, his last year with the A's, Baker was frequently among league leaders in batting average, on-base percentage, and slugging percentage. He carved out a Hall of Fame career by using a diverse set of skills. But during the 1911 World Series he would become known simply as "Home Run" Baker.

In the sixth inning of the second game Baker belted a two-run home run off Rube Marquard. Baker's blast broke a tie game and, coupled with fine pitching by Eddie Plank, Philadelphia earned a 3–1 victory to even the Series. Baker's shot caused a stir. Marquard was not easy to hit. In fact, in 1911 he was every bit as effective as Christy Mathewson, and at 24-7 Marquard had a more impressive record. Don't think the Colossus was unaware of this fact.

Supposedly, a ghostwritten newspaper column under Matty's byline the next day blasted Marquard: "Marquard served Baker with the wrong prescription," as the column as been regularly quoted over the years. "That one straight ball . . . right on the heart of the plate, came up the 'groove' . . . [and] was what cost us the game." John Wheeler, Matty's ghostwriter, wrote that Marquard had violated manager McGraw's instructions. "Rube was especially warned not to pitch low to Baker. Rube pitched just what Baker likes."

Of course, as Norman Macht's research has shown, the historical record allows a clear-as-charcoal portrait. *Baseball Magazine* called the pitch a "fairly high ball, with a little curve, and breaking a little below the shoulder." Wheeler, in his memoirs, said Matty told him Rube's mistake was pitching inside. Baker said it was a fastball inside, without saying if it was high or low. Fred Lieb called it a low fastball above the knees. The 1912 *Reach Guide* called the pitch a low fastball, perhaps based on what Mathewson had written. Three years after the event, Mathewson claimed Collins, on second at the time, tipped Baker that a fastball was coming. "I had instructed Marquard not to pitch a high fastball to Baker, but he forgot," McGraw said in *My Thirty Years in Baseball.* "He put one in that spot and Baker whammed it into the stands." In a 1947 *American Magazine* story, another writer called it a curve inside.

Whether the pitch broke, sank, traveled underground, or made curli-cues in the air between the mound and home, Mack is said to have posted Matty's column in the A's clubhouse the next day at the Polo Grounds. Game 3 would be one in which Mathewson would have the chance to show the proper way to pitch to Frank Baker.

The game started in a drizzle but the precipitation went away and eventually the sun peered through. Going into the ninth, Mathewson was working on another shutout. He was a machine: wind him up and he pitches World Series shutouts against Philadelphia. Or so it seemed. The score was 1–0 when Matty retired the first Athletic in the ninth and Baker stepped to the plate. On a 2-1 count, Mathewson threw a high curve that Baker slammed into the right-field stands. Another dramatic homer. Giants fans were shocked. They were not used to mortal mo-ments from Mathewson.

Meanwhile, Jack Coombs was tying up the Giants' bats, pitching two-hit, one-run ball through ten innings. In the Philadelphia half of the eleventh, Eddie Collins pushed a one-out single to left. Baker followed with an infield single. Collins went to third and scored on consecutive errors. Harry Davis drove in Baker with another single. In the last of the eleventh, an A's error permitted a second Giant run, but the rally died when Beals Becker was cut down trying to steal second.

The next morning, as the story continues, Marquard returned the fa-vor: "Will the great Mathewson tell us exactly what he pitched to Baker . . . Could it be that Matty, too, let go a careless pitch when it meant the ballgame?"

Baker's homer was more than a crucial run in a World Series game. It seemed to break a spell. Until that point, Mathewson had pitched 44 Series innings against the A's and had allowed a total of one run. Again, speculation was intensely focused on pitch selection. Again, the pitch was a fastball-curveball on the outer-inner half of the plate just above the knees and just below the belt. Depending on one's point of view.

Eventually a writer had the temerity to ask the man who swatted the pitches. "If you believe what Marquard and Mathewson are saying, I can't hit the ball only in one spot," Baker told the *Philadelphia Evening Times*. "Taking it all in all, I'm a lucky guy to be in the league at all, after they get done telling where I hit 'em and where I miss 'em. You want to know the kind of balls I hit for those two homers? Marquard gave me a fast one on the inside. Matty handed me a curve about knee high. It didn't look a bit different than the other curves he handed me all through the series."

Charles Bender must have delighted in the exploits of his teammate and friend. Bender and Baker had a lot in common: Both had rare talent to play baseball, and neither wanted much attention away from the field. They also shared a love of hunting and took many trips together. One story Bender often told was about a hunting trip he made with Baker, who had eyed a particular bird and shot four times, hitting the bird each time. "But the only way he could kill the duck was by rowing out and cracking it over the head with an oar," Bender said. After baseball Baker lived a quiet life on his farm near Trappe, Maryland, where he was born. But he and Bender remained friends. Baker would serve as a pallbearer at Bender's funeral.

About as soon as Baker's blast landed on the other side of the wall, he was dubbed "Home Run." In consecutive games he had hit meaningful homers against two different future Hall of Fame pitchers in the biggest spotlight in sports. By the start of Game 4, A's street vendors were selling "Home Run" Baker's bat, tied with a ribbon.

The momentum was with the A's. They had two dramatic wins under their belt. They had deconstructed Mathewson, and Bender, well rested and Series tested, was ready to pitch.

But then a nor'easter blew in and it rained. For six days.

Game 3 had been played on October 17, and Game 4 wouldn't be played until October 24. With nothing legitimate to report during the rain-soaked interim, writers racked their minds to come up with ways to write about the condition of the field, saying that Shibe Park "looks like a Jersey cranberry bog." "Pickerel is biting at Shibe Park," the *North American* said, "bass is also plentiful."

The break between the third and fourth games was so long Philadelphia center fielder Rube Oldring's sister died and he was able to go home, attend the funeral, grieve, and not miss an inning. Drainage systems in those days were not advanced. Even when the rains subsided, Shibe Park remained a swamp. Crews used everything from sponges to sawdust to soak up water.

Conventional wisdom held that the Giants stood more to gain from the weather. For one thing, Philadelphia's momentum would be squelched. For another, the Giants had the more top-heavy pitching staff. By the time Shibe Park was drained McGraw would be able to send a rested Mathewson back to the mound. Mack's starting pitcher, Bender, hadn't pitched in a live game in eleven days. As he was handing him the starting assignment, Mack told Bender: "I think you're going to win this one, Albert." But it wouldn't be easy. A pitcher, especially one like Bender, appreciated rest. But there is such a thing as too much. He would be susceptible to overthrowing and might struggle to find his control.

Nothing discouraged that line of thinking in the first inning, when New York scored two big runs. Josh Devore started the game by whacking one back through the box. The ball caromed off Bender and trickled to shortstop Jack Barry. Barry threw to first but the speedy Devore was already there.

The field was in better condition than most expected; the infield was fairly firm and the base lines offered good footing. But the outfield turf was treacherous. Doyle followed Devore by sending a liner to center field that, had the field not endured a meteorological phenomenon in the days before, Oldring likely would have been able to cut off. Instead, Oldring slipped, the crowd groaned, and Devore raced all the way around to score as Doyle pulled into third.

The game's first out produced the game's second run as Snodgrass lifted a long sacrifice fly to Bris Lord in left field. Bender then induced a ground ball from Murray and struck out Merkle on three pitches. Bender had not been hit especially hard. But given Matty's mystical powers over the A's, a 2–0 lead loomed large.

But in the fourth Home Run Baker—one paper the next morning called him "the demoniacal slapsmith of the series"—continued to show he knew something about Mathewson that hitters in the National League did not. He laced a double into the left-field gap, between Snodgrass and Devore, to start a rally. Murphy followed Baker and first popped a foul ball that Meyers, despite a headfirst dive, could not reach, and then slammed a ball over Devore's head to plate Baker.

New York expected the next batter, Davis, to bunt, but instead the veteran tricked the Giants defense by popping a double down the line in right. The third consecutive two-base hit allowed Murphy to run home with the tying run while, as the *North American* said, "the fans got on their feet and went daffydillish."

Mathewson appeared dazed and the look alarmed McGraw. He instructed Marquard, Red Ames, and Hooks Wiltse to warm up in the bullpen as Matty stalled for time. As he did the crowd just got louder. There was a noticeable delay before Matty threw another pitch. The anticipation swelled.

When play resumed Barry punched a sharp one to Herzog at third, who made a brilliant stop. Davis took third on the throw to first and scored when Ira Thomas hoisted a sacrifice to Murray. When Davis stomped on the plate the A's had a lead they would not relinquish.

Mack had urged his charges to jump on Mathewson's first pitch and the A's obliged, often with success. Baker drove in another run in the fifth, with another double off the fence, a knock that just missed being a home run. That wasn't needed. He already had the nickname. Things were so unpleasant for Matty that by the time Baker came up again, he walked him intentionally. Philly fans didn't know whether to whoop or sneer.

Mathewson was pinch hit for in the top of the eighth. By this point he had allowed ten hits and four runs—one more than he had allowed against the A's in five previous starts combined.

Rather than toil to find his release point, Bender began to find himself in the second inning when, after allowing a one-out single to Fletcher, he retired nine straight batters. Bender generally retired the first man to face him. When runners did reach base it was often with two outs. With two down in the fifth Bender was so sure he struck out Devore he started toward his team's bench only to be corrected by umpire Bill Dineen. Devore wound up flying to left.

Bender got out of a minor jam in the sixth and in the seventh Meyers fouled one back into the upper pavilion. Bender did not want to serve Meyers a fresh ball and so he motioned for the ball to be returned. The fan held on. Meyers hit the clean one hard, but right to Collins for an out. After the inning Bender and Harry Davis lectured those in the crowd about the merits of the tenth man.

But Bender didn't need much help. The next day the *North American* said, "Bender, after an unfortunate start, was unhittable after the second inning. His sweeping curves blinded the New York batsmen." The Giants tried to rally in the ninth, and Merkle doubled. But he was stranded as Bender kept firing into the strike zone. Herzog hit a hot shot to Baker who fielded it cleanly. Fletcher popped to Collins and Meyers grounded to same. The final score was Philadelphia 4, New York 2. More importantly, the A's were two games up in the Series and the Giants were on the brink.

Bender had held the Giants scoreless, and allowed only five hits, over the final eight innings. He struck out four and walked two. Only five balls were batted to the outfield, none with particular authority.

As New York lamented the tarnish of Mathewson's mark—a headline in the *Tribune* remarked that the "Athletics Win Again as Matty Fails Giants"—Philadelphians celebrated their pitcher. Bender had finally beaten Matty.

"To Chief Bender belongs the lion's share of the laurels for this victory, which was considered the crucial one of the series," the *North American* said. "[Bender] out-pitched the great Christy by a considerable margin."

Before the World Series sportswriters frequently mentioned that more than most pitchers Charles Bender needed to be "handled properly." What is proper handling? Whatever Connie Mack says on a given day. If Bender were to be held out for five games at Mack's behest, well, then, that's how much rest Bender required. Generally speaking, those who thought much about such matters believed Bender couldn't be pushed. Even in a pinch. If one was going to err with Bender, he should err on the side of too much rest. James Isaminger said that Mack "nursed the willowy Chippewa" and said Bender was as "delicate as Dresden China."

By the time the Series ended such received wisdom would be questioned. In Game 5 the Athletics allowed the Giants to escape from apparent death. A third-inning three-run homer by one Rube, Oldring, off another, Marquard, provided the only scoring through 6½ innings. Jack Coombs was mowing down the New Yorkers, and with every out the game looked more and more like a Series finale. But the Giants crept back with one run in the seventh and two more in the last of the ninth to tie the score. During that inning Coombs severely strained his abdomen and Eddie Plank replaced him in the tenth. Plank was tagged with the loss in a 4–3 game as Larry Doyle led off with a double, took third on a missed fielder's choice, and scored on Fred Merkle's fly to deep right.

When Bender shuffled to the middle of the diamond for Game 6 the Shibe Park crowd displayed mixed emotions. Some fans were thrilled to see the team's moneyman for what would be a crucial contest. Game 4 had been in Philly, Game 5 in New York. Were there to be a Game 7 it would be in the hostile Polo Grounds. And, suddenly, the Athletics' deep pitching corps had thinned. Philadelphia undoubtedly would be without Coombs's services the rest of the Series—during Game 6 he would be at home in bed—while during a potential seventh game the A's would have to face a reasonably rested Christy Mathewson. So if the A's were to win the Series logic said Game 6 would be their best chance.

For that reason Bender's presence on the mound caused other fans to feel somber. They had read the newspapers. They knew Bender's reputation was not built on a foundation of iron. What's more, he had been sick most of the season.

Despite a 12-strikeout performance against Washington in late April, Bender struggled during the early part of 1911. He had won just two games near the end of May and his performance reflected his team's. Philadelphia did not play like a club poised to defend its league title. The Athletics lost six straight at one point and in the early portion of the schedule Eddie Plank was their only reliable starter.

By early June Bender had a sore shoulder and was seriously ill. "Chief Bender will not be used in the games except only in dire necessity," one newspaper reported. "Bender is suffering from a rheumatic arm. He warmed up last Thursday and told Mack that it would be a long time before he could pitch."

Ten days later, on June 14, pitching for the first time in nearly a month, Bender outdueled Ed Walsh 2–1 of Chicago in ten innings. On June 20, Bender pitched well in a 6–2 win but was booted from the game. With two out in the ninth, Washington had filled the bases with a walk by Jack Lelivelt that came on a pitch that Bender thought crossed the plate. Bender argued the call and was tossed.

Three days later, still in the same series, he received another ejection. "Bender's departure from the game furnished the big excitement of the day," the *North American* said. With one out in the sixth inning, the A's were down 2–1. Bender had two strikes on Wid Conroy when someone threw a ball onto the field. The ball had been hit foul and the patron was returning it, which was not unusual. Bender picked up the ball, looked at it, and threw it over the pavilion. The umpires took umbrage. Bender explained the ball was not in good shape and that he had not intended any misdeed. He was nonetheless ordered off the field.

In early July, Bender was 5-3. But on July 26 he started to put something together as he allowed five hits and struck out six—without issuing a walk—helping the A's to a doubleheader sweep of Cleveland. Later in the month he contributed a shutout in a doubleheader sweep of Detroit. He scored the only run of the game in the eleventh inning and scattered eight hits while striking out six.

"His control was so perfect that not a man walked on him," the *North American* said. "Bender struck out Cobb the first two times. The Indian got a great hand for the feat."

But by mid-September health again became an issue. "Charles Albert Bender is an ailing Chippewa, and will not be found in a Mack box score for at least two weeks," the newspaper said. "While Connie Mack professes that Bender's illness only embarrasses the A's temporarily, the fans receive the news as a blow. Bender has been ill with the grippe for three days and yesterday his physicians ordered him to keep to his bed. It is not expected that he will be at Shibe Park for ten days."

Some believed matters were so severe that Bender might not pitch in the World Series. But Mack denied the rumors. "The Chief will be in the Series," the manager said. "He will be as good as he ever was. He has been pitching great ball and I did not care to force him too hard when he had the stuff."

When he was able to pitch during the second half of the season, Bender was sharp as he won 12 of his last 14 decisions. Fortunately for the A's, they didn't need much more from him. Coombs went 28-12, and Plank's record was 23-8 with a 2.10 ERA. More than pitching, though, it was the lineup that carried Philadelphia. From top to bottom the Athletics had the strongest offense in the game. Philadelphia led the American League in runs, batting, and slugging. Eddie Collins hit .365 and Baker hit 11 home runs and drove in 115.

The A's trailed the Tigers until the first week of August, then pulled away for a 13½-game margin as Detroit played .500 ball in the latter portion of the season. Philadelphia had been slow out of the gates and had trailed Detroit by 12 games at one point during the first half, but by the end of the season the offense was on such a roll—winners of 20 of 22 during one stretch—that the A's wound up with a 101-50 record.

In the early part of the 1911 regular season, one paper had said of Bender's signing with the A's eight years earlier that "Mack made the greatest discovery since Christopher Columbus' find."

In the 1911 World Series the baseball world would find out something else about Charles Bender.

Plank was the obvious choice for Game 6, but Mack also had Bender warm up. As the umpire asked Mack for a lineup, noted *Sporting Life*, Bender pleaded with his manager: "Get a new ball out of the bag for me, Connie."

Mack didn't come to the park intent on pitching the right-hander. But he was swayed and sent Bender to the mound at the last instant. "In the warming up period Strongheart displayed so much strength that the shrewd Mack picked him to end the Series," one newspaper said the next morning. That's right. After the display that was to follow Bender would be referred to as Strongheart more than once. Sportswriters would pack away the fine china analogies.

Josh Devore, the first hitter of the game, was surprised when he dug into the batter's box and looked up and saw Bender heaving the ball toward him. Devore smashed a grounder back to Bender, who speared it with his bare hand and threw Devore out at first. It would be an apt metaphor for the day.

In the second inning, with a runner in scoring position, Collins made a brilliant stop of a hit by Meyers and whipped the ball across the diamond just in time. The play saved at least one run, and as Bender walked to the Athletics' dugout he wore a large grin.

The game was 1–1 in the fourth when Home Run Baker continued one of the more impressive performances by a position player in the short history of the World Series. He started a rally by hitting a single to center. Murphy followed and poked a single to left on a hit-and-run. John Mc-

Graw drew his infield in and Harry Davis pushed one to Doyle, who made the critical miscue. Instead of immediately throwing home, he hesitated and by the time he uncorked, as the *North American* reported, he "didn't have as much chance to catch Baker as the emperor of China."

Baker slid home safely. Barry then bunted in front of the plate, and New York pitcher Red Ames's throw grazed Barry's head, and the ball rolled into right field, allowing Murphy to score. Murray backed up the wild throw and cut loose with an errantly aimed toss of his own; he was trying to get Davis, who was headed to third. Not so much. The throw was so off the mark that, not only did Davis score, Barry did, too, and the rout was on.

The rest of the game was a gallop into history. Bender made the first and last outs of the seventh inning. In between Philadelphia scored seven runs on seven hits. John McGraw burned through three pitchers during the afternoon and no matter who stood on the mound the Athletics kept belting balls all over the yard, making thirteen hits.

McGraw once remarked that no championship club is great unless it can repeat. By the time, late in the game, Connie Mack sent the injured Stuffy McInnis to first base for sentimental reasons the Giants had suffered an historic drubbing and the Athletics were able to claim greatness under McGraw's definition. The 13–2 score was finalized when Baker gathered in reserve catcher Art Wilson's ground ball.

The score masked Bender's dominance. Both runs scored off him were unearned. The Giants scored in the first inning on a two-out outfield error. "Some pitchers might have been worried by this, but not Bender," the *Cleveland Plain Dealer* said. "He just smiled his famous smile and a moment later caught Murray napping at first base."

New York pushed across another in the ninth aided by another outfield miscue. Bender allowed just four hits and struck out five batters against a pair of walks. He was in control most of the afternoon. Despite pitching on two days' rest, he looked like he could have thrown extra frames if necessary. "Bender pitched Thursday with brain and nerve rather than with brawn," the *Philadelphia Press* said.

The *North American* said, "Bender surprised everybody with an unexpected exhibition of stamina by beating the Giants and saving the championship, although it was the frail Indian's second game in three days.

"New York is still shaking at Bender's sardonic grin, a little more creepy than Mephisto's, that giggle of the Chippewa."

The A's outscored New York 27–13. Bender, Coombs, and Plank each had sub-2.00 ERAs and held the powerful Giants lineup to a .175 batting average. Only Doyle (.304) and Meyers (.300), among nonpitchers, batted above .200. "I have been in baseball for twenty-five years, and have never in that time played with, managed or even seen a gamer, braver set of boys than mine, and I am proud of every one of them, from the greatest star down to the lowest substitute," Mack said. "It is their triumph, and to them goes the glory."

Bender and his mates received $3,654.59 each for winning the Series, easily the highest player share in history to that time, and Bender had earned his dough. During the Series he went 2-1 with three outstanding starts and a 1.04 ERA. He allowed three earned runs and 16 hits in 26 innings, struck out 20 men and allowed eight walks.

"Bender," McGraw said, "pitched three of the best games ever seen in a World's Series, excelled, perhaps, only by Matty's work in the series of 1905."

Bender's heroics in that Series placed him, in the eyes of some baseball observers, as the best pitcher on the best team in the game—and this was a time when pitching was the thing. In those days there wasn't a World Series Most Valuable Player Award, but had there been Bender likely would have claimed the honor, even considering Frank Baker's performance. With that achievement came rare acclaim.

The A's had started to attract more attention everywhere they went, including from young, vocal women, not an otherwise large baseball constituency in those days. Soon after the Series, Bender, Rube Oldring, and Cy Morgan, attired in mufti, hopped on a train for New York, as they had signed to tour with the Pearl Sisters in a vaudeville act called "Learning the Game," which required the players to sing and dance in uniforms. Morgan, who had a lot of theater experience, was the star performer. Bender was basically there to flash his smile.

Soon after the show Bender, inexplicably, became a movie star of sorts. Moving pictures were different then, much shorter and, of course, silent. But "The Baseball Bug," a comedy-drama produced by the Thanhouser Company and released in late November 1911, included what may have been the first examples of guest star appearances in a non-documentary baseball picture, as Bender, Oldring, Morgan and Jack Coombs had roles.

The word *bug* was a synonym for *fan*. The film, according to *Thanhouser Films: An Encyclopedia and History*, was the tale of a haughty small-town ballplayer served a plate of crow by his wife, who arranges a match between her husband and several professionals.

The movie drew the attention of various periodicals. Reviews included one in the *Moving Picture News*: "Bender! Coombs! Morgan! Oldring! They're picture players! Now let the hearts of all fans rejoice, for the four stars of the Philadelphia Athletics will be with them once more, though the season is over. And it will be a diversion to see them as actors—to see if they face the cameras confidently as they did Mathewson. In advance, let it be said that they did. They enacted their roles at the Thanhouser studio with the precision of veteran photoplayers."

The *Moving Picture World* wrote glowingly about Bender, even as they made mincemeat of his biography, and called him "a highly educated man" who is "known in baseball as one of the cleverest pitchers." The periodical also published a detailed synopsis of the film: "A little frog who splashes into a tiny puddle sometimes thinks he has created a commotion in the Atlantic Ocean. A young clerk in a small town was like the little frog, as local tryouts on an amateur baseball team convinced him that he was really a wonderful player and far superior to the men in the big leagues. Glory came to him, that is to say, his name was a household word in the small village where he lived, but he got no money for it. More than that, he neglected his regular work in a store and was endangered of being discharged. For he thought baseball, drank baseball, and dreamed baseball. He was a nuisance to his friends and a trial to his family, and his wife worried greatly as to what the future would bring.

"The wife had a distant cousin, Big Chief Bender, the noted twirler of the world champion Philadelphia Athletics, and she decided to confide her troubles to him. She figured that a man who could pitch three out of the six past seasons' games against the Giants, win two of them and miss the third by a fluke, must be resourceful enough to help her. She judged correctly, and her appeal was not in vain."

Other publications, such as the *New York Dramatic Mirror*, were not so kind about the story's merits. Unfortunately, no footage of the film is known to survive. The reviews don't raise questions as to whether Bender deserves a posthumous Oscar. But less than fifteen years after he left the reservation for the last time, there was little doubt Charles Bender stood on a once unfathomable rung on the ladder of celebrity.

Chapter Seventeen. By the 1914 World Series opener, Bender's prominent stature on baseball's best team and his place in the dominant culture seemed secure. In the fourth inning, he again faced the minimum. Joe Connolly singled to right, but Possum Whitted grounded into a double play, pitcher to shortstop to first. Butch Schmidt then grounded out. Leaving aside that second inning, only one hitter had reached, and as Bender headed back to the Philadelphia dugout the crowd roared. Shibe Park was only six years old, but by this time the sight and sound were familiar.

The summer Shibe Park opened the Athletics were locked in a pennant race with the Detroit Tigers. In August 1909, the A's slipped out of first after a fierce, physical series in Detroit. Ty Cobb headlined the Tigers' offense, not only with his bat but also with his spikes. The well-after-the-fact stories have it that Cobb was flying around the bases trying to hurt people. Alleged incidents involved Frank Baker at third base and Eddie Collins at second.

By the time Detroit came to Shibe Park in mid-September for a four-game series, Athletics fans had spent the weeks in between revving their engines. Newspaper articles in the *Philadelphia Bulletin* and elsewhere amplified the anticipation. As Bruce Kuklick wrote, before the series numerous notes had threatened Cobb that if he played someone would shoot him. Mack called for extra protection. Cobb was escorted to and from the park by police. During the series hundreds of officers, including detectives, were on hand. Some wore street clothes among the masses, and uniformed men stood in a line in the outfield, between Cobb and the fans. Cobb had thick skin, but Philly fans rattled him so much that at one point he "jumped at the backfire of a car in the street."

Charles Bender relished pitching in front of large crowds, and after the teams had split the first two games of the series, on Saturday, September 18, 1909, the largest crowd in baseball history filled Shibe Park. Or so claimed the newspapers. "Official figures give the attendance at 35,409," the *Philadelphia Inquirer* said, "but several thousand additional persons viewed the conflict."

This continuation of the A's-Tigers clash, a crucial late-season contest between the league's two heavyweights, offered a marquee pitching matchup: "Wild" Bill Donovan versus Bender. By this time, Donovan had twice won 25 games in a season, and on this day he threw the ball as well as he ever did. Donovan allowed just four hits and two walks. But he wasn't the best pitcher in the joint.

The Tigers had the American League's top offensive team. Their lineup was explosive. They led the circuit in batting average, on-base percentage, and steals. They were second in slugging. They could give a pitcher and a defense fits. But on this day Detroit was, the *Inquirer* said, "helpless" against Bender.

The fans, many of them clad in straw hats, were "dippy," the newspaper said. "Every play, no matter how trivial, evoked some expression from the enthusiastic crowd."

Through the first eight innings, the Tigers had fallen "before his deadly darts," having managed just four base runners off Bender, three on singles and another on an error. Neither hit was bunched and Detroit had just one runner reach as far as second.

The game stood at 2–0 A's when Davy Jones, batting for Donovan, led off the final inning and promptly struck out. Matty McIntyre then walked, the only pass Bender permitted on the afternoon. At that point Bender "grinned so boldly," the *Inquirer* said, "the faithful believed he only issued the free ticket to prolong the misery of the Royal Bengals."

With the count 3-2 on shortstop Donie Bush, Bender kicked, whirled and fired a heavy fastball. Bush swung the bat, but too late. It was Bender's ninth strikeout of the game.

But for all his fine work through 8⅔ innings, Bender was still one pitch away from trouble with none other than Ty Cobb stepping into the batter's box. Cobb rarely needed external motivation, but if he wanted any Philadelphia fans had offered him a hearty helping. Bender put the first pitch over but then threw two balls.

"Bender apparently was not worrying," the *Inquirer* said, "for he grinned defiantly at Jennings and his bunch, and then heaved a fastball toward the plate."

Cobb connected and the sound made a crack. The ball headed quickly toward right field along the ground. But Eddie Collins dashed over, gathered it in, and nipped a sliding Cobb at first.

"The reason I used Bender is that I knew almost to certainty that we would win," Mack said after the game. "I always use the Chief on just such occasions, and he has never failed me.

"The club has been in some big crises, and Bender has often been called upon to do work which would have taken the nerve out of a great many pitchers, but he has always pulled us through with flying colors."

Said the *Inquirer*, "Too much credit cannot be given Bender for his part in the victory. He was the very embodiment of coolness." The newspaper described the Cobb at-bat by saying "Chills swept through the fans as the Indian served up a ball to Cobb."

The first game of the 1914 World Series presented a similar scene, as Bender stepped out of the Philadelphia dugout to start the top half of the fifth inning, the mechanical scoreboard in Shibe Park reading Braves 2, Athletics 1.

Chapter Eighteen.

Charles Bender helped the Athletics win games even when he wasn't pitching. His eyes were so sharp Connie Mack made him a regular in the coaching box. When a right-hander was on the mound, Bender would coach third base. When a southpaw was pitching, he would coach first. All Bender needed was the chance to study a pitcher and invariably he would pick up something that told him which pitch was coming. Often, in fact, he could tell what the pitcher was going to throw before he started his windup.

It went something like this: Bender would coach at third and Harry Davis would be stationed at first. Bender would study the pitcher and pick up tendencies. He might notice that whenever Christy Mathewson served his fastball he preceded the delivery by holding the ball in his right hand with his arm hanging loosely at his side. Either Matty was calling his own pitches, or he had a habit that tipped them. Bender would pick it up in an inning or three. Then, from the coaching box, he'd call out something such as, "Come on, Frank, old boy. Hit 'er out." Words would be tied to which pitch was coming. Or he'd signal to Davis in the opposite box, who would relay signs.

In the seconds between pitches a pitcher makes several motions that are almost unnoticeable to the casual observer but which often have meaning. Teams usually reached the conclusion that Bender or some

Bender's eyes were so sharp he helped the A's win games even when he wasn't pitching. National Baseball Hall of Fame Library, Cooperstown NY.

other member of the A's—captain Davis was also said to be excellent at
noticing subtleties—was stealing the catcher's signs. So in mid-game they
would inevitably change them, to no avail. Teams were worrying about
the wrong problem.

New York Giants catcher John Meyers suspected the A's were stealing
his signs during the 1911 World Series. "They're getting our signs from
someplace," Meyers told manager John McGraw. "That coach on third base
. . . is calling our pitches. When he yells, 'It's all right,' it's a fastball."

"He must be getting them off you," McGraw said.

Meyers knew they weren't but he told his pitchers to pitch without signals. Didn't make a difference. Davis still yelled, "It's all right," when a
fastball was on its way.

Bender, *Baseball Magazine* noted, picked up on how Ed Walsh, the no-
torious spitballer of the Chicago White Sox, tipped when he was going
to throw his fastball. Before delivery Walsh put his hands to his mouth
as if to wet the ball. But of course he actually only applied saliva when
throwing the spitter. Bender's eyes could see when Walsh was bluffing.
The A's would let those nasty spitters sail by and wait for a fastball. Hitting a baseball may be the most difficult thing to do in sports. It's a tad
easier when you know what's coming.

Teammate Cy Morgan and Bender used to walk together down the
street. "Way off in the distance we would see a small lettered sign which
I could not make anything out of, and I have pretty good eyes," Morgan
said. "I'd point it out to Bender and he would read it easily."

Morgan, himself a spitballer, came over to the Athletics in a 1910 trade
with the Boston Red Sox. Immediately after Morgan put on an A's uniform, Davis called him over and told him to correct a subtle habit that
tipped his pitches. Morgan saw both sides; he was both victim and bene-
ficiary of the Athletics' brainwork.

Philadelphia was long accused of theft, but the team's methods were
shrewd and legal. Bender was not the only Athletic responsible, but his
eyes were clearly an integral part of the club's success. "There can be no
secret signals when Bender is on the assignment," the *Cleveland Leader*
said. "There is absolutely no method which the wonderful sleuth can be
double-crossed."

Baseball Magazine said, "with the cunning characteristic of his race he sees a lot of things that escape the eye of the Caucasian."

In a 1912 interview Morgan further explained the ways in which Bender's eyes and the Athletics' wits were used to win games.

"I know a lot of people who believed we had some system of getting the catchers' signs, but it was not true," he told *Sporting Life*. "We do study the pitchers all the time, and whatever ideas we get about what is being pitched we get from them and not from the catcher's signs. We scared the Giants a lot in the World's Series by making use of our reputation. When one of the boys got on second he would make a lot of bluff motions and the catcher would yell something. Then [New York catcher John] Meyers would run in and confer with the pitcher and switch signals.

"We sit there in a row on the bench and study the pitcher, and if we detect any difference in his motion we watch to see what kind of ball it means. Bender gets up on the coaching lines for a while, and . . . he comes and tells us what kind of a ball that motion means. Then we all know it and remember it."

Mack liked intelligent players, and the nucleus of his early pennant winners was loaded with brains. No question the A's won championships because they had a terrific infield, a fine pitching staff, and a lineup of quality hitters. They also won because they were the smartest team in the circuit. This was no coincidence. Mack recruited players who had at least some education, and his roster often had several college boys. That's probably part of the reason why Bender was such an attractive player to Mack. He could think for himself, and he noticed the little things that helped his team win championships.

But in the 1914 World Series, Bender's powers of observation would be countered by the Boston Braves. The Athletics were facing a club prepared not just to beat them on the scoreboard but also between the ears. In the days before the Series, the Braves solicited the help of fellow National Leaguers. Phillies catcher and soon-to-be manager Pat Moran provided Boston with A's scouting reports. Christy Mathewson instructed them on how to pitch to Philadelphia. By this time Matty had pitched against the A's in three World Series. He also happened to be one of the brightest men in the game. Giants manager John McGraw, no tactical slouch, also offered tips.

Boston also was aided in no small way by former Athletics Danny Murphy and Rube Vickers. Newspapers reported the pair had been chumming with the Braves for several days leading up to the Series and possibly provided Boston with inside dope.

"Bender can come pretty near to getting anybody's signs," Murphy said. "Harry Davis is another wizard in this line. I could mention at least one of the $100,000 Infield that wouldn't hit .200 if his fellow players didn't furnish him advance information from the coaching lines."

A day before the Series began, as Bender was greasing his arm in Shibe Park, the Braves were working out in Baker Bowl, the Phillies' home park. Dick Rudolph and Hank Gowdy warmed up together for a long time as George Stallings, exhibiting tenacity as though the World Series had already begun, kept his eyes planted on their every move. The manager stood some distance away, about where the rival coach would stand, and craned his neck to see whether Gowdy's fingers conveyed his intentions to the pitcher. Stallings knew all about the Athletics' sign-stealing abilities, and he made sure his players kept their pitches and plans shielded from the querying eyes of Charles Bender.

Stallings's preparation paid immediate dividends. Through four innings the A's had managed only one run, and that run might not have scored without a multiple-base miscue in the field.

No, the Braves were not having trouble with Bender's brown eyes, which looked up to find hefty Hank Gowdy poised in the batter's box to start the fifth inning.

As Bender stood with the ball on the mound, Stallings sat rooted in his spot in the dugout. Many baseball men are superstitious, but few were as paranoid as Stallings. If the Braves started a rally, he would move as much as a mannequin. He also became annoyed with disorder. As Norman Macht pointed out, Stallings particularly disliked scraps of paper around the dugout. When opposing fans and players learned of this idiosyncrasy, they often left a mess near his spot on the bench. As Bender wound, flinging his left leg up, Stallings sat still, legs crossed. In a section in the lower pavilion behind first base, the Royal Rooters—who had filled seven train cars on their way from Boston—sang "Sweet Adeline" and a breaking ball whistled toward the outer half of the plate.

Gowdy jumped on it, blasting a triple to right center.

Maranville followed with a single over McInnis's head, and Gowdy jogged home. Once again, Deal hit into a double play. This time, the feeble-hitting third baseman tried to bunt, but he couldn't manage to keep the ball on the ground, popping to Bender, who doubled off Maranville at first. Bender then struck out Rudolph to end the inning. But Boston had scored another run.

Each time a Brave crossed the plate the Boston dugout celebrated as though they had just won the game. Then again, few teams could say they posted three runs on Charles Bender in a span of five innings during a critical game.

But Bender had shown vulnerability before, and Philly fans had only to consider the World Series that took place one year earlier to convince themselves that Bender would quickly correct his flaws.

Chapter Nineteen. Before the first game of the 1913 World Series, Connie Mack called Charles Bender into his Shibe Park tower office. "Albert, I am depending on you to win this series." Mack paused. "By the way, how much do you owe on the mortgage on your home?"

"I believe that's a personal question," Bender said.

"All right," Mack said before Bender slipped out of his office. "We'll talk about it later."

During Bender's tenure with Philadelphia the Athletics won the American League pennant five times and on three such occasions they faced the New York Giants in the World Series. Philadelphia and New York were the two best teams of the first half of the second decade of the twentieth century, and when they faced one another the contrast between the team's respective leaders became glaringly obvious.

In many ways John McGraw and Connie Mack served as each other's doppelgänger. McGraw was forceful and controlling. A former star player, he asserted himself, harrying umpires and directing action from the dugout. Mack, the even-tempered former journeyman catcher, didn't yell. He also didn't swear much. He prepared his charges before games and, aside from an occasional wave of his scorecard to adjust his defense, sat mostly still during them. He allowed his players to use their own minds.

"They were different types," Bender said years later, after serving a stint

Though they had their differences, Connie Mack was a father figure to Charles Bender. National Baseball Hall of Fame Library, Cooperstown NY.

as a coach for McGraw, "but both were real leaders. Mr. Mack was the fatherly, soft-spoken type while Muggsy was the hard-boiled, swashbuckling hell-for-leather type."

As early as 1905 the local press began referring to Connie Mack as a "genius," so it's not as if the accolades missed him entirely, but because of his demeanor, Mack's skills as a strategist are perhaps underappreciated. In baseball it's the managers who make themselves part of the story who usually receive most of the ink, and credit, for their team's success. Managers like, well, McGraw.

Mack wasn't without ego, but he wasn't demonstrative and he preferred to work behind the scenes. Besides, he was too busy preparing. One of the first managers to chart opponents, Mack instructed his players how to pitch to and position themselves against various hitters. His notes were supposedly so detailed that "not only did he record how a man might hit the curveball," baseball historian Donald Honig wrote, "Connie refined it to how the man might hit Chief Bender's curveball." Doc Cramer broke in with the Athletics in 1929, and in one of his early appearances in the Philadelphia outfield Mack waved him into shallow center with heavy hitter Goose Goslin at the plate. Goslin hit the next pitch on a line that Cramer grabbed because of his unorthodox positioning. When Cramer returned to the dugout he asked for an explanation. "Just a hunch, boy," Mack said. "That's all it was. Just a hunch."

In 1913 Mack quietly made a different type of adjustment, one that if applied ninety years later would cause hysteria from the live-inside-the-box baseball establishment: he abandoned a rigid rotation and instead used his top two pitchers whenever and wherever they were most needed.

The move was borne partly of necessity. The third member of Mack's three-pronged pitching assembly, Jack Coombs, was ill for nearly the entire 1913 season. So Mack had to make an alteration of some kind. He had several young pitchers of promise, and he could have plugged one of them into Coombs's spot in the rotation. Instead, he decided to try something different.

Though nothing like a modern rotation was used, teams during the Deadball Era usually relied on four or five starting pitchers. Several of the game's most adept pitchers, including Bender, were used both as starters and relievers, and managers started relying on relief pitchers more than they ever had. At the start of the Deadball Era pitchers completed almost 90 percent of their starts. By the end, they finished them about half the time. For his career, Bender completed 255 of the 334 games he started, a rate of more than 76 percent.

In 1913 Mack threw Bender 236⅔ innings, and yet he started only 21 times. Meanwhile, a trio of youngsters—twenty-six-year-old Boardwalk Brown (35 starts), twenty-one-year-old Byron Houck (19), and twenty-year-old Joe Bush (16)—received nearly half of the team's starts. Instead of using a conventional rotation, Mack often started one of his young pitchers and then had Bender or Eddie Plank pitch in relief. The strategy made sense. Mack's lineup was potent and so on many days his young pitchers worked with a healthy margin of error. When the game was close he could bring in Bender, who would be fresh in the third, fifth, or eighth inning. He might pitch six innings one day, two the next. The radical change in job description was exemplified in Bender's pitching line. He won 21 games *and* tied the Major League record for saves in a season (retroactively calculated) with 13.

The more decisions a manager makes the more difficult his job. When in spring training you wind up a starting pitcher and tell him that, barring injury, he'll pitch every fourth or fifth day, the plan takes little further thought to execute. The shift in strategy for 1913 placed a greater burden on Mack for his team's performance. He would hand Bender starting assignments—and wave him in from the bullpen—when the time was right. He would have to pick his spots well.

Bender was pounded in his first couple of starts of 1913, and some wondered whether he hadn't shaken the ills of a dubious 1912 season. Bender said he wasn't worried by his early struggles, however, because his velocity was still there, and on April 24 he recruited believers. That day he tossed a six-hit, eight-strikeout complete game at the New York Yankees.

On May 13 he shut out Chicago on a six-hitter. Six days later he threw seven shutout innings—allowing just four hits and one walk while striking out five—in relief of another young arm, twenty-one-year-old Weldon Wyckoff. Bender started a game on June 1 and pitched six innings of shutout baseball before being sent to the showers. The Athletics were running away from New York that day and the manager didn't want to waste innings. Good thing, too. Two days later Bender threw five shutout frames in relief. At one point during the season Philadelphia writer James Isaminger said Mack was "revolutionizing the handling of pitchers."

Whether or not he was leading a revolution, Mack usually pushed the right buttons. The A's, customarily slow starters, played well from the start in 1913. On June 5 they were 32-10, then won six of their next seven. At one point during the season they won fifteen in a row. Mack's plan went swimmingly. He used thirteen different starters and every pitcher was expected to relieve regularly. His top six pitchers made 90 appearances in relief combined.

Of course, it didn't hurt that the A's had a great offensive team—as late as the second week of August there were seven Mackmen hitting .300-plus. The A's offense in 1913 may have been the best of any during the decade, led by one of the most dynamic all-around players in the game. Eddie Collins reached base at an exceptional .441 clip. "Collins is the greatest ball player I've ever had," Mack said, "and is playing the best ball of his career this season."

Bender had also taken his performance to a new level, and newspapers took notice. His previous high for appearances in a season was 36, but in 1913 he appeared in 48 games, and most of the pitches he threw carried pennant-race consequences. If the game was out of hand, he was generally out of the game.

"Bender is now an Iron Man," the *Philadelphia North American* said in an about-face. "Last year he disappointed, but this year he has showed that his impersonation of the iron man in the big games was no flash in the pan."

Bender threw a two-hit shutout at St. Louis on June 10. His five strikeouts helped the A's win their fourteenth straight. He threw a complete game despite the fact he hadn't started a game in several weeks. Few balls were hit hard against him and he allowed just one walk.

On June 13—a Friday—in 1913 Bender pitched thirteen innings to beat Cleveland 2–1. The newspapers called it Hoodoo Day and the Athletics scored the winning run on a Cleveland error. There was no sign of a black cat, but Bender was frighteningly good. He allowed only six hits and missed a shutout only because of a wild throw by Frank Baker in the ninth inning.

The A's were 55-19 on July 10, and by July 25 they led the league by 9½ games. At the end of the month Bender had two complete-game wins, and the balance of the regular season became mere formality. Philadelphia led the American League for all but five days and rarely suffered anything close to a losing streak. The surprising Washington Senators—propelled by an amazing season from Walter Johnson (36-7, 11 shutouts, 1.14 ERA)—finished the season 6½ games out, but the race wasn't even that close. By the end of September the tension had subsided, and Bender began to fool around. Newspapers noted that he had a "new delivery" that "astonished" hitters in practice games. In those days, delivery was a synonym for a pitch. The pitch Bender started delivering was a "half-speed" fadeaway.

The timing of this addition to his repertoire—in advance of the 1913 World Series—was hardly coincidence. Seeing as how the A's were about to once again face Christy Mathewson, the fadeaway's most celebrated practitioner.

"I learned how to pitch a fadeaway watching Matty," Bender later said. "It took quite a time to master the delivery, but I finally made it with constant practice and fine control."

New York fans "howled" when it was the Giants' turn to bat in the bottom of the first inning. There wasn't a more deafening crowd in the game than the one that frequented the Polo Grounds, and at the start of the first game of the 1913 World Series the fans were hungry. The Giants had lost the previous two World Series. It was inexplicable they would lose a third straight.

The New Yorkers were not attired in black uniforms this time. Instead, they wore white while the Athletics wore the butternut uniforms, with blue trim, that had been their away outfits since Mack brought the team into the American League. Before the game Mack had spoken to his charges.

"Think of more than the money," he told them. "Look to the honor. Long after what we win in this series is done, we will be remembered as the heroes who triumphed, or the team that should have won but lost. Our grandchildren will make their boasts, if we come through again."

McGraw's club was clearly the class of the National League. The Giants overtook the fast-starting Philadelphia Phillies on June 30, winning 101 games and the pennant by 12½. Their lineup was essentially the same and still featured terrific pitching: Mathewson, Rube Marquard, and Jeff Tesreau combined to win 70 games and throw 876 innings. The highest ERA of the three was Marquard's 2.50.

"New York is credited with having a far better pitching staff, but I can't see the logic of that argument," Mack said before the Series. "I have two first-class veterans in Bender and Plank. I don't want a better pitcher than Bender. There may be some who can stand harder work during the season, but there is none who can do better work.

"I only use Bender in important games, games that I must win, and he wins those kinds of games for me."

Eddie Collins's column appeared in newspapers each day during the Series. "This has been an extraordinary year for Chief because, besides taking his regular turn," Collins, who did not use a ghostwriter, said before the first game, "he has been compelled to respond to more than numerous calls of assistance from fellow twirlers. To these he has responded nobly, and this new role of rescuer Chief has done a world of good to our club that few outside of his team know. He has saved many a game for us that the records give to someone else. And the beauty of it is that he improves with it all."

Collins continued: "John Coombs was our original 'Iron Man,' but Chief has upheld the title well during Coombs's enforced absence. Right here I want to go on record as saying that I never saw Bender in better shape in his life. . . . The Chief is the coolest man under fire I have ever seen. He is also absolutely indifferent to the crowd. Hostile howling does not disturb him."

The man-made wind in his face, Bender stepped onto the diamond, which had been kept in perfect shape, protected all morning by tarpaulins. The day was dark, misty, always looking like it was about to rain. Bender stopped and said a word to his catcher, Wally Schang, then shuffled toward the mound. "He was," the *North American* said the next morning, "perhaps the coolest man in the stadium."

During the prime of his career there were many games in which Bender seemed to find another ounce of ability under conditions when every ounce was required. In several such instances he pitched brilliantly and won with a comfortable margin, not having to toil through the middle innings with the opponent ready to ruin the day. When you make something look easy people believe you. Bender's performance in Game 1 of the 1913 World Series was impressive for a different reason. That he dangled at the edge only demonstrated his resolve.

There was nothing especially unusual about the first four innings. He faced the minimum in the first, left a two-out base runner stranded in the second. The nickel curve was tight. His control was sharp.

In the last half of the third the Giants touched him. Merkle sent a playable ball to Jack Barry that the shortstop wasn't able to field. The pitcher, Marquard, laid down a sacrifice. With two outs Larry Doyle "galvanized thousands of throats" when he smoked a single to right, scoring Merkle with the first run of the game. The lead was meaningful, as Marquard was not having trouble finding a path through the Athletics' lineup.

But Collins responded in the fourth with a long triple that, had it not been played well, might have been an inside-the-park homer. Frank Baker then lashed a single to right. Tie game.

The reaction was surprisingly loud, as there were a number of Philadelphians in the crowd. Most of them had begun their day with a visit to the Somerset Hotel, headquarters of the Athletics. Several players greeted fans in the lobby, though Bender was not among them. He remained in his room and slept a long time. Players lunched and dressed at the Somerset. A mob had blocked the street to see the A's make their start for the park in automobiles.

With Baker at first, McInnis was instructed to lay down a sacrifice. Amos Strunk then hit back to the pitcher, who nipped Baker at third. But Barry revived the rally with a double to left and Schang followed, belting one. The flight of the ball fooled center fielder Tillie Shafer, who took so long to recover that by the time the ball was retrieved Schang was on third and the A's had a 3–1 lead.

Philadelphia added two more in the top of the fifth. Collins walked and stole second. Then Baker harkened memories of 1911. He threw his right hip open and exploded on the ball squarely. Those in the Polo Grounds knew right away that the grounds were not long enough to contain the shot. Baker, said one newspaper the next morning, was a "pitcher murderer."

Collins didn't wait for the ball to clear the field. He trotted home and stood until Baker joined him. The two embraced at the plate and walked lockstep back to the bench. In the dugout the A's flipped their bats in the air, a customary reaction to Baker homers. There was enough rejoicing in the stands that if you closed your eyes you might be fooled into thinking the game was being played in Philadelphia.

Philadelphians who could not be in New York physically were there emotionally. During the two hours and six minutes Bender battled the Giants, more than 40,000 people called the *North American's* phone service, Walnut 750, to ask for updates. About the same number called in the hours following the game to learn the final score. Thousands stood outside Philadelphia City Hall plaza and watched an electric scoreboard flash the tallies. Many others viewed the game on the "Nokes Electrascore" at the Forrest Theater. There were various versions in other major cities across the country. By this time, people in many major cities throughout the country were able to follow baseball games on large mechanical scoreboards such as the one in Philadelphia. Newspapers often erected these scoreboards outside their buildings during the World Series. Large groups of fans would stand or sit outside watching a baseball diamond that was plotted using light bulbs and simple sound effects. Different colored lights would flash throughout the game, signifying different outcomes—outs, balls-and-strikes, runs—allowing fans to learn results quickly.

The idea of staring at a board for hours, waiting for it to light up basic facts about a game, may sound mundane, but the scoreboards were wildly popular. Newspapers sometimes sold tickets because there was more interest than room. Thousands surrounded the boards, reacting with shouts and whistles, as if they were watching live action.

On the surface, there is something peculiar about turning a portion of one's happiness over to a collection of ballplayers, and perhaps more peculiar still is concerning oneself about ball games played decades before one's birth. But there is a reason to remember why people stood in front of an electric board while Bender was exhibiting his wiles in New York. Indirectly, he was enhancing the lives of men and women whom he would never meet. He didn't provide necessities, economic or otherwise, but rather something subtler, and possibly as powerful: pride.

By 1913 remote scoreboards of the kind watched by Philadelphians were common on the East Coast. But it was a new technology out West. Before the Series began more than fifty American Indians in Washington and Oregon traveled as far as 150 miles to Portland, Oregon, where they would view the returns of Bender's, and John Meyers's, performance. Newspaper wires were quick enough in those days that American Indian fans could have received the news the next morning at some location far closer to home. But they couldn't wait that long.

There may have been a sense of déjà vu as Bender carried a 5–1 lead to the mound to start the bottom of the fifth. But the Giants weren't paralyzed by the familiarity of Baker's blast or by the luster of Bender's right arm. In the last half of the fifth they inflicted more damage on Bender's World Series résumé than any team had up till that point.

Fred Merkle began the inning with a single to center and Moose McCormick, batting for Marquard, followed by doing the same. Bender induced a ground ball from leadoff man Tillie Shafer, but it was to the right side and both runners advanced. Larry Doyle hit a bouncing ball to shortstop Jack Barry, who fielded it and promptly threw it away. Merkle ran home and McCormick took third. Art Fletcher then hit a ball off Bender's foot that caromed into the outfield, driving in McCormick. Baker made a fine play on a hard-hit ball off the bat of George Burns, but he could only turn the ball into one out, not two, and Doyle scored. Suddenly New York was a run away.

Bender was facing a great team in front of a hostile crowd in one of the most crucial games of the season. Clearly he didn't have his best stuff, and because of what happened in the fifth he had to be second-guessing himself. The Giants had posted four runs on him in five innings. If ever he was going to break down, if ever he was going to be mortal and have a subpar outing in a money game, this seemed to be the time.

There was another thing working against Bender, this one under his skin. In the days leading up to the 1913 World Series rumors spread that a group of gamblers had offered him $25,000 to throw his World Series games. During Bender's career baseball had an unsavory relationship with gambling and gamblers. The fix in 1919 was a disease, the symptoms of which had begun to spread years before. In fact, while the Giants were in Philadelphia during this Series, detectives were distributed throughout the crowd in an effort to suppress open betting.

There was no foundation to the story that Bender was trying to throw games—after all, he'd wind up winning the only two he pitched—but that didn't mean he was oblivious to the noise. He tried to squelch the rumors and he could only do that with his performance. He threw as hard as he could, perhaps at times he overthrew. Even if he had been on the level he knew a poor outing would have looked suspicious. Sometimes too much motivation can overwhelm.

There are usual reactions to pressure, but few of them applied to Charles Bender. He had a unique relationship with adversity. When the New Yorkers raised their voices to another level, when the situation was slipping out of control, Bender's reaction was not to become more serious, restrained or tense. Instead he looked into the face of pressure and winked. During the fifth-inning rally McGraw tried to nag him, whipping invective from the bench. But Bender took steps toward the New York dugout, smiled, and held his hand to his ear, mockingly, urging McGraw to make his remarks louder so he could hear them.

In the sixth, the score still 5–4, Bender started to shush McGraw and his team. He retired Murray on a groundout to Collins. Meyers tried to bunt, but Bender pounced and made a fine throw to retire him. The Giants were set down in order after Bender whiffed Merkle.

Bender again faced trouble in the seventh but again found a way out. With runners on first and third and one out, when a hit or a long fly ball would have tied the score, the speedy Fletcher was up. Mack had a decision—play the infield in or set up for a possible double play. He elected to have his fielders play back. Fletcher drove the right kind of grounder to Barry, who started a 6–4–3, aided by a stretch from McInnis.

The A's celebrated their infield's fine play by adding to their margin in the eighth as a light rain began to fall. McInnis's only hit of the game was a double that scored Collins, who went 3-for-3 and reached base four times. Bender allowed a two-out single in the eighth, but was not again threatened.

Before the 1913 World Series, a pastor at a New York church supposedly took to the pulpit the subject of "Who will win?" and cited Christy Mathewson as "the finest illustration of the well-pressured man." During

Game 1 Matty was not called upon. Instead, he sat on the bench, where he watched another well-pressured man beat his team. Before the ninth inning Matty saw Bender sitting next to Connie Mack while Danny Murphy and Collins swarmed the pitcher, offering advice. A team trainer was "fanning him with a towel throughout the recess and mopping him with a sponge," Mathewson said. "The Indian went back and won on his gameness."

Bender's final inning may have been his sharpest of the afternoon. Merkle grounded to second. Larry McLean popped to second. By the time Bender struck out Shafer to end the game he had recovered from near disaster in the fifth to pitch four straight shutout innings.

"In my opinion," Mathewson said, "he did not use bad judgment, but was just dangling on the ragged edge, ready to slip over and let go. The wonderful Indian went through the last two innings on his nerve alone, putting all that he had on the ball and applying every bit of his craft to win."

In fact, despite his troubles in the early half of the game, Bender's control was outstanding. He didn't walk a batter. Bender, Matty added, was "spinning the ball over with everything he had."

They couldn't see him with their own eyes, but upon learning that Bender had won, the American Indians who were huddled in downtown Portland, according to a wire story widely published two days later, "literally whooped at news of his victory."

That night, Bender returned to the Somerset and found a crowd reliving the game. Loud, competing voices. Jostling. Pushing. Shouting. People tried to hear one another "above the din," *Sporting Life* said. Though dozens wanted a piece of him, Bender—who had "waltzed through the McGraw horde as a whirlwind rips through the unprotected alfalfa"— walked into the hotel and never broke stride. He took his key from the hotel clerk "with as much emotion as would a toothpick" and went to his room.

He came down a few minutes later, ate some supper and headed for the train that would take the A's back to Philadelphia. His teammates also hopped aboard, jubilantly singing and celebrating. Bender sat in the corner reading a magazine. A newspaperman walked over and asked him how he felt. Bender reached into his pocket and pulled out a red piece of paper, folded, its edges tattered.

"Remember that?" Bender asked.

The newspaperman nodded. He recalled the story written in 1910 that Bender would not measure up when he faced Chicago in the World Series.

"Well, I couldn't let the Cubs beat me after that, could I?"

Bender then reached further into his wallet, pulled out another clip and smoothed out the wrinkles on his knee. He pointed to one of the sentences he had underlined: *McGraw knows he can beat Bender, and hopes that Mack will start with the Indian.*

"A friend sent that to me a week ago," Bender said. "So when I got into the box I thought of the clipping, and that was enough. And the Giants will not beat me in this series."

Three days later Bender had a chance to prove the claim when he was on the mound for Game 4. The A's had a 2–1 Series lead. The Giants won Game 2 in Philadelphia when Christy Mathewson drove in the winning run with a single in the tenth inning of a previously scoreless game. Giants injuries—including those to Fred Merkle, Fred Snodgrass and John Meyers—were a factor in the Series as they forced McGraw to try peculiar defensive alignments. In the second game the New York manager used pitcher Hooks Wiltse at first base and, shockingly, it worked to New York's advantage. The A's managed to put two runners on base with none out in the bottom of the ninth. Wiltse threw both out at home. Before Game 3 in New York, Bender warmed up and felt so good he tried to convince Mack to pitch him. Almost worked, too, but Mack decided against it before the first pitch.

Instead the manager went with rookie Leslie Ambrose Bush. Prior to the 1913 season Bush's big league career amounted to a total of eight innings, but in 1913 he was surprisingly effective as he went 15-6. Bush joined the Athletics two seasons before Bender would leave them, but the two became fast friends and were often associated with one another for geographic reasons. Bush was raised in Brainerd, Minnesota, the son of a railroad conductor. Young Leslie supposedly learned to pitch while throwing rotten apples at outhouses.

Bender wasn't from Brainerd but sportswriters often wrote that he was. It seemed inconceivable two pitchers for the same pennant-winning team came from the same small town in northern Minnesota, not exactly a renowned manufacturer of baseball talent. In fact, several miles and eight years separated their births, but the two had a lot in common. Bender and Bush's friendship lasted long after they stopped sharing a dressing room. In the off-seasons they hunted together and at one point they bowled on the same team. Bush's friends called him Bullet Joe, and the nickname, ascribed by a newspaper in Missoula, Montana, wasn't drawn from a hat. Bush was wild but he threw hard. He carved out a fine Major League career, and, like Bender, one of the highlights was throwing a no-hitter against Cleveland. In Game 3 of the 1913 World Series Joe Bush pitched the best game of his young life, allowing five hits in an 8–2 win.

Bender followed Bush by baffling the Giants for six innings in Game 4 as the A's built a 6–0 lead at Shibe Park on another overcast day. After Game 1, Eddie Collins had written in his column that he thought the Giants had received all of the breaks and still didn't win. As the fourth game unfolded Collins looked correct—the A's were outplaying the Giants and about to take command of the Series. Bender had allowed just two hits through six innings when George Burns opened the seventh with an infield hit. Tillie Shafer then popped to second. Red Murray singled to left, moving Burns to second. Art Wilson struck out but on the final pitch of the at bat Burns stole third and Murray second. Then Merkle blasted a three-run home run.

After the game, it was Murray's at bat, not Merkle's, that most bothered Bender. "I pitched bad to Murray in that seventh inning," Bender said to Collins while the two were in the shower. "I had him two strikes and nothing and I got the next ball right in the groove."

The Giants wanted back into the game and Series, and in the eighth they proved the point more forcefully. The score was 6–3 when Buck Herzog singled to open the inning. Larry Doyle replaced Herzog at first by hitting into a fielder's choice. Then Fletcher replaced Doyle by doing the same thing. But Burns provided life for a rally, hitting a double to left, scoring Fletcher. Shafer followed with a triple to right, the Giants' sixth hit of the two-inning spree, making it a one-run game with the tying run on third.

On the bench, Mack was concerned. He instructed captain Danny Murphy to walk onto the field and talk with Bender, who assured Murphy he was all right. Most pitchers would have been yanked before this point. Bender clearly was not throwing his best pitches and Mack considered pulling him. But Mack had a rare level of trust in Bender. For one thing, his demeanor illustrated a portrait of control. Newspapers noted the next day that Bender smiled throughout the game with an "inscrutable smile." For an opponent, even one dishing out a bundle of hits, it was unnerving.

Sporting Life said Bender's troubles were due to his "carelessness, or rather his cynical contempt for his opponents." But he escaped when Murray grounded to Collins and he got serious in the ninth, putting "everything he had on the ball," according to *Sporting Life*, retiring pinch hitter Doc Crandall, Merkle, and pinch hitter Eddie Grant in order. "It was some game comeback on Chief's part," Collins said.

Bender used five strikeouts, fine control (he walked one, the only one in eighteen innings during the Series), and his mettle to push Philadelphia to the brink of its third title in four seasons. Which the A's won the next day in New York when Eddie Plank dominated New York, Christy Mathewson made his World Series curtain call, and the Giants became the second—and most recent—team to lose three straight World Series. The A's, *Sporting Life* said, were "one of the greatest base ball teams ever organized."

Half a country away, northern Minnesota celebrated the victory as fervently as did Philadelphia. After the scores were made known, northern Minnesotans lit bonfires to celebrate the win and the achievements of Bush as well as Bender.

"There was not a store in Brainerd that did a nickel's worth of business after the returns began to come in," said William McKenzie a northern Minnesota resident at the time. "The interest was so intense that everybody deserted business and flocked to the telegraph office to get the news hot off the wire."

Bender was also admired in his adoptive hometown. "The *Philadelphia Bulletin* the other day said: 'On Broadway they rave about Mathewson being the greatest *money* pitcher in base ball—but only on Broadway,'" *Sporting Life* reported. "Right here in this town where we boast of the greatest ball club of all time we boast of the greatest *money* pitcher—the greatest of all. That hurler is Charles Albert Bender."

In addition to the acclaim he had earned, and the satisfaction he must have felt, there was a tangible reward. His cut of the player's share was $3,244, or "$14.61 for every heave he made" in the Series, *Sporting Life* noted. Soon after the World Series Bender packed up and took a vacation—a hunting trip (what else?)—with Jack Barry at Weldon Wyckoff's home in Williamsport, Pennsylvania. But before he left Connie Mack called. According to one version of the story, it was the night the A's clinched, and Bender had already consumed at least one celebratory glass of wine.

"Do you remember that conversation we had before the series started?"

"No, I don't," Bender said.

"Well, be in my office tomorrow morning."

After he appeared Mack presented his money pitcher with a check for $2,500—the amount needed to pay off his house.

Chapter Twenty.

Charles Bender and Connie Mack also had a conversation before the 1914 World Series, but this one wasn't as cordial. In the latter days of the 1914 regular season, after the A's made a mad dash through the American League, Mack began to prepare for the World Series. He sent Bender, his bright pitcher with the eagle eyes, to New York to scout the Boston Braves. But, according to one version of the story, while Bender was supposedly in New York Mack ran into him on a Philadelphia street corner.

"I thought you had gone to look over the Braves," Mack said.

Bender shrugged him off. "What's the use of wasting a perfectly good afternoon looking at that bunch of bush league hitters?"

Like most with greatness inside, Bender was confident. Often written about as "stern," "cool," and "impassive," some of the commonly used terms had prejudicial overtones. But the stoic descriptions were not entirely inaccurate. Bender carried himself with an air that told the world that he was in control of the situation. He was not boastful, but he was purposeful. He always seemed to believe he would succeed, and never was his confidence higher than before the 1914 World Series. Three months later George Stallings wrote in the *Boston Daily Globe* that Bender demonstrated his bravado in the moments before the first game when

Bender, said sportswriter F. C. Lane, was "the coolest pitcher in the game."

he "got thoroughly warmed up then kidded with the crowd by throwing the ball underhand."

To the observer, the tension of baseball games rarely seemed to touch Bender. People tend to look for, and find, details that reinforce their views, and by 1914 there was plenty of evidence to support the notion that Bender was unflappable. Given his many clutch performances, few had to stretch their imaginations to see that he was a calmer character than most. Bender likely enjoyed the reputation he had built—maybe he even tried to play it up—and at some point probably believed the hype. He could slip into his uniform and resume being brilliant when being brilliant mattered most.

Perhaps, too, his outward shows of calm came from knowing something his teammates and those watching from the bleachers could never know. Maybe he did not get rattled in big games because he knew a greater strain than the World Series. When pressure is unyielding the word means something different to you.

Grantland Rice said Bender was one of "the greatest competitors I ever knew." Rice recalled their golf games. "I never saw Bender worry over any type of shot—a bad lie in a bunker or a four-foot putt."

Bender was so even-keeled Rice once asked him if anything ever bothered him.

"Why should it?" he said. "I'll tell you how I figure those things. When something like this shot into the trap takes place, I look on it as a problem. It is a new problem that has to be worked out. It has to be studied and played correctly. I don't face any ordinary shot. If I play it well, I get a kind of kick out of it. If it doesn't come off . . . well, what difference does it make?"

Bender seemed to see tough luck as an opportunity, a challenge, something to be excited about. "What's a six-foot putt? You either hole it or you don't," he said. "The only thing to consider is to play it right—not hurry the stroke, move the body or lift the head.

"I get a kick out of getting in tough places. When you have a tough shot and play it well, that's something to remember."

For all the athletic intelligence Bender used while toeing the rubber, perhaps the thing that most distinguished him from his contemporaries was his rare ability to compartmentalize, a word that wasn't yet used but could have been invented for him. Those who managed him, played with him, played against him, and wrote about him noticed this ability to focus on the task at hand. It was a useful skill for a pitcher—and almost a necessity for a man trying to find his place in an unwelcoming world.

Bender's methodical approach was evident to Rube Bressler, a Philadelphia A's rookie pitcher in 1914 who roomed with Bender on the road. Bressler quickly began to look up to Bender and Eddie Plank. Unlike some acclaimed stars, Bender and Plank didn't put on airs or act coolly toward the young player, instead sitting on the bench next to Bressler, offering advice gratis. "I used to try to get near them and listen to what they were talking about," Bressler told Lawrence Ritter, "and every question I'd ask they'd pay attention and tell me what they thought. I used to put sticks behind my ears so they'd stand out further. Boy, I wanted to hear what those guys had to say."

The tutorials continued away from the ballpark. Bressler learned from Bender not only how to approach hitters but how to manage the successes and failures of life. One time Bressler said he had been matched against Walter Johnson in a game in Washington. The Philadelphia Athletics on that day became one of 110 teams shut out by Johnson during the Big Train's career, a hard fact to which opposing clubs were accustomed but young players were reluctant to accept. Bressler pitched about as well as he was capable that afternoon, but his effort wasn't good enough as the Athletics lost 1–0, Bressler said in *The Glory of Their Times*. By the time he reached their room that evening Bressler was still kicking air.

"Gee, that sure was a tough one to lose," Bressler said.

"Are you talking about today's game?" Bender asked.

"Of course."

"Did you hear the boys yelling when we came into the hotel?"

"What boys?"

"The newsboys."

"Oh, I guess so."

"What were they saying?"

"They were saying 'Washington Wins, 1–0.'"

"That's right," Bender said. "It's a matter of record now. Forget about that game. Win the next one."

That regular season, Bressler went 10-4 with a 1.77 ERA. Following the

1914 World Series, he resumed a seven-year career pitching for Philadelphia and later moved on to Cincinnati. For the rest of his career he was 16-28 and three times had an ERA greater than five runs per game. "I forget who my roommate was [two years later]," Bressler said. "But I'll tell you one thing: it was not Chief Bender."

Rice placed Bender in a group with Walter Hagen and George Gipp as the three athletes who were the best at relaxing while under heavy pressure. "Tension is the greatest curse in sport," Bender told Rice. "I've never had any tension. You give the best you have—you win or lose. What's the difference if you give all you've got to give?"

It's hard to know how much of Bender's comments were an accurate assessment of his views. Bender may also have wanted others to think he managed pressure, and so he often laughed at the concept. The more one appears in control, the less one is bothered with probing questions.

In any event, when the bench jockeying came fast and fierce, he had the habit of smiling in the face of his opponent—and there may be no greater insult to an enemy than a wide, toothy grin. For example, in 1903, the Athletics were playing the Browns in St. Louis. After a collision at home plate in which he had been run over Bender and Browns hitter Bobby Wallace exchanged words. Next time Wallace came to the plate Bender drilled him in the ribs. Wallace became furious. Players had to intervene.

"It wasn't the act of hitting me that riled me up," Wallace said, "but 'twas the grin Bender wore that set me wild."

Bender's calm was revealed to opponents with another weapon in his arsenal: humor. While on the mound he would talk to a batter or holler at the opposing dugout. "No use trying to get the Chief's goat," said all-star bench jockey John McGraw. "You can't get under his thick skin, and he'll wind up kidding the shirt off of you."

This wasn't a lack of professionalism. Rather, Bender used jokes like some pitchers use the brushback—to disarm. Make no mistake, when there was a big game Bender was serious about wanting the ball. "Chief Bender exemplifies, in a high degree, the invincible calm of the Indian," F. C. Lane wrote in *Baseball Magazine*. "The whole list of the game's casualties offers nothing that can disturb, to the slightest degree, the Chief's composure. . . . Even when that most disheartening of all possibilities, a ninth-inning rally, had wrested from his hands a sure victory by the score of 5–4, he left the field with that same quiet, unruffled dignity, as though nothing in the world had happened. The Chief feels defeat as well as the next man. He is cool, that is all. His coolness nerves him to fight with undiminished energy for victory. It also nerves him to accept defeat with stoicism. Bender is the coolest pitcher in the game."

The *North American* was not beyond the racist depictions of the day, but it covered Bender's career as well as any rag in Philadelphia. "Bender," the newspaper said, "is one of the rarest characters the game has ever known."

Especially early in his career Bender was not given much respect by the press. But over time some of the writers who saw him daily came to realize that there was something different about this man. The prevailing stereotypes did not apply to him. He was refined, articulate, esteemed—not some easy target for teammates' jokes. That Bender received deference from men the writers themselves revered was worth noting.

"He commands the respect of all, and while he is entirely inoffensive, they understand that a man of Bender's blood could brook no insult," the *North American* said. "With his keen eye, hair-trigger brain, steady nerve and tremendous strength, Bender would prove a formidable antagonist if ever put to a test. Ballplayers know this and let him alone."

Coverage did little to discourage the one-dimensional view of the kind espoused by the chants and catcalls. But eventually it was difficult not to acknowledge how far that simple-minded view missed the mark.

"It is always amusing to those on the inside when the crowds in other cities attempt to guy the highly polished and cultured Carlisle graduate. 'Where's your tomahawk, Chief?' 'Back to the wigwam,' and other sallies are hurled at him when he goes to the [coaching] lines by persons who are distinctly his inferiors," the *North American* said. "But up to date there is no record of anybody offending in this manner at close range. If anybody ever had such an intention, one glance from those sinister, steel eyes would be enough to cow him. It must not be inferred that Bender is a recluse, who shrinks from the society of his teammates. His attitude is that of a master."

Bender's explanation was simple. "All games were the same to me," he said. "I worried about each pitch and that was all."

Players said he had ice in his veins, especially during moments when everyone around him was nervous. He had, Christy Mathewson said, "a cool head and a fine arm and plenty of courage." That's the rich irony of his nickname: Despite its ridiculous etymology Bender carried himself as though he was a chief, with a lowercase C.

Which is why the sixth inning of the first game of the 1914 World Series was so shocking. No one had ever seen Bender unravel before. Not in such an important contest. Not in such a complete manner.

Herbie Moran began the inning by hitting a looper. Shortstop Barry raced toward the foul line and made a desperate lunge to spear the ball with his bare hand inches from the line. Barry's momentum carried him almost to the fence, and he had to struggle to keep on his feet. It was the kind of catch that people would have talked about later if the play had mattered.

But then Johnny Evers slammed one through Bender's legs that no fielder could prevent from being a single. Bender threw four balls to Joe Connolly. And, after taking a ball, George Whitted hit a triple that scored two. In the stands the Royal Rooters were celebrating as though the game was over. But the Braves weren't done. Butch Schmidt hit a single to left and Whitted waltzed home.

In 79⅔ previous World Series innings Charles Bender had allowed a total of 22 runs. He had started nine games and finished all of them. His performance on this day was something Philadelphia fans hadn't considered possible. Bender had fallen behind in the count most of the short afternoon, and when he tried to battle back with fastballs, Boston pounced. And it might have been worse; the A's had turned three double plays in Bender's 5⅓ innings of work. For the first time in his World Series career Bender looked toward the Philadelphia dugout and saw Connie Mack standing up, waving his scorecard, calling him in.

"That's enough," Mack said.

The manager instructed captain Ira Thomas to replace Bender with Weldon Wyckoff. Bender ambled off the field with his head down. He was dejected and he stepped slowly. Philadelphia fans didn't know it, but this was the last time they would see Bender in an Athletics uniform.

After he reached the bench Bender stopped to take a drink of water.

Mack turned to him. "They don't hit too badly for bush leaguers. Do they, Albert?"

Bender mumbled words not printed in the newspapers and headed for the showers.

Chapter Twenty-One. Dick Rudolph shut down the Athletics the rest of the afternoon, throwing slick, darting riddles over the plate that Philadelphia hitters never figured out how to solve. Rudolph's control was not outstanding early, but after the first two innings the Mackmen, the *North American* said, "were as weak as jellyfish." The Athletics made only five hits, didn't score an earned run, and struck out eight times. Rudolph, Stallings said in the *Boston Daily Globe*, "went out and pitched the game of his life." The final was 7–1.

The crowd inside Shibe Park was stunned by the team's poor performance, and it seemed the A's had lost more than a game. The fans seated on porches and rooftops, as well as those who followed the game on scoreboards outside newspaper buildings and in theaters, were also disillusioned. Their moneyman had been abused and their hitters were swinging boat oars.

The next morning James Isaminger pulled out his thesaurus: "Boston beat, whipped, licked, tormented, maltreated, belabored, walloped, smashed, gashed, bruised, mangled and wrecked us, to say nothing of inflicting other indignities too multitudinous to be itemized." He also said that the A's "didn't exhibit any more enthusiasm than a missionary being led up to a cannibal king's soup pot," that the Boston "vandals ruined Mack's masterpiece in bronze," and that Bender was a "mortified Indian."

Hugh Fullerton said Boston "swept the Athletics off their feet, out played, out generaled and out gamed them." The "Mackmen were doing their best, but seemed nonplussed by the Braves' system of attack and defense. The Braves were assaulting Bender viciously and without regard to the rules of warfare.

"The Chief looked good. His fastball was hopping and his curve was breaking fairly well. But when he got the smoke going he lacked control and when he slowed down to second speed to get the ball over the Braves waded in and hit the tar out of it."

Stallings did not act like anyone but himself: "The victory in the World's Series is no surprise to me," he told *Sporting Life*. "I never had the least doubt we would beat the Athletics." In other articles he said Bender didn't have his best stuff but that his team would have beaten him even if he had. His players did something no other team had done—they got under the pitcher's skin. "Every hitter went up to the plate and had something to say to Bender, and so did the players on the bench." The Braves knew Bender was not right and that he knew it, too.

"He came back at two or three of the hitters, which is a sure sign," Stallings said. "Usually, when right, he says nothing, only smiles."

Stallings added: "He did not wear his customary smile long."

The thought entering the Series was that the Athletics would walk over the Braves and calmly pick up their World Series checks. But instead the momentum Boston used to win the National League carried them to the championship. In the second game at Shibe Park Boston pitcher Bill James gave up only two hits, out-dueling Eddie Plank, 1–0. James won the first Fenway Park game as well, throwing two scoreless innings in relief of George Tyler. It had been 2–2 after nine innings, and each team scored two runs in the tenth. Boston won, 5–4, in the twelfth when A's pitcher Joe Bush threw wildly past third base after fielding a bunt with two on and none out. Rudolph was almost as good in Game 4 as he was in the opener, and the Braves won 3–1. Boston, not Philadelphia, had a clean sweep.

"We didn't take that first defeat seriously," Bender said years later. "We said to ourselves, 'We'll win tomorrow.' But tomorrow never came."

Bender's outing in 1914 was the only one of ten World Series starts
he didn't complete. Source unknown.

Instead, the opposite. The A's were stifled by three hot pitchers. The premiere team in baseball hit .172 for the Series, scored just six runs, and produced nothing more substantial than a double. Frank Baker batted .250, Eddie Collins .214, Stuffy McInnis .143—and several regulars hit worse.

"Ten days ago, if anybody predicted such an easy triumph," Isaminger said, "he would have been hauled off to the lunacy court."

How do you explain the event that caused your life to spin into free fall? Answer: in every possible way. A 1950 Associated Press poll of sportswriters called the Boston Braves' victory in 1914 the biggest sports upset of the first half of the twentieth century. Bender was asked about Game 1 and the Series periodically during a span of about forty years, and over time the loss was attributed to a laundry list of reasons.

Poor scouting. "The men who scouted the Braves for us came back with the wrong reports. They told us to pitch high/inside to Hank Gowdy and you know what he did to high/inside pitches. He murdered us."

Inflated craniums. "We had lost respect for the National League. We had beat them 12 games out of 16 in three prior series. In short, we got fat headed."

Illness. Bender was feeling ill, with "vertigo and trouble with my gall bladder and stomach."

Opponent's fine play. "Rudolph and James were great in that 1914 Series. They had perfect control. Both had spitballs they could throw through the eye of a needle. It was uncanny how they both kept the ball low and away from our men." And "Johnny Evers and Rabbit Maranville hit our pitchers as if they owned them. We pitched wrong to them, too."

Attitude. "It was the Braves' spirit, as well as the way we pitched to them, that carried them through. Spirit is something you cannot buy or cannot learn. It is infectious, like a tonic. You don't know where it comes from when you have it and you don't know where it goes when you lose it. The Braves had that kind of spirit that year. It wasn't mere combativeness. It was confidence and determination mixed. And that is a hard nut to crack."

Stallings's preparation. "Another thing that played a part in our inability to hit was the fact that we couldn't get their signs. Much of our success in batting had been due to our ability to get either the catcher's or the pitcher's sign and to know what to expect at the plate. If fellows like Stuffy McInnis knew what was coming, they could murder the ball. Stallings was too smart for us. The Braves had read the series of articles written by Eddie Collins in one of the magazines telling how we stole signs. They were prepared.

"Rudolph and James 'covered up' their spitters and fastballs in perfect fashion and the catchers used combination signs. We didn't get to second base often enough to learn what they were using."

The better team won. "We had no alibis. We didn't get any bad breaks. The umpiring was perfect. The weather was magnificent. They just outplayed us from the first pitch.

"The Braves beat us because they were the better club."

Lack of beer. At the time, players thought a proper amount of barley and hops was an important element of training. "There is quite a story about that series that has never been published—a yarn that carries a lesson to every athlete," Bender said. "We got off to a great start that year and played fine ball to take a big lead. With six weeks to play, it looked like a cinch. Such a cinch that Connie called us together one morning to make plans for the rest of the season and the World's Series. 'It looks like we're going to win,' he said. I can remember his words as if they were yesterday. 'And I want you to do something for me. I want you to give up drinking—even beer. I don't want the fans to be able to say one word against anyone.'

"We all agreed and kept our promise. This means that I, for example, who had been used to stopping on the way home from the ballpark for a glass of beer to relax my nerves, went straight home. The rest of the boys did the same. We became stale . . . and then took a shellacking from the Braves.

"Every athlete has to relax. If he doesn't, he goes into a slump, gets stale, and can't do a thing."

The irony of the beerless defense is that many believed the converse was true. As long as there have been ballplayers there have been ballplayers who have imbibed, and perhaps that was never more the case than during Bender's career. The nature of the game was conducive to recreational drinking; since games were played during the day and half of them were played on the road, players often had evenings free and no commitments that prevented trips to watering holes. Pitchers such as Bender had even more time on their hands than did position players. Although he was not used exclusively as a starter there were certainly days Bender went to the ballpark knowing there was little chance he would enter the game.

Happenings related to ballplayers' favorite after-hours hobby were not often reported in the press. When a star player was too hungover to play his manager winked at the newspapermen and the newspapermen would either write that the player was ill or they wouldn't write anything at all. An examination of box scores during Bender's career shows numerous unexplained, prolonged absences, periods when he mysteriously didn't pitch for weeks at a time. In fact, Bender suffered a series of illnesses, those unrelated to alcohol, and he also endured arm problems, some of which may have been caused by rheumatism. But by the 1914 World Series it was also no secret to anyone close to the team that Charles Bender was a drinker of some repute.

In early September of 1912 Mack indefinitely suspended Bender and his pal, outfielder Rube Oldring, for what newspapers referred to as being "out of condition," a common euphemism. "The suspensions of Bender and Oldring did not come as a surprise to those who have been hearing tales nearly all season of the doings of certain members of the Athletics," the *Philadelphia Telegraph* said. "The only surprise is that manager Mack did not act sooner."

Mack tolerated Bender's drinking for some time before the suspension. He hoped the pitcher would sober up and that the Athletics would return to contention. Mack's team won the pennant four of five years but it was 1912, the year he didn't win, that he thought he had his best team of the five. Frank Baker had a monster season, batting .347 and leading the league in home runs and RBI. Eddie Collins hit .348 and stole 63 bases. The Athletics had won in 1910 and 1911 and there was no excuse for them not to win in 1912. They were relatively healthy and every member of the team's nucleus was in his prime.

Repeatedly, Bender's and Oldring's erratic performances and absences were explained as illness. Once it became obvious the A's were not headed to another World Series there was no reason to finesse the situation. Besides, the excuse was no longer being taken seriously. One writer who began to devote column inches to the situation was James Isaminger, who believed Bender drank because he was fat and happy after back-to-back World Series victories.

"With their [World Series] check in their pockets," he said, "suddenly they imagined they were in the Guggenheim and Morgan class. . . . Boys who should have been resting in their cabins instead of lushing in the cabarets."

But Mack, Isaminger said, will "have the last giggle on the bottled-in-bond boys" at contract time. "Lo, the rich Indian. Then came the fall."

Added Isaminger, "Connie Mack's Christmas gift to Chief Bender will be a brochure called 'The Rise and Fall of Louis Sockalexis.'"

Bender was publicly rebuked for his drinking, but Mack did not give up on him, not in 1912 anyway. It's not known what conversations took place between the two men, but perhaps Mack also tried to sway his star pitcher through the press, which would have been a willing mouthpiece. "Bender really is a man of intelligence," Isaminger said. "The Chippewa is a gentleman and the mental superior of the average tosser. He is well read, plays fine billiards and is a crack shot. He loves these sports dearly, and will go two seasons without a break of any kind. But once in a while he will get into a rut and then he is inclined to forget about his obligations to the club.

"Bender is by no means hopeless. The Indian is shooting redbirds and saying nothing. If Mack chooses to give him another chance and not trade him elsewhere he may come back in 1913 and pitch winning ball. It's up to him."

Looking toward 1913, Mack used Bender in the final day of the 1912 regular season. Then Bender pitched in an intracity series exhibition game, coming on in relief and striking out six Philadelphia Phillies in six innings.

Of 1912 Mack told sportswriter Arthur Daley late in life, "I sent [Bender and Oldring] ahead of the rest of the squad from Washington to New York and they never did show up. That happened in mid-August and ruined our chances. So the next year I sent Bender a contract for only $1,200. Goodness gracious, but that was mean of me. His wife tore it up so he couldn't sign it.

"A few days later he came to see me, 'I don't know anything else but baseball,' he blurted out. 'I'll sign and I'll behave.' So he signed at that ridiculous figure."

Three seasons prior Mack had cut Bender's salary in half in a message about the manager's views of his habit. In 1913 Mack wasn't going to mess around. He wrote into Bender's contract that he would be paid a full salary only if the pitcher "refrains from intoxicating liquors." (The oft-told tale of Mack's generous World Series bonus following the 1913 World Series may have been partly Mack's making up the difference after Bender had made good on his word rather than an act of pure kindness.)

Bender's drinking may have been tolerated more loosely on other teams. Not on Connie Mack's club. Fred Lieb said he was not "an absolute teetotaler." He enjoyed a celebratory glass of wine, and as a player he had consumed a beer now and then. But Mack had a strong will and unabashed honesty. Whether or not he read Aristotle, he subscribed to the philosopher's theory that a wise man practices moderation in all things. Bender was no longer a moderate drinker.

After Bender's and Oldring's suspensions Mack spoke about his frustrations. "Booze and baseball don't mix, never did and never will. . . . Once in a while you hear of some marvel who can stay out all night, drink all the breweries dry, wreck a few taxicabs and otherwise enjoy himself, and then step into the box and pitch a wonderful game of ball," he said. "Players who haven't any more sense point to Rube Waddell and Bugs Raymond and that brand and say, 'Ah, these were the good old days! None of your high-priced managers and their red tape then.' . . . Well, look at Waddell—one of the most remarkable pitchers nature ever produced. But Waddell, with all his talent, couldn't stay in the Major Leagues. Why? Because he stood there and pitched himself to Old Man Barleycorn, and finally every one he threw was slammed over the fence. And that's the way they all go. Is it so wonderful, after all?

"No, sir, the day of the stewed ballplayer has gone, and it won't come back. If the members of my team want to drink, all right. But they can't drink and play ball at the same time. That's settled. They can do whichever they prefer, but they can't do both. There are no exceptions to my rule, either. Any manager will tell you the same: A short life and a merry one— that's it. And the merrier it is the shorter it will be in the big leagues."

By the conclusion of the 1914 World Series Connie Mack didn't have any more patience for Chief's benders.

On the morning of the first game the *North American* had printed a plea at the top of the first page—above the fold and displayed more prominently than an advance of the game—from William A. Sunday. Billy Sunday had been a professional baseball player on a team of big-league drinkers in the 1880s. He was a terrible hitter but ran like a man chased by wolves. He stole 71 bases during a season in which he reached base just 133 times. One Sunday afternoon, or so goes the story, Sunday and some teammates had left a Chicago saloon when they ran into a gospel wagon that included a preacher, brass band, and hymn singers. Sunday stopped and listened. A few minutes later he turned to his teammates and said, "Boys, I bid the old life goodbye."

In the years that followed Sunday learned to move his lips as fast as he could move his feet and he became a well-known fire-and-brimstone evangelist. He held a fundamentalist view, delivering passionate sermons against political liberalism, evolution, and perhaps his most famous sermon was "Booze, Or, Get on the Water Wagon," which convinced some to give up drinking. His efforts would later become a major social influence leading to the adoption of Prohibition. In 1914, he had already begun to fight.

"The issue is booze or no booze," Sunday said. "I call upon you in the name of God, home and native land to support the men and the political party who are against the saloon. Now is your chance to show your colors and to hit old John Barleycorn a knockout blow."

The culture was heading in that direction, but Charles Bender wasn't buying what Billy Sunday was selling. According to Norman Macht's research, Bender may have arrived at Shibe Park only some fifteen minutes before Game 1. Bender was supposedly so late that he missed the presentation of a new automobile to teammate Eddie Collins, most valuable player in the American League. Shag Thompson, an Athletics reserve, later called Bender's game-day illness not one of Bender's periodic maladies but rather an old-fashioned, head-spinning hangover, the result of Bender's and Rube Oldring's drinking the night before.

In fact, later press accounts mentioned that several of Mack's stars—

unnamed—had been out to the wee hours of the morning. *Sporting Life* reported that Bender was so "absolutely confident" that he became "careless as to his condition" and "physically unable to check the enemy." Why bother worrying about rest? They were only facing the lowly Boston Braves.

There were also sketchy, loosely detailed reports that after the first-game loss Bender tanked up on "firewater." According to the rumors, Bender was rebuked by Mack, who feared using him again in the Series.

Did Charles Bender show up for a World Series game either drunk or hung over? Or was his illness just a poorly timed appearance of the many he suffered throughout his life? It's unlikely a certain answer will ever be known.

But the distinction is not necessarily crucial. He drank because he was sick. He was sick because he drank. Either way, the cause was probably the same.

The body can only take so much stress before the inner illness reveals itself. As a young man Bender thought he had made a bargain with himself, and before the 1914 World Series that bargain seemed to have worked. Despite the hostility the world threw at him, he had seemingly found his place. But that bargain was a false question. He thought he had chosen the best path, but the paradox was that there was no right course. He had been heading for a moment like this one from his earliest days, and there was little he could do to prevent the inevitable.

Whatever the full explanation of Bender's particular actions, something went seriously wrong between Mack and Bender in what appeared to be a short span of time. The strategy before the World Series was to use Bender in the first and fourth games and Plank in the second and fifth. Bender would have three days rest between starts and, if the series went that far, he could still be used in Game 7. Before Game 4, newspapers reported that Bender was the likely starter. Many expected him to take the mound. Before that game the *North American* said Bender is "frothing at the mouth for another chance" and projected, perhaps encouraged by subtle hints from Mack, that he would pitch. But the manager started Bob Shawkey and relieved him with Herb Pennock. Mack had no intention of using Bender ever again.

The sweep was the first in the short history of the World Series and because a favored team was the first to be swept, theories developed. The most severe of these involved the idea that members of the Athletics—a team almost as heavily favored to win the 1914 World Series as would be the Chicago White Sox five years later—were paid not to win by gamblers who had placed large bets on the underdogs.

Usually, writers and historians convey this notion with a sentence that says something along the lines of this one: *Suspicions linger that "corrupt play" tainted the 1914 World Series.* It's an easy, fence-riding statement, of course, and since it doesn't prove anything little harm is done. Except that once the idea pops up, it's likely to be repeated, and with each repetition it is perceived to have more credence. Yet the evidence never changes. Only the view of that evidence changes.

One piece, according to Mack's biographer, Macht, is an alleged letter written by Mack to a friend in which Mack "supposedly voiced suspicions." Macht said the letter is apparently in the archives at Notre Dame University, but no one there can locate it. Jim Peterson, a former Philadelphia pitcher and friend of Mack's, told historian Lee Allen that Mack believed the 1914 Series was fixed and that Bender had a hand in the plot. But Allen apparently did not believe Peterson's story.

Another item that some have used is the fact that because George M. Cohan, a friend of Mack's, supposedly won a lot of money betting on the 1914 Series (as well as the 1919 Series), he must have had inside dope.

The rest is conjecture. Charles Bender usually pitched brilliantly in the World Series. Yet this time he was pounded. The A's were runaway favorites. Yet this time they lost four straight. Must be something to that. Or so goes the line.

In fact, when a similar level of logic is applied to the other side the circumstantial case becomes a bit more flimsy. For one thing, betting on the Series was light. A week before the *Boston Daily Globe* reported that an affluent man had tried to bet $1,500 on the Braves at 2 to 1 odds, but the best he could find was 10 to 7 or 10 to 8. As Macht's research has shown, the A's were consistent favorites and there was never any sudden or unexplained shift as there would be if heavy betting on the Braves showed up. The *New York Tribune* later reported that among the biggest losers in Wall Street betting circles was none other than Arnold Rothstein. Rothstein was reported as giving 8–5 odds and betting heavily to recoup losses from when the Giants lost the pennant. So if there was a fix, no one told one of the key figures behind the fraud of 1919. In fact, *Sporting Life* noted in its coverage of the Series that the Boston Royal Rooters lost money because even they didn't bet on Boston.

So few people seemed to make much money, the very motivation for a fix. The play on the field also didn't offer any substantive clues.

If you're going to throw a World Series you either have to buy off multiple pitchers or several fielders. Aside from the lopsided loss in Game 1, the other 3 games were decided by a total of 4 runs, including a 12-inning affair and a 1–0 loss. What's more, the fielding of both teams was fine; Philadelphia made a total of 3 errors in 4 games, a low total for the era.

It's also important to note that the rumors of a fix came after the fact—years later—and evidence has not, at least so far, been pegged to contemporary sources.

Instead, the outcome may be explained by the nature of the game. Boston's four-straight victory is one of several surprising sweeps in baseball history. In 1954 the Cleveland Indians, despite winning 111 games, were swept by the New York Giants. The 1990 Athletics, then in Oakland by way of Kansas City, were swept by the supposedly substandard Cincinnati Reds. Nearly any outcome is possible in a short series. Baseball is a game in which upsets are not only possible, they are probable—especially when a hot team with outstanding pitching is part of the equation. Clearly the Braves figured something out as their staggering second-half run attests. Is it possible the 1914 World Series was fixed and Charles Bender had a role? Within the confines of reason, it is. But if such a loose definition is the standard, one could justify similar accusations about scores of performances.

Conclusive evidence is unlikely, so one can't make a set-in-stone statement either way. But simply raising the question over and over, perpetuating an after-the-fact rumor that's not based on empirical evidence, also doesn't mean that the question becomes any more valid.

Over the years, Mack was asked, and his public response was always the same. "That doesn't mean the club threw the series to the Braves," Mack told the *Saturday Evening Post* in 1938. "Our players were simply more bitter against one another than interested in the series."

Another plausible rumor: Suspicions linger that inferior play cost Bender and A's the 1914 World Series.

Whatever the circumstances of their defeat, in effect, the Philadelphia Athletics were like a cream-filled balloon; after they popped, there was a mess. In the weeks that followed the World Series debacle, rumors about player departures circulated, until Mack ended the speculation with a series of actions that flummoxed the baseball world and sent Charles Bender reeling.

In late October wire reports announced that Mack had asked for waivers on his top three pitchers, Jack Coombs, Eddie Plank and Bender. Coombs had been a fine pitcher for Mack, but a bout with typhoid had permitted him to start a total of just four games over the previous two seasons and so his ouster was not shocking. Plank and Bender were another matter.

The pair combined for a 32-10 record in 1914 and both were veterans, on the wrong side of thirty, sure, but leaving aside Bender's outing in the World Series there were no signs either pitcher had thrown his last effective season. They were two of the top pitchers in the game. But Mack's decision was not purely a baseball one.

There were other factors, and Danny Murphy was linked to them. Murphy, a key player in several Philadelphia A's league championships, had been Connie Mack's captain, the guy who willingly changed positions to make room for a better player, the guy once dubbed "Old Reliable" for his steady play. Murphy got off to a fast start in 1912, batting .323 through 36 games. But then, according to Doug Skipper's research, he broke his kneecap during an attempted steal, an injury that may have included structural damage to the joint. "His playing days were not over," Skipper wrote in *Deadball Stars of the American League*, "but his skills were severely diminished." A sore arm developed in spring training of 1913, which didn't help matters, and in the spring of 1914, Mack released him. A week later Murphy signed with the Brooklyn team in the Federal League as both an outfielder and as a "scout." The Brooklyn Feds were backed by the deep pockets of the Tip Top Baking Company's Ward family. Mack, while guiding his A's to another pennant, soon learned that his former player's job description during the 1914 season was to lure star A's players, including Bender and Plank, to the Federal League.

Murphy didn't bring any players of significance to Brooklyn, but damage was inflicted nonetheless, and he was blamed for his role in ending the Philadelphia dynasty. "Danny Murphy, who had been one of my standbys, became an agent of the Federals, and he began to operate among my players," Mack said. "Murphy offered my players three times what they were getting from me."

Mack would later call the 1914 season "a nightmare" because this courting of his players by the upstart Federal League, which lasted from preseason to postseason. In an effort at damage control during the regular season the Athletics tore up several contracts. Mack even gave Eddie Collins and Frank Baker multiyear deals—the type of security players at the time seldom received. But the Feds kept raising their offers, kept extending the length of their contracts, and with the carrot in view several A's became frustrated with Mack's pay scale. The team divided into factions, one loyal to the Athletics, the other ready to jump. Some players had supposedly gone to Mack and told him they would finish out the 1914 season with him, but that the following spring they would be wearing Federal League uniforms. The Federal League "wrecked my club by completely changing the spirit of my players," Mack said.

By the start of the World Series, Mack was aware that Plank, at least, was on his way out the door and that Bender, maybe others, likely would follow. "I felt it was the most unhappy season I ever experienced," Mack said. "In the view of conditions which existed on my ball team, the beating we took from the Braves . . . was not surprising."

The players weren't wholly unjustified to ask for more. In 1914 Mack was considered a wealthy man. As historian Bruce Kuklick has pointed out, magazines of the time reported that Mack's share of the team's profits rose steadily each year, as he commanded a salary well beyond that of even his core players, and by 1913 the Shibes had already made in excess of three hundred thousand dollars. Such reports may not have been entirely accurate, as it's doubtful writers had access to the team's financial ledger, but the point is that many believed that the A's were the most profitable team in the American League and they were probably right. Mack was making a tidy sum.

There was irony in the Federal League's role in the destruction of Mack's machine. During his playing career Mack had been an eager member of John Montgomery Ward's Brotherhood of Professional Baseball Players, a group that formed the Players League in 1890, an early effort in which players fought for more rights, including a more equitable share of the revenue pie. In 1914 Mack sat on the other side of the table, as he was the man clenching his fists, fighting players seeking what he sought twenty-five years before.

But unlike other owners with deeper pockets, baseball was Mack's lone source of income. He had a large loan to pay off for his share of the team, and, besides, he wasn't in the habit of paying players more than necessary. In the first week of July, Mack had turned down Baltimore Orioles owner Jack Dunn's offer to sell him a pitcher named George Herman Ruth, saying he didn't have the money. If Mack wasn't willing to pay for the Babe he wasn't going to give Bender the kind of raise he could command in an open market, certainly not with the headaches that might accompany such an extension.

As the decades passed Mack's view of 1914 softened. "I was pretty sore at the time—awfully sore," he said. "I felt the players were letting down both me and the club, and that we had paid them as good salaries as baseball then could afford and made it possible for them to get into four rich [World Series]. Today, over perspective of the years, I feel a little differently. The players were taking advantage of a baseball war to get all they could, just as I took advantage of a baseball war to raid the National League when we first put a club in Philadelphia. I long have forgiven the players who gave me those 1914 headaches, and most of them have been back with me in some capacity."

But at the time, Mack's treatment was harsh. Following the World Series he quietly tried to find an American League team that would take Bender and Plank, rather than lose them to the Federal League. But Tigers manager Hughie Jennings leaked the story to the press and so Bender learned his days with the A's were over in the same manner as did the average A's fan.

"I guess Mr. Mack was quite disgusted with all of us . . . I know I was quite disgusted with myself," he said long after the fact. "I decided to go hunting and forget it. I was in the Texas Blockhouse in Williamsport, oiling my gun one morning, when Jerry Donovan dropped a paper in my lap. 'Hey, look at this, Chief,' he said. Across the top of the sports page was the banner line: 'Mack Asks Waivers on Bender and Plank.' I felt as if someone had hit me with a sledgehammer."

But in public at the time, Bender seemed less concerned. The Williamsport *Gazette and Bulletin* asked for a reaction. "I haven't heard a thing about it, therefore I have no statement to make," Bender said. "Tell Jerry Donovan to bring up a head of Limburger cheese."

Bender wasn't being shown the door—he was being kicked out of it. Men who were teammates earlier that month suddenly treated him like a stray cat. "Both of them are bothered a whole lot with rheumatism," A's pitcher Bob Shawkey said of Bender and Plank, "and will probably never again pitch winning ball in the American League."

Bender was livid about the way he was told. "I worked faithfully twelve years for the Athletics, gave them the best there was in me and do not think the summary way I was treated a month ago [was] the right kind of treatment for my years of labor."

He long maintained that it was only after Mack put him on waivers that he became serious about the Federal League. At least one news report in October 1914 stated as much. "It has been said that we were flirting with the Federal League before the series and weren't prepared to give our best, but that isn't true," Bender said years later.

But it defies logic that he would not have received an early offer from the Federal League, which was trying to lure players with his kind of star appeal. Bender's explanation also doesn't jibe with Mack's version of history. "We knew Plank and Bender already had signed Federal contracts," Mack said, "so we gave them their release."

That wasn't all. The team's best player, Collins, was sold to the Chicago White Sox for $50,000. Over the next two years Mack sold Barry, Baker, and other players for about $130,000. It was an astonishing fire sale. "If the players were going to 'cash in' and leave me to hold the bag," Mack said in his autobiography, "there was nothing for me to do but cash in, too." (The fact that Mack didn't sell Bender has been offered as circumstantial proof Bender did something sinister. This rationale is puzzling. After all, as long as Mack had decided to cut bait, what difference was the method going to make? Whether or not Bender threw his start, the wave-or-sell decision doesn't support either side of a "fixed" Series argument.)

Mack was criticized for breaking up the A's—years later. Fred Lieb later wrote that he was "accused of valuing dollars ahead of the Quaker City's baseball welfare." But at the time, Mack's hand was forced by the Federal League, and given the circumstances, he thought he was making a wiser baseball move than most realized. Though Bender's record in 1914 was flashy—he led the league in winning percentage—his performance, as Chris Jaffe's research has shown, wasn't as impressive as it seemed. Mack clearly used Bender against the weakest teams that season. For example, Bender did not make a single start against second-place Boston. He also didn't start against fourth-place Detroit. Three times he pitched against third-place Washington. Each one of his other twenty starts came against second-division teams with losing records. That kind of pattern didn't happen by accident, certainly not in the Deadball Era.

Over the previous two seasons Mack had raised a stable of fine pitchers in Shawkey, Joe Bush, Rube Bressler and Weldon Wyckoff. They were younger and cheaper. In short, Mack thought he could develop new Benders, Planks, and Coombses to reload for another run. "When you win," Mack said, "you have a general rise in all expenses. When a club is behind, salaries are low, so are expenses."

Mack had summarily broken up the game's first dynasty, and his actions have fueled speculation. Why would he get rid of his stars unless they had committed a greater sin than losing a Series? Rather than a supposed fix, however, this may have been about money—not just how much Mack would have had to pay to retain veteran players but his view of money's powers to corrupt. His complaint was already thirty years old, and it would be repeated a few hundred thousand times in the following century. "They started to think only of money," Mack said, "instead of baseball."

Had Bender received a serious offer from Mack it seems logical he would have accepted it, but by this time Mack was not in the mood to do Bender any favors. The manager was upset with Bender's performance, but even more he was frustrated by Bender's drinking. The Feds. The booze. The loss. Mack didn't feel as though he had a decision. By outward appearances his thinking had shifted radically in a short amount

444

4444

44444

444444

of time. In less than a month Bender had gone from ace in the hole to dog in the house. But the stunning World Series loss made the decision appear more dramatic. The reality was that Bender's release was the culmination of factors raised over the course of seasons.

Nineteen-fourteen was "one my best and most unlucky years," Bender said. "If I had had someone to advise me I probably would not have accepted [the Federal League offer], but I thought the waivers meant that Connie was through with me. It was the biggest mistake of my life."

Chapter Twenty-Two. Connie Mack's dismissal would push Charles Bender down a deep valley, but it would take time before he reached bottom. In fact, 1914 wouldn't be the last time Bender found fingers pointed at his chest. On the night of February 17, 1917, Bender drove toward Philadelphia with a friend, Harry Weikel, sitting in the car's passenger seat.

The pair had been to New Jersey, where Bender had taken part in a clay target shoot in the afternoon. He broke 94 out of a possible 100. At this time Bender's abilities with a gun had perhaps exceeded his abilities with a baseball. The move to the Federal League had been a disaster.

Fans of capitalism could scarcely argue with a player's decision to explore the alternative league. While consuming baseball's delicious history it's easy to overlook the fact that for the first several decades of the modern game, up until the advent of free agency in the mid-1970s, the players who generated the drama, inspiration, and pleasant memories were essentially indentured servants. They served the big business of baseball as both skilled labor and product, and yet they held precious little power over the terms of their employment. The Federal League, which claimed Major League status in 1914, was attractive because it offered players larger salaries and greater security. The league signed players to multiyear deals that included salary increases. Players would receive notice by September 15 if their contracts would not be reserved for the following season. The league even offered free agency to those with ten years of service time.

The Feds certainly acted big league, building eight new parks, including the park currently known as Wrigley Field, and quickly acquired star power. According to baseball historian Harold Seymour, during the Federal League's existence 81 of its 264 players came from Major League rosters. Included were a number with established big-league track records, such as Mordecai Brown, Joe Tinker, Hal Chase. Charles Bender, the renowned "brainy twirler," as the newspapers always wrote, was another drawing card.

As Bill James pointed out in *The New Bill James Historical Baseball Abstract*, the Federal League was well financed and well conceived, copying the format of the other major leagues with eight teams playing 154-game schedules. The venture may have thrived, but officials picked possibly the single worst time to start a league—as the game went into an economic slump. Said the 1915 *Reach Baseball Guide*, "External causes of decline [in baseball include] the political unrest and revolution in the nation; the constant harassment and depression of the country's big and little business; and the incessant distracting and disquieting exploitation of social, individual and financial theories, which had become . . . a national mania."

The business of baseball was in a downturn on December 4, 1914, when Bender signed one of the Federal League's "square deal" contracts for a term of two years. His contract, which called for a salary of $7,500 per season, was with the league, not with a specific team, but it was agreed Bender would pitch for the Baltimore Terrapins. Compared to his earnings with Connie Mack—his top salary with the Athletics was about $4,000—he thought he had made a steal for the few years he still had in his arm. Shortly after signing the contract Bender talked to Ty Cobb.

"For the first time in my life I am getting a fair recompense according to the modern salary standard. And just think, Ty, I have provided at least [two] golden years. I scarcely expected to last that long."

"But, Chief, are you sure you have left no loophole of escape for your new employers in case they should wish to get rid of you before the term of your contract expires?"

"Nothing doing. I have feathered my nest. My contract is so good that if the league exploded tomorrow I wouldn't worry. But it isn't going to explode."

So what happened? The league exploded. And Bender was equally combustible. Pitching for a last-place club, he was ineffective, compiling a 4-16 record and a 3.99 ERA, nearly a full run above league average. Baltimore, a preseason pick to win the pennant, managed a .305 winning percentage. In the end, the Federal League didn't attract enough customers to remain viable, and it folded after the 1915 season, one of several casualties of the baseball recession.

Team officials didn't like what they were receiving from Bender for their money, and that pregnant phrase "out of condition" was being used again. Not only did the league not honor the second year of Bender's contract, he was released outright during the first week of September. The letter came from Carroll Rasin, president of the Baltimore club: "I beg to notify you that at a meeting of our board of directors, held last week, they notified me to advise you of your unconditional release. This action, as you may surmise, is due to your failure to keep in the condition necessary for you to properly perform your part of the contract. You are now a free agent and can sign with any club which may desire your services."

Bender filed suit of alleged breach of contract in U.S. District Court against the Federal League, seeking to at least recover the salary owed him for the rest of the 1915 season. "The allegation that the Chief was not in condition to give his club his best services is absurd," argued Edmund Kirby, Bender's lawyer. "On the spring training trip he contracted some intestinal trouble, which bothered him during the season. He pitched his best and was given a bad deal when released. Bender was not paid for the last two weeks he was with the club, while he has not received any salary this month. . . . I have not the slightest doubt that Bender can recover. His contract contained no '10-day release' clause and no means whereby he can be released before the end of 1916. We consider that the Federal League has dealt unjustly with him." The precise settlement is not clear, but no matter how the Federal League was advertised, Bender was dismissed in the same fashion he would have been from any other circuit.

Once the league folded, clubs in the American and National leagues bid for the available players. Bender hoped Connie Mack would make an attempt to bring him back, but that never materialized. Instead, the Philadelphia Phillies acquired him. The 1916 Phillies had a strong team, finishing second to the Brooklyn Dodgers in the National League, but Bender was not relied upon heavily. Used mostly as a long reliever, he started just 13 games and posted a 7-7 record with an ERA more than a run above league average. There was speculation the Phillies would let Bender go after 1916, and in fact he was released temporarily. But at some point they decided to bring him back during the 1917 season.

That winter evening, Major League spring training was a few weeks away. It was about six-thirty, and Bender's car was moving through the dark winter streets of Philadelphia. The roadways were wet and lights projected shadows as Bender drove northbound on Broad Street near the corner of Poplar Street. By the time the figure appeared before his car, by the time Bender tried to swerve, it was too late. Bender's car struck a thirty-two-year-old man named John Curran, who died later that night at St. Joseph's hospital.

The precise events of that night are steeped in mystery, and immediately there were conflicting reports about what Bender did in the moments after striking Curran. Did he stop—or did he flee?

Bender's version of events: "The man, who was standing near the curb, staggered in front of my car. I was operating the machine carefully, and was going at a moderate speed, but I was unable to stop the car in time to avoid striking the man, because he walked directly in front of my machine.

"I swerved the car around, but it struck him and knocked him to one side. I drew up on the other side, but by that time the motorcar which followed mine had stopped and the injured man was placed in it and taken to St. Joseph's."

According to reporting in the *Philadelphia Public Ledger*, Lt. James Scanlin of the detectives bureau said that authorities were searching for the driver of the car more than four hours after the incident and then, around eleven, James Robinson, the superintendent of police, called City Hall and told him the culprit was Bender and that Bender "has been apprehended." Scanlin said that after the accident Bender drove to Robinson's house. Bender, the paper reported, was a friend of Robinson's (an article later in the spring noted that the two shot at the traps together).

One person who came forth as a witness was a policeman named Baker. Baker said the car that struck Curran did not stop but instead turned around and went south on Broad Street. According to Baker's story, he went into the Metropolitan Opera House to telephone for an ambulance. When he came out he found that Curran had been removed from the street. Baker said a passerby informed him a car took Curran to the hospital.

Scanlin, according to the *Public Ledger*, said the car was Bender's. Hospital officials said Curran had been delivered by a crowd of men who quickly disappeared.

The next morning Baker's story changed somewhat or, at least, the reporting of it was different. Baker then said he found that Bender, after striking the man, had turned his car around and brought it to a stop on the other side of the street. According to the *Philadelphia Evening Bulletin*, Baker said he went over to Bender, took his number and was talking to him. He said he did not know who Bender was at the time, and while he had intended to place him under arrest, did not state that clearly.

Baker said Bender remained there about ten minutes. Baker then went to where the injured man had been and sent him to the hospital. When Baker returned, Bender was gone. It was explained that somebody had said, "Go ahead," and Bender believed the remark was meant for him and he departed. Baker jumped into another motorcar and went as far as Broad Street Station but could not find Bender. It was shortly after that Bender telephoned the home of the superintendent of police and said he would give himself up whenever wanted. He was told to appear at the station the next morning.

There was and likely always will be uncertainty about Bender's precise actions. "After I stopped, a policeman came up to me and took my name and number," he said. "I did not try to get away. The policeman could have arrested me then if he had wanted."

Throughout his adult life, Bender did not have an especially fortuitous relationship with the horseless carriage. Not long after he was released by the Athletics, he was in a one-car accident when his car struck a rut in the road near Sunbury, Pennsylvania. He was tossed against the windshield and received several cuts on his face and hands, narrowly escaping serious injury. The accident in 1917 was in another category.

Bender was initially charged with manslaughter and was held in jail for about a day before being released on bail. Harry Davis, former captain of the Athletics, the man who nurtured Bender during his first days as a professional, bailed him out.

According to newspaper reports, there was conflicting testimony about the location of the accident. Curran's widow contended her husband was in a crosswalk. Bender asserted the man was struck north of the crossing. He testified that on the night of the accident the street was wet and that lights near the street corner had cast shadows. In court a witness testified that Curran had been intoxicated.

"I was looking straight ahead at the time of the accident and was driving very slowly," Bender said. "The man must have been hidden from my view by the shadows on the wet street, for I did not see him until he was directly in the path of my car."

Nine days after the incident, Bender was exonerated. He did not, at least publicly, talk about the matter again. Instead, he would do as he had always done when life presented him with taxing situations: he tried to move on, he kept his mind on other things, and he grabbed his gun. The day before his name was officially cleared Bender entered and won the silver trophy at a large shooting tournament.

In 1917 he must have looked like he was through. But he would soon pick up a Major League baseball once again. For all his other talents and interests, all his life he was drawn to the game. Almost as if it's where he belonged.

Chapter Twenty-Three. Imagine if your performance at work was judged within the context of your race. *Jones, you offer surprisingly effective customer service for a grim-faced child of the forest.* Or that those upon which your stature in the community depended held a litany of harsh, unjustified views about your ancestry. *We thought your stoicism masked the burning rage of your race, but you are a pleasant surprise.* The mind reels. There is no plausible way to deny that a mountain of prejudice remains to be conquered. But most human beings have reached the progress point at which such overtly racist descriptions are considered absurd. A person in the current century who speaks in those tones is summarily marginalized from mainstream society. At the turn of the previous century, however, not only were such racist perceptions permitted, they were printed on broadsheets and distributed in the public square.

Charles Albert Bender played every game of his career while managing a type of pressure few players ever face. Most must bend their minds just to begin to understand an ounce of it. It's true he was afforded acclaim and privilege other American Indians of the time were not. Bigotry sometimes makes exceptions. But that is altogether different than saying he dodged its callused hand. The cruel irony is that for the incalculable additional pressure heaped on Bender's shoulders during his playing career, his legacy lacks any comparative respect for the achievement. In his time Bender wanted to be judged strictly as a pitcher, but he wasn't. In perpetuity he should be remembered as a pioneer, but with rare exception he is remembered strictly as, well, a pitcher.

So contemplate the legacy. How good was Charles Bender at his craft? To frame an answer, it's worthwhile to consider how he stacks up numerically against his peers, and the natural place to begin such analysis is at his bronze bust at the National Baseball Hall of Fame. There are flaws with using the Hall of Fame as the game's gold standard. Benchmarks for induction are subjective, voted on by a fluctuating constituency whose justifications have shifted throughout the shrine's history. In one sense the only thing anyone can say with certainty about a player's candidacy is that he's in the Hall of Fame or he's not. Much of the rest of the debate is people talking past one another in different languages. Yet, for better or worse, the Hall is the coin of the realm. Everyone knows about the most famous museum in sports, and baseball fans on barstools everywhere debate players' greatness in a Hall of Fame context. The Veteran's Committee handed Bender a Hall pass in 1953. He *is* a Hall of Famer. But does he belong?

Numbers alone do not paint a black-and-white picture. Bender won just 212 Major League games during a time when high victory totals were not the achievement they are today. A pitcher's win-loss record is a dubious way to judge performance, but outside of extenuating circumstances— such as the injuries sustained by Sandy Koufax—contemporary voters don't seriously consider a pitcher who finishes with so few wins. One comparison to Bender is another Minnesota-born player, Jack Morris, who compiled several sensational regular seasons during the mid-1980s and early 1990s. Like Bender, Morris's World Series starts usually were outstanding. Like Bender, his career totals are underwhelming.

Morris finished with 42 more wins than Bender, pitched 807 more innings, and had 193 more starts. The comparison isn't perfect, but it is useful. There's an argument to be made that Morris deserves induction, but he's been on the ballot several times and he hasn't been inducted. In fact, he hasn't come close. Bender, who played on several of the best teams of his era, was blessed with excellent run support. Based on the offense that backed him up, he probably won as many games as he should have. It's not as if he toiled on losing clubs, missing out on victories he otherwise would have received.

Only once did Bender pitch more than 250 innings, a feat regularly achieved by other frontline pitchers during the Deadball Era. He never led the league in wins, ERA, or strikeouts. Never placed in the top ten in innings pitched. He led the league in winning percentage three times, which is impressive but in no small way a function of his teammates' abilities.

Bender's rate stats are excellent. As of 2007, there were 70 pitchers in the Hall of Fame. Among the 60 who played in the white Major Leagues, Bender ranks fifteenth in winning percentage (.625), seventeenth in hits allowed per game (7.89), and eighth in career ERA (2.46). But those numbers are tempered by the era in which they were posted. Bender pitched during several seasons of historically low run scoring.

There is a belief, perpetrated by various esteemed baseball men over the years, that Bender was used almost exclusively against the best teams. Not so. In dispensing pitching assignments Connie Mack was judicious. He wisely used his best pitchers as both starters and relievers and tried to place them in high-leverage situations. Mack thought certain pitchers performed well in certain circumstances, against certain teams, and he trusted Bender to throw crucial games, late in the regular season and during the World Series. But Mack didn't reserve all of Bender's starts for the Detroit Tigers.

One objective way to measure a player's career is by using Baseball-Reference.com's Hall of Fame Candidacy quotients, which stem from the work of baseball authority Bill James. One is Hall of Fame Standards, used to measure overall quality. The benchmark number for a likely Hall of Famer is 50. Bender ranks at 51.0. Hall of Fame Monitor is how likely a player was to make the Hall. The benchmark for a likely Hall of Famer is 100 and Bender was at 119.0. Baseball-Reference.com also has a tool for comparing players across time. Of the six pitchers numerically closest to Bender, four are in the Hall of Fame: Jack Chesbro, Ed Walsh, Mordecai Brown, and Stan Coveleski. A fifth, Eddie Cicotte, is not eligible because he helped fix a World Series.

The lag on Bender's cumulative totals: he didn't post outstanding seasons after he turned thirty. At that point, Bender's career marks projected to inner-ring Hall of Fame material. By the time Bender peaked at thirty, he was numerically similar to Grover Cleveland Alexander at the same point, and by thirty-two he was at a level that would rank him close to Greg Maddux. Through his age-thirty season Bender had been in the top ten in strikeouts per nine innings ten times. Seven times between 1907 and 1914 he was in the top ten in ERA. In fact, Bender's ERA dropped for seven straight seasons, from 1904 to 1910. That's not easy to do. Thirty-six of his 40 shutouts came by the age of thirty. Five times he was in the top four in fewest walks allowed per nine innings. Five times he was in the top ten in fewest hits allowed per nine.

"There is no question in my mind that an All-American league team would be incomplete without the wily Indian, Bender," John McGraw wrote in 1923. "The game has produced very few such pitchers. In addition to his natural strength, his wonderful speed and curves, Bender made an intensive study of batters. It was seldom that he made a mistake."

Many pitchers decline after thirty, but Bender didn't just fade away. He burned out. The question is why. Of course, he wasn't the first pitcher whose star fell from the sky in a flash, and he wouldn't be the last. One could conclude he was just another in a long line that could not sustain excellence. If accurate, it's hardly condemnation.

But there's a more salient explanation: race. It's acknowledged that during Bender's lifetime—he was sent to boarding school the year after the Wounded Knee massacre—a slew of bad things were done to American Indians. But there is a failure of capacity to understand and recognize the depth at which those things personally and deeply affected American Indians. That was a hundred years ago, or so goes the thinking, let's move on. Just because it was a "different time" doesn't mean the spears of racism that rained from the bleachers, the jaundiced coverage in the press, the racial stereotypes that were spewed from opposing dugouts, the cool treatment given by some teammates, didn't tear Bender apart.

Though large groups of people endured prejudice of the kind dealt Bender, the truth is that every person experiences pain in unique ways. There's simply no way to know the manner in which the racism hurt him or the depth of which it altered his very being. It's only certain to say that it must have affected him in profound ways.

Bender's drinking, which likely limited his longevity, was a manifestation of the culture that enveloped him. Personal choice? Perhaps. That's the easy answer. No one held a gun to his head, but society did the next closest thing. When forced to live between cultures—on one hand Bender was told in ways subtle and not that he was racially inadequate and on the other that he was unable to fit into white society—the rational choice is to seek a salve. In that sense the decision to drink seems altogether sensible. So flip the question around: It's not unbelievable Bender flamed out. It's hard to believe he didn't flame out sooner. That Charles Bender performed at such a high level for twelve seasons with the A's is radically underappreciated.

Despite those factors, a case can be made that Bender was fully capable of reviving his career. Many pitchers who thrive in their thirties do so only after working through the inevitable adjustments that age, and the accompanying loss of velocity, demands of the position. Roger Clemens is an example. The Rocket had a losing record and an ERA of nearly four and half in his age-thirty season. Over a four-year period in his early thirties he went 40-39. By the time Bender's performance regressed, circumstances weren't conducive to a Clemens-like return to previous levels of production. Though he may have been poised for such a comeback.

In 1917 Bender's Major League career was nearly finished, but during that season he wasn't an aging veteran hanging on to a roster spot because a team owner had an inkling to cash in on past glory. He wasn't playing out the string. He was pitching as well as he ever had.

For most of his Major League career Bender was fortunate to pitch with some talented men. Rube Waddell. Eddie Plank. Herb Pennock. Jack Coombs. When he landed back in Philadelphia in 1916 Bender joined another talented staff, this one led by Grover Cleveland Alexander, who can be found on more than one short list for greatest pitcher of all time. Few pitchers can claim a one-year level of production to rival Alexander's 1916 season as he threw 389 innings of 1.55 ERA baseball, winning 33 games, 16 of them shutouts. Eppa Rixey was the Phillies' second-best pitcher, and in 1916 he had the finest season—22 wins, 1.85 ERA—of a career that, mysteriously, landed him in the Hall of Fame.

In July of 1917 Bender was an afterthought on the Phillies pitching staff. He wasn't starting games, appearing only in spot relief and not doing even that job all that well. In fact, after one outing, the *Philadelphia North American* said, "Chief Bender pitched the last three innings and was as weak as the Kaiser's excuse for devastating Belgium." There was a lot of rain on the East Coast that summer, and the Philadelphia schedule quickly filled with double-headers. Manager Pat Moran eventually had to use additional arms, and Bender was inserted into the rotation near the end of the month. He made his first start on the final day of July, allowing four runs and seven hits in seven innings.

He was given another opportunity August 5, and he won his first game of the season when he allowed two runs in nine innings in a 6–2 win over the Chicago Cubs. In his second start of the month, August 13, Bender threw a four-hit shutout over Boston, a 3–0 Philly win.

Five days later, pitching what the *Philadelphia Inquirer* called "masterly ball," he threw a shutout on Pittsburgh as Philadelphia again scored three runs. Bender allowed just three hits and didn't walk a batter. The Pirates earned one scratch hit in the first inning, and not another man made a hit until the seventh, when Chuck Ward reached on a clean single to left field. Bender retired 27 of 31 batters.

"The wily redskin," the *North American* said, "never looked better."

The hyperbole would soon be trumped. Three days later, on August 21, Bender threw a one-hit shutout—in a 6–0 win over Chicago—his third shutout in eight days (in those 27 innings, he had allowed just eight hits). Pete Kilduff made the only safety, a two-out, two-strike knock in the second inning. It was a legitimate hit that sailed on a line over second base and fell at the feet of Phillies center fielder Dode Paskert. Bender walked Larry Doyle twice, but no runners reached second base. He fanned five Cubs, including all three to face him in the fifth. When Max Flack flied out to Paskert for the final out of the game, fans demonstrated their enthusiasm as Bender "showed his delight by running off the field with the stride of a college pitcher after winning his first varsity game," one paper said. He was congratulated by teammates; Alexander was the first to extend his hand, as Bender approached the clubhouse gate.

"The Chief completely flabbergasted all scoffers," the *Inquirer* said.

Bender had allowed just 15 hits in his previous 42⅔ innings pitched. And he wasn't done.

On August 25, the Phillies were scheduled to have a doubleheader with the Cincinnati Reds. Before the start of the twin bill, Reds manager Christy Mathewson insisted that his two hot pitchers, Fred Toney, a year away from a 24-win season, and Pete Schneider, who would finish sixth in the league in ERA, could beat any two pitchers on Moran's roster. Moran picked Alexander in the first game and Bender in the second, and Philadelphia won both. Bender allowed only one Red to reach base in the first five innings and held Cincinnati to six hits for the game. He nearly earned his fourth straight shutout in a 3–1 win.

After his fifth win in as many starts, the *North American* prominently published Bender's mug over this caption: "The wonderful redskin [is] among the pitching princes of America again."

Bender won his sixth game in as many starts in the month on August 30, beating Boston 4–3. He helped as much with his bat—he hit a homer and had a clutch single—as with his arm. Philadelphians must have rubbed their eyes and wondered if it was 1910 all over again. Bender, James Isaminger said, is "the amazement of baseball this year."

The *Inquirer's* "Old Sport," a well-read column written under a pseudonym, said "the comeback of Chief Bender is the decided sensation of baseball."

Added Old Sport: "Seemingly the Chief's days as a big league twirler had ceased last fall, when Moran released him and now that he has shown that all this dope was mere fallacy, the greater has become his fame. His wonderful work has possibly helped more to put the Phils back into the race than any other of Moran's warriors' efforts. . . . They can now depend upon the Chief as much as they have upon Alexander."

In six starts during the month—he also relieved three times—Bender had as many wins (six) as runs allowed. He nearly stretched his streak to seven in a row, but on September 5 he lost to the Giants despite a six-strikeout, two-runs-allowed effort. He carried a shutout into the eighth and lost on a home run by Benny Kauff.

Meanwhile, Bender became popular with his teammates, and he and Rixey became buddies. Ballplayers spend a lot of time in clubhouses and hotels doing nothing much of anything, and during such down times Bender and Rixey often engaged in friendly wrestling matches. One night, however, things got out of hand. As they were grappling the six-foot-five Rixey threw Bender heavily against a windowpane. His arm went through double plates of glass. He suffered a long sharp gash in his pitching arm and bled profusely.

Mike Dee, the Philadelphia trainer, patched the six-inch wound and planned to have Bender see a doctor the next morning after the team had traveled to Boston. They managed to induce Bender into bed, but he wasn't able to sleep. During the night, as the Phillies' train rolled along the tracks the pain grew and the arm swelled, Bender said, "like the head of a rookie pitcher after a no-hit game." When the arm began to get blue Bender started to worry.

He climbed out of bed and sought Alexander, the peculiar, and often inebriated, right-hander. Bender explained his trouble, produced a pocketknife, and asked if his friend wouldn't mind performing a minor operation. Sure, why not?

They sterilized the knife and applied tourniquets to Bender's arm. Alexander then slashed Bender's arm with the penknife, the infection was allowed to drain, and the swelling went down. The next day, Bender told an astonished doctor of Alexander's operation on that train in the middle of the night. The physician admitted he couldn't have done a better job himself and said Alexander may have saved Bender's life.

At least that's the tale told throughout the years, an anecdote impossible to confirm. What's without doubt is that immediately following a run that had harkened his best stretches with the Philadelphia A's, Charles Bender was on the shelf for nineteen straight days. Newspapers didn't explain much about the absence, but mentioned he had a "barked elbow," as the result of a fall.

Bender made and won two starts near the end of the season, one of them a 2–0 shutout at Pittsburgh as the Phillies were playing out a season in which they finished a distant second. He went 8-2 with a 1.67 ERA, nearly a run better than the league average. His Major League career was effectively over, but few who saw him in the summer of 1917 could argue he didn't deserve a Major League job in 1918.

But there were other matters to tend to that season.

After the United States entered World War I, the U.S. government mandated, under a work-or-fight order, that able-bodied, draft-age men either report for military service or find employment in an occupation essential to the war effort. Major League Baseball played on in 1918, but Bender didn't play professionally that year. He went to work.

He reported to an area southwest of Philadelphia along the Delaware River, where the government contracted a company to build ships and a shipyard. The area was called Hog Island, supposedly because early local residents had allowed pigs to roam free. At the time Bender worked there, Hog Island was the largest shipyard in the world. "Hog Islanders," cargo ships and transport ships, were not pretty to look at, but they were robust. The vessels Bender had a hand in building were not, in fact, used in World War I, but several were around for use in World War II. At the time, they were some of the greatest ships in the world.

Bender pitched for the Hog Island nine, and made outings for an area semipro team in the Delaware County League on Saturdays. But he was not at Hog Island as a figurehead. Like most Americans, he was swept up in patriotism and believed it was more important to work on behalf of soldiers than to resume his pitching career. Proof: The New York Yankees claimed Bender, and instead of accepting the offer to return to the majors, he remained in the shipyards. Besides, Bender made more money there than he could heaving a ball.

"I was not particularly glad when the announcement was made that [Yankees manager Miller] Huggins had paid [Phillies owner William] Baker of the Phillies . . . the waiver price for my release," Bender said. "I am sore that Baker got any money for me, for he has never treated me right, and I think it was foolish for Huggins to take that kind of a gambler's chance.

"And it is a chance, too, for unless I receive a willing release from those in charge at Hog Island and their assurance that I can resume my work in the fall after the ball season is over, I will continue as I am.

"Baseball is a secondary consideration with me and while I realize that the fellows who are doing their bit over here need amusement . . . I also realize that we need ships and all the men we can get to build them. I made all this clear to Joe Kelly, the Yanks' scout, when he was over to see me, and I presume he reported my attitude to Huggins. . . . I have stated my case to the officials at the shipbuilding plant, and it is up to them to say whether I shall stay there and help build ships or play ball with the Yankees."

Perhaps the reason Bender didn't return to the majors was that he simply didn't want to face it all again. Around this time, the *Washington Post* noted that Bender had been taken to the hospital after suffering a nervous breakdown, which may have been caused by his drinking. Contemporary newspapers cited overwork from time spent in the shipyard.

Whatever his motives, Bender bounced back quickly. A day after the *Post* story ran, the same newspaper said "Bender Fools Doctors" by showing up and outscoring many contestants at a gun club. He continued to build ships, and he was so efficient he was placed in charge of a crew of riveters. It was tough work; he spent his days swinging a sledge. After a few months he got into better physical shape than he had been in years.

"I weighed 195," he said, "and was as hard as nails."

In June of 1919, Ben Wilson, owner of the Richmond team in the Virginia League, asked Bender to manage his team. There were two weeks to go in the first half of the season, and the team finished last. But under Bender's direction the team won the second half. He usually pitched Mondays, Wednesdays, and Saturdays, and he hurled three double-headers.

Bender was facing minor league hitters but his performance regularly made headlines anyway. He won 29 games and lost 2. His ERA that season is not an established fact, but one source in Bender's file at the Hall of Fame lists it as 1.06. Richmond fans were so pleased that at the end of the season they passed the hat and bought Bender a new car. Wilson also handed him a $2,000 bonus.

Bender was asked how he had such a stellar season. "What's bothering me," he said, smiling, "is how did those young bushers ever win two games from me. I must be slipping."

He was so effective for Richmond that Major League scouts came to see him pitch, and at least one team, the Cincinnati Reds, offered him a contract for the rest of the 1919 season. Pat Moran, Bender's manager when he was with the Phillies, had taken charge of the Reds, and in mid-August one of Moran's scouts saw Bender dominate a Virginia League game and tried to persuade him to leave for the Reds immediately. At this point Bender had pitched 23 games and won 21 of them. He was also manager of the team. In those days Bender was likely making almost as much money in Richmond as he would have been in Cincinnati. He turned down the Reds' offer. "I thought better of it and stayed with the boys while they won the pennant," he said. Bender told Moran he would join the Reds after the Richmond season ended in early September.

But in mid-September Bender broke a bone in his ankle at Vineland, New York, while pitching for semipro Millville. According to contemporary newspapers, near the end of the game he was trying to beat out an infield single and slid into first base. In doing so, his foot became entangled in the bag and his ankle was wrenched. After a runner had been substituted for him Bender was brought to the hospital. The ankle was so swollen doctors could not immediately determine if the bone was fractured. (When Bender was taken home his wife met him at the door, one newspaper noted, her left arm in a splint. The day before she had been shopping and while descending from the third floor to the second of a department store lost her balance, falling down the entire flight.)

The injury may or may not have prevented Bender from pitching for Moran's Cincinnati Reds in their march to the World Series. Bender never threw a pitch for the Reds but he did help Moran in that Series with the Black Sox. Moran brought Bender in to prepare pitchers and to scout. In mid-September, Chicago came to Philadelphia to play the A's and Bender, who knew many of the White Sox, including old friend Eddie Collins, then the Chicago second baseman, was allowed to pitch batting practice.

"A valuable aid to Moran in the series will be old Chief Bender," Christy Mathewson said in his column.

"Some of the big league scouts who saw him working at Richmond said he was never better in his life. However, the Chief will render assistance from the coaching lines and he is about as clever a man in such a position as I know of. We used to think that he got the signs of the other club. I am not certain that he did, but his very presence gave us something to worry about besides the game."

There were whispers that Bender was brought in to steal signs. In his column Matty denied that Bender stole signals during the 1919 Series, as if that were a crime, or even against the rules.

"Bender is a student of baseball and a deeper student than many fans and writers are willing to admit," Matty said. "His presence on the bench or the coaching lines would naturally mean much to a ball club, for I have never met a player who could grasp situations as quickly as the Indian."

For whatever it's worth, Reds pitchers threw better in the 1919 World Series than they did during the regular season. It's suspect to give a part-time pitching coach credit in any eight game-series and especially one in which several members of the opposing team were trying to lose. But the Reds did believe Bender was there to help—if not with his right arm, at least with his head and his keen eyes.

Baseball language is conveyed in numbers. Numbers provide a permanent record of a player's achievement, magnifying or shrinking his place in the long-running story of baseball. In that way, numbers are arbiters of history; they provide the punctuation of a legacy. Charles Bender did not throw another meaningful pitch in the big leagues after 1917. Illness, self-induced and otherwise, stole wins and innings from his peak years. One can safely speculate that with minor alterations to history he easily could have compiled heftier raw totals. But his career line is what it is. There are bright individuals who spend their time considering these matters who believe Bender is a Hall of Famer who doesn't deserve the honor.

Perhaps Bender's candidacy was boosted by his ability as a clutch pitcher, a reputation aided in no small way by the single most common quote ever written about him. "If I had all the men I've ever handled, and they were in their prime, and there was one game I wanted to win above all others," said Connie Mack, who managed Lefty Grove, Herb Pennock, Eddie Plank and Rube Waddell. "Albert would be my man." In the early decades of the Hall of Fame, sabermetric analyses were not performed on candidates. The reputation of respected baseball men often held greater sway than numerical milestones.

After all, who was going to argue with baseball's Methuselah?

But in order to run a proper statistical analysis of Bender's career, one would require qualitative tools that are not likely to be invented. For example, judge this player's cumulative totals: 1,518 hits, 137 home runs, 734 RBI, 197 stolen bases. Based on those statistics alone you would likely say this was a good player but certainly not a Hall of Famer. But if told the player's identity—Jackie Robinson—your vote would likely change. As just a ballplayer, Bender was a borderline Hall of Famer. As just a ballplayer, Jackie Robinson was, too.

Of course, the Robinson-Bender analogy has flaws. Robinson was hand-selected to knock down a wall that had stood prominently and embarrassingly for a half century. During Robinson's career blacks were considered a threat to whites while during Bender's career American Indians were supposedly a dying race. Bender didn't integrate baseball—according to Jeffrey Powers-Beck, James Madison Toy in 1887 is believed the first American Indian in the game—and he wasn't the game's first prominent player of Native descent. Louis Sockalexis had a dynamic personality and rare ability. He also had a desire to see the bottoms of whiskey bottles, and in the 1890s drank himself out of baseball. Sockalexis's story, which played out in front of people with inherent prejudice, created a climate in which there was doubt about whether American Indians were reliable enough to succeed in the big leagues. In John Meyers's first game in organized baseball, for example, he signaled for a fastball and the pitcher fired a spitball that hit the catcher in the gut. After the pitcher crossed him again, Meyers quit signaling and just caught whatever the pitcher threw. Just as for decades black football players weren't thought capable of playing quarterback, some white pitchers didn't take orders from nonwhite catchers.

Bender threw his pitches not just to avoid the bats of American League hitters but also into the face of this kind of prejudice. There is no way to measure the magnitude of racism's influence on his career. But it is naïve, if not irresponsible, to dismiss the topic from the discussion. If the measuring stick is cumulative totals, Bender's case is on the margin. But if the Hall of Fame is supposed to be a record of the great human achievements in the game's history, it's hard to fathom a shrine that excludes Charles Albert Bender.

Then again, during second half of his life, he was still searching for something more earthly than immortality.

Chapter Twenty-Four. After Charles Bender checked into a Carlisle hotel, children crowded around him in the street as though he had returned from conquering a distant land. Bender's exploits in the Major Leagues had been closely followed in Carlisle newspapers throughout his career. "Bender's success may be attributed to hard work and correct habits of life," the *Carlisle Evening Sentinel* said twenty years earlier. "His career is a lesson not only to members of his own race, but to all who hope to be a star in the world of sports." On August 28, 1930, there were still people in town who remembered Bender from his days as a student at the Carlisle Indian School, which had closed a dozen years before, and the prep school at Dickinson College. Those folks waited, too, to greet one of Carlisle's favorite sons.

Bender had made a pit stop in Carlisle in 1916, but this was the first time in twenty-eight years he had been back in any meaningful way. Marie and two friends accompanied him. One of them, Edmund Kirby, was apparently one of Bender's dearest. The two were so close that Kirby and the Benders purchased a cemetery plot together around the time Kirby's young wife died in 1927. An attorney, Kirby served as Bender's counsel in various affairs, including representing him in his lawsuit against the Federal League.

The day began with an honorary luncheon sponsored by the Carlisle

Rotary Club during which Bender spoke. He also toured the old Carlisle school grounds, harkening memories of a place and people that in no small way shaped his life. Bender's face was highlighted with satisfaction. "This visit brings back memories I have carried with me ever since I left Carlisle," he said.

Inevitably, in some corner of his mind Bender could hear the echoes of Richard Henry Pratt's voice. Indeed, he had stuck to it, sir. He hadn't reached his destination quite yet, but he hadn't given up and he never would.

A baseball player's life follows a cruel arc in that by age twenty-five or thirty he has reached his professional climax. With rare exception, after a ballplayer hangs up his spikes he climbs aboard a buggy that slowly travels along the periphery of fame. Sure, some fans will remember the player's achievements the rest of their lives, but the nature of retirement is that everything you did that people cared about happened ten, twenty, forty years ago. Hey, didn't you used to be Chief Bender?

A player in the contemporary game can make more money in a season than most people make in their lifetimes. That's no knock on the modern player, as in most cases he's receiving what market forces command. When great players retire in the twenty-first century some find second careers to occupy their time, but few need to do so. This was not the case in Bender's era. There are greater tragedies in the world than a pitcher who no longer can strike out the side, but such a life does present a sudden, unkind decision: What do I do when my greatest employable skills have left me?

Some men never find a personally satisfying answer to that question. Bender wasn't one of them. He left the spotlight but he didn't linger in the shadows. He enjoyed life. And he kept pitching. Even after his Major League career had ended, baseball was still very much a part of his daily life.

The minor leagues during Bender's time were much different than the organized, affiliated leagues in the decades that followed. For the most part, they were independent, and rosters often contained players who were of Major League caliber—or at least once were. Players, especially those with name recognition, could make a decent living kicking around for five or ten years in places such as Richmond and Erie. The trajectory

Bender pictured with Frederick Fegan at Biddle Field, August 28, 1930, the day he returned to Carlisle. Cumberland County Historical Society, Carlisle PA.

of Bender's career was such that he didn't play an inning in the minor leagues before he rose to the big leagues. But after he left the majors he spent a lot of time in the middle levels of the game, and during the 1920s became one of the great drawing cards in minor league baseball.

After he lit up the Virginia League in 1919 George Weiss—who would later preside over the New York Yankees in a career that earned him induction into the Hall of Fame—hired Bender as pitcher-manager for the team he owned in New Haven. Bender said he made $8,500 that season. "I'll bet it was the highest salary George Weiss . . . ever paid an Eastern Leaguer," he said.

Whatever the stipend, Bender earned his dough. He pitched in 47 games, was the winning pitcher in 25 of them, and had an ERA of 1.94. He struck out 252 batters and walked just 71 in 324 innings. Weiss received multiple offers for Bender from Major League teams, but was more concerned with winning his league's pennant than returning Bender to the bigs. Besides, Bender's salary made sticking in the minors perhaps a more lucrative option, and of course it was a more stable one.

Bender and fellow former Major League star Ed Walsh, manager in Bridgeport, Connecticut, ruled the Eastern League not only because they still had some life in their arms but because their baseball IQs were so much higher than those of everyone else in the league. In the early half of the season Bender supposedly cased all the clubs, stole their signs, and kept them secret. One day Bender was dealing a no-hitter in the ninth against Bridgeport when Walsh inserted himself as a pinch hitter and fought off a two-strike pitch for a single. But Bender got even. The next time he faced Walsh and Bridgeport, in late August, he took another no-hitter into the ninth and that time finished it off.

"I had a lot of fun in the Eastern League," Bender said. "One day in Albany, Evert Nutter . . . tried to steal third base with none out and [he represented] the winning run. He was thrown out by ten feet. I was coaching and as he saw the look on my face, he reached for his leg and cried out: 'It's broken!'

"I shook my head. 'Tch-tch-tch—that's too bad,' I said." Bender signaled for help from the dugout. "We lifted Nutter in our arms, carried him half way to the bench—and then with the crowd straining to see what was happening, we dropped Nutter flat on his back. He never tried to steal third with none out again."

Bender was without question the best pitcher in the Eastern League in 1920, so Weiss brought him back for 1921. His ERA (1.93) and winning percentage were as good, though his workload was lighter as he threw 196 innings.

In 1922, Bender managed the Reading, Pennsylvania, club in the International League. The next season he pitched for the International League team in Baltimore and followed that by making a return to New Haven in 1924. During the 1920s Bender coached the U.S. Naval Academy team and in 1925–26 served as a coach with the Eddie Collins–managed Chicago White Sox. In 1925, Collins brought Bender, then 41, in to work the ninth inning of a late-season blowout game against the Red Sox—the club he had beaten for his first Major League victory. Bender was able to retire three batters, but not before allowing two runs on a walk and a home run. It was his last appearance in the Major Leagues, eight years after his previous one, but Bender wasn't done with competitive baseball.

Two years later, and twenty-five years after entering organized baseball, he won 7 games against 3 losses and posted the lowest ERA (1.33) in the old Middle Atlantic League. That season, 1927, an ownership group with deep pockets purchased the Johnstown club and decided to raise the team's profile. First they signed Babe Adams, well-known ex-Pittsburgh pitcher, as manager. But he didn't pan out so the owners turned to another famous former Philly pitcher, Bender, whose arrival coincided with a prosperous period in Johnstown baseball history. Bender managed the team, leading it to the playoffs, and was its main attraction.

In nine seasons as a minor league manager Bender had four first-place clubs, one second, one third, and a fourth. He had great fun running a team, but he regularly found himself in fierce arguments with umpires, likely because he had not gotten control over his drinking.

One night while managing the Erie Sailors, according to one story, Bender went out partying with a couple of scouts. He was still in a spirited mood the next afternoon when the first game of a June double-header began. He was ejected from the game for throwing a ball still in play into the stands. An intense argument ensued and tensions rose between his players and those of Dayton. A brawl started and benches cleared. Police officers jumped onto the field and Erie officials held Bender responsible for the conditions on the field. He was summarily fired.

The team began searching for an interim replacement, but in the hours that followed, Bender, a fan favorite, conferred with the Erie heads one more time, and they "rehired" him after he expressed remorse. (That was not the end of embarrassing incidents. At the end of the 1923 season, in which he pitched for Baltimore, manager Jack Dunn dismissed Bender and catcher Lena Styles after the two "disgraced" the team at a banquet attended by the mayor and other Baltimore city officials.)

The minors were rough, and problems arose that were not self-induced. While managing in Johnstown and still pitching—he threw a one-hitter at age 43—during a series in Fairmont, fans were all over Bender and his team. Eventually, one boisterous fan procured a megaphone and started to make fun of Bender and his club. He became irritated and finally appealed to the umpires to eject the fan from the park. But his pleas went unanswered.

Bender, however, continued to protest. At the time his team was batting, but after his hitters were retired and set to take the field, he ordered his players to remain on the bench until the fan had disposed of his megaphone. The umpires became angry and threatened a forfeit if he didn't place his team on the field within five minutes. A Fairmont team official, however, spared that step by persuading the fan to give up his megaphone. Bender had made his point. He sent his team onto the field.

After he became a baseball star Bender rarely returned to Minnesota for so much as a visit. Though for a number of years he owned his allotted property on the reservation, he had left at such a young age that he hadn't a chance to form the kind of bond children usually have with their parents. And whatever faint tug came from northern Minnesota over the years had abruptly ceased two months before the day he was feted in Carlisle.

After Bender's parents separated, Mary married Arthur Cooley, a red-haired, bewhiskered forest settler, and the couple moved to his place south of the present Norris Public Campground, about as far north as one can travel on land in Minnesota and remain in the contiguous United States.

Art Cooley, a worker at the local sawmill, was a storyteller who smoked a cigarette in a long holder. Bender's mother was well known and liked in the area and friends called her Squaw Mary. In mid-July, 1930, Mary, Arthur, and Mary's daughter, Elizabeth, had taken Elizabeth's husband, Henry Roe Cloud, a Winnebago, to catch a train in International Falls. Arthur, who was learning to drive, was behind the wheel of a Cadillac when he lost control near the point at which two small highways join not far from Spooner.

Neither Elizabeth nor Arthur was seriously injured, but the tiny Mary was thrown through the windshield. One of her broken ribs pierced a lung and she sustained head injuries. Elizabeth, one of the first American Indian women trained as a nurse, cared for her mother in the days that followed. But there were limits on what could be done. There was no hospital in the vicinity, so Mary was brought home, where she died days later.

Mary Bender Cooley's funeral was held in the forest — friends made wreaths and flowers, and one person brought a moccasin flower—and she was buried at Wildwood Cemetery, south of the campgrounds. Years later, a collection was taken, and a stone was purchased for her grave. As an adult Charles Bender apparently never got close to Mary. After his tenure with the Philadelphia A's ended he mentioned in a handwritten letter to a third party that he did know how to reach his mother.

Bender's father did not remarry, and in 1922 he died of cancer. There's no record that after Charley ran away he and his father ever spoke again.

Though he had many brothers and sisters—at least ten who lived beyond infancy—Bender also didn't have especially close ties to most of his siblings. In many cases, their lives did not intertwine. Several of them attended the Hampton Normal and Agricultural Institute, at least four of them were born after young Charley left home, and more than one had died at a young age. Charles and Marie were close to one sister, Emma Bender, a nurse who married and divorced, and Emma's daughter. They even shared a house in Philadelphia for several years.

Elizabeth Bender, four years his junior, is the most well known of Bender's siblings. She was a highly educated, spirited teacher and philanthropist. Elizabeth married Henry Roe Cloud who, Stuart Levine wrote, was "among the most eloquent and best trained" of early white-educated Indian leaders. Roe Cloud was extremely intelligent and wanted young American Indians to have the same opportunity he had received. The first American Indian to graduate from Yale University, he was a lightning rod in that he shared a belief that Indian assimilation into white society was coming, like it or not. Roe Cloud became a leading reformer for the rights of American Indians, and one such effort was the opening of the Roe Institute, later renamed the American Indian Institute, in Wichita, Kansas. The nonsectarian missionary school aimed to provide Christian-based college-prep education for American Indians. Goals included moving beyond vocational education and promoting self-reliance; students were pushed to give their lives in service of their race.

Elizabeth was closely involved with two nationwide organizations—the Society of American Indians and the National Congress of American Indians—and devoted her life to the cause of American Indian education. Franklin Delano Roosevelt appointed her as a delegate to the 1940 White House Conference on Children and Youth. She would be selected Mother of the Year, the first American Indian so honored, in 1950. Qualifications cited were her success as a mother as shown by the character and achievements of her children as well as her spiritual honesty.

Elizabeth and Henry Roe Cloud met when Elizabeth was teaching at Carlisle, though their first meeting may have been during a conference for missionaries in Wisconsin, and they were married in 1916. The ceremony was performed at Charles Bender's house.

Aside from his relationship with Emma, most of Bender's siblings had scattered to different parts of the country. By 1930 Charles Bender didn't have much of a bond with his family of origin. In effect, his life began at Carlisle, and this day was Carlisle's chance to remind the world of that fact.

Of course, there had to be baseball. Bender promised to pitch for the Carlisle community team against a club of workers from the Pennsylvania Railroad. After taking a long time to limber up, he pitched seven innings on Biddle Field and allowed four hits, striking out seven. Bender pitched well for six innings, then he allowed a single run in a 1–0 loss. But this wasn't a day about victories and defeats.

Major Sullivan, a former big-league player, caught Bender during the game, and between innings kids crowded around. Everyone wanted—and received—an autograph. Wearing an old Philadelphia A's uniform, Bender was the picture of a well-aged man, still slender, and he greeted the children with wide, warm smiles throughout the day. This was his day but he made it theirs.

"It has been twenty-eight years since I pitched in Carlisle," Bender said. "My legs are gone and my arm is gone by my eyes are still good."

Before the game started in the afternoon about two thousand fans gathered. State senator Leon Prince addressed the throng, welcoming Charles and Marie back to Carlisle. "Every town, great or small, shines in the reflected glory of celebrated persons or events associated with its history," Prince told the crowd. "Carlisle boasts the prison of Major Andre, the birthplace of General Armstrong, the ancestral home of James G. Blaine, the burial ground of Molly Pitcher and the schoolhouse of Chief Bender.

"There is an ancient feud between his people and ours. But if the white man conquered the red man with the rifle-ball, the red man has conquered the white man with the baseball. Chief Bender holds priority of place in sport as other world figures hold it in science, industry, and art. There is only one Edison, only one Henry Ford, only one Douglas Fairbanks, only one Chief Bender.

"Carlisle has expanded and improved since the Chief dwelt among us. . . .

"In days of old when knights were bold it was the amiable custom to present the keys of the city to distinguished guests in a token of hospitality. We have no keys because we have no gates. We have no gates because we have no walls. But we assure Chief Bender and the gracious lady who adorns his name and who shares his merited popularity of our affectionate pride in his notable achievements, and we extend to both our heartfelt welcome to the old home town."

That wasn't the last game Bender threw. Hardly. He pitched two or three games per week in independent ball through 1937, when he was fifty-three. He threw a 5–0 shutout in a semipro game on June 24, 1937, in what may have been his last game. At that point he had been pitching for thirty-eight years. And the sportswriters had said he had no stamina.

Along the way Bender regularly added lines to his coaching and managerial résumé. John McGraw hired Bender in 1931 to coach one of his pitchers, a hard thrower with a wild streak. Bender managed the eastern club of the independent House of David, a barnstorming team, during the 1930s. That didn't end well. Supposedly one day in 1933 a bat slipped out of the hands of a House of David team member and flew into the bench where Bender was sitting, injuring his kneecap. The injury put Bender in bed for a few months. He claimed that not a penny in salary or medical bills was paid him from the time of his injury until he filed suit with the team for lost wages.

Among other stints, he managed Erie of the Continental League in 1932, Wilmington, Delaware, of the Inter-State League in 1940, Newport News in the Virginia League in 1941, and Savannah in the Sally League in 1946.

During these years Bender, of course, made time to pursue his various off-field hobbies. He also stayed close with some of his teammates and enjoyed himself. He bowled a lot in midlife, often scored in the 200s, and at one point he organized a team that consisted of Jimmie Dykes, Wally Schang, Bing Miller, and Joe Bush. Bender thought the sport allowed him to regain his arm strength. "Five years ago I couldn't break a pane of glass at fifteen feet," he said at age forty-nine. "Then I began bowling and after a time I regained most of my old-time speed."

In his early thirties he had organized the Bender Sporting Goods Company of Philadelphia, located at 1306 Arch Street. (A newspaper advertisement said, "The Chief knows what's what in baseball and baseball toggery! Everything you get here you can bank on will be O.K.") Time spent at that venture was among many years Bender worked in retail, first in sporting goods and later in men's clothing departments, becoming an expert in textiles and tailoring. Sometimes, Bender managed the store baseball team. "Say, I'm only fifty-four," Bender said. "I've got at least another quarter of a century before I stop tossing them up to the plate. And I don't know that I'll quit then."

Though he spent those years engaged in various jobs and hobbies, baseball was always part of his identity. In 1939, *Time* magazine noted that Bender was on hand at the Franklin Institute in Philadelphia when a new flexible safety glass for cars—"billed as the best ever"—was unveiled. A young woman stood on one side of the glass when Bender whirled and fired a baseball at the pane, which stopped the ball. The glass was such an invention Franklin Roosevelt sent a congratulatory telegram. If Bender couldn't throw a ball through the glass must be safe.

Charles Bender became a baseball star during his years with the Philadelphia Athletics. But maybe the reason he never left the game was because at some point baseball—the backslapping camaraderie, the feeling of a well-thrown ball, and the anticipation of another afternoon in the sun—became more meaningful than the collective memory of the glory years. Indeed, throughout his life baseball provided Bender with something more permanent than a paycheck and more valuable than a collection of greatest hits from the World Series.

"Thirty-eight years may seem long to you, but to me it has gone too fast," Bender said. "I love baseball. I love working with the youngsters. The game was good to me. It had its heartaches, but they were but a drop in the bucket compared to the fun I had and the friends I made."

Chapter Twenty-Five. A confluence of baseball's past and future dotted the Shibe Park infield. Mickey Mantle, Yogi Berra, Phil Rizzuto, and other New York Yankees spread across the first-base line as Eddie Joost, Ferris Fain, and the Philadelphia Athletics stood in attention along the third-base side. Clark Griffith, then president of the Washington Senators, was on hand. Hank Greenberg, Cleveland's general manager, was there, too. Several former A's were in attendance, including Rube Oldring, Lena Blackburn, and Ira Thomas. Frank Baker wouldn't miss it. Of course, neither would Connie Mack. Present were Hall of Famers, future Hall of Famers, all-stars, former teammates, respected Philadelphia community members, and business leaders. Casey Stengel managed the Yanks. Of the top fifteen vote getters for that year's American League Most Valuable Player Award, seven were on the field. It was a rare collection of gems that had turned out for Chief Bender Night.

A crowd of 31,424 buzzed in the Shibe Park grandstand. Following an easy win on this day, September 4, 1952, the Yankees would roll to the fourth of five straight World Series victories. No threat in the American League pennant race, the Athletics would finish in the first division for the first time in four seasons. But this otherwise ordinary Thursday night in the latter stages of a predictable campaign had been transformed into the celebration of a unique American life. The game was unremarkable.

But Charles Albert Bender carried the mental snapshots captured before the first pitch to his grave.

A baseball sailed toward the plate. One pitch. Whack. Then a second. Whack. Still lanky, even if the years had added a few pounds, he reached back, rotated his hips and pushed his way toward home plate. The arm was slower. The famous kick was gone. So, too, was any semblance of velocity. That was no longer the point. Whack. Charles Bender eventually stopped trying to retire hitters, but he never stopped pitching. Even if pitching meant throwing batting practice to young, eager players, at least some of whom didn't know what he once meant to the city in which they lived. Whack.

Bender's employment in baseball did not end in the minor leagues. Even in his sixties, he pitched to the Athletics, serving as the oldest BP pitcher in the game. "I don't know if I've been of much help to them," Bender said, "but I give them thirty to forty minutes work every day the team is home.

"A good batting practice pitcher has to have speed—something I ran out of a long time ago."

As the decades passed the ice between Connie Mack and Bender melted, and over time the two once again became close. In the late 1940s the Yankees hosted an old-timers game billed as the "American League's All-Time Stars." Joe McCarthy managed the Yankee greats; Mack directed a team of AL stars that, in his honor, was liberally represented with Philadelphia Athletics. A lump raised in the Tall Tactician's throat watching Bender shuffle to the mound, head down, the way that had excited fans in another generation.

"It's surely like old times, Albert, having you pitch for me again," Mack said.

Bender smiled. "It's good to be pitching for you again, boss."

At one point Bender served as an instructor at Connie Mack's baseball school in West Palm Beach, and Mack formally welcomed Bender back into the Athletics family in 1938 by signing him to a contract as a scout. He was thrilled to be back in the fold, to see his baseball life come full circle, but he wasn't necessarily enamored with the job description. Scouting, he said, was lonesome work. When Bender entered Major League Baseball in 1903 he was noticeably introverted; he chose every word carefully and generally kept to himself. Human beings sometimes change personalities during the course of their lives, and by the time Bender became a World Series star he had changed his—or at least his true self had become more evident. As he aged and mellowed he became even more of a people person, and scouts often are not allowed to be one of those.

"You can't get friendly with people," he said, "and if you do meet people who know the idol of a certain town, you can't promise anything definite."

Except for a brief stint as a coach with the New York Yankees in the early 1940s, Bender remained on the Athletics payroll and, despite constant pain that comes from a lifetime of illness, remained active to the end, serving as scout, minor league manager, school pitching instructor, roving coach, and Major League coach. As early as 1921 some had believed Bender was destined to be a Major League manager. He was certainly bright enough for the job, but he was never given the opportunity, either because of his race or because a lot of outstanding baseball men never are.

Before the 1951 season Bender was brought in to help A's pitchers under manager Jimmie Dykes. In those days, teams didn't have "pitching coach" as a formal title, but that's essentially the job Bender was hired to do.

"As a scout and coach Bender has developed many young pitchers," Dykes said. "His experience should help our pitching staff produce in the manner they're capable of producing."

Said Bender of his hiring: "I'm tickled to death."

Bender was a patient teacher. He would stand beside the mound studying his pitchers. He worked with each one, just teacher and student. When he spoke, he spoke softly. Sometimes he would back up his words with a demonstration. But usually he'd step back in calming silence. No loud lectures.

Great athletes often struggle to teach those with lesser abilities. It's not easy to relate to someone learning "Chopsticks" when you once played Rachmaninoff to a crowded house. But Bender didn't demand that his pitchers perform as well as he had. Instead of radical mechanical changes, he tried to make modest adjustments and instill a fresh approach. While

Bender with old friend and former battery mate Ira Thomas.

standing behind them he would count silently under his breath, and then he taught them to do the same. The idea was to calm them down, to show them how to be cool and composed, between pitches. He knew something about that.

"A guy doesn't throw the ball right back at the catcher in a regular game," Bender said. "Or, at least, he shouldn't. The idea is to put the batter on a spot, too. Make him wait—let him stew for a moment over what's coming. . . . The batter starts wondering whether he's going to get the fast one or the curve. Or maybe a slider or a change-up. He begins thinking and—who knows?—maybe he'll get himself all confused, and the pitcher's problem is solved."

Of course, Bender stressed control. He recalled that his own control developed only when he exhausted himself in pursuit of the skill, so he worked his pitchers harder than they had worked before. He made them throw in batting practice, and when they weren't throwing they were running. Tired pitchers, he said, throw fat pitches. "When I took this job, most of the fellows were half-licked before they started to work," he said. "They not only lacked confidence, but control. Without either, a pitcher might just as well stay in bed."

Joe Astroth, an Athletics catcher at this time, had met Bender a few years before, when Bender served as a coach in the A's minor league system. Bender, Astroth said, was easy to talk to but also quiet. "He was a very learned man," Astroth said years later. "A well-versed man. Straight as a stick." Bender was always "holding court" with the young players, Astroth said. He was "soft spoken and would never lose his temper. He always had a good word for young pitchers, always trying to encourage them."

One day at Shibe Park, Astroth came up and nonchalantly slapped Bender on the back, as ballplayers do. Bender turned "with a fire in his eye." Astroth said the players didn't know about the cancer but the catcher understood not to do that again.

"He was sick for a long time but no one knew it," Astroth said. "He never showed the pain. He didn't say anything. He kept it to himself."

Bender also provided comic relief. He was talking pitching one day at spring training when a young woman approached him, seeking an autograph. Thrusting a pen in his hand, she flashed a pretty smile and asked, "Do you mind?"

"Right here," she said. "On the back of the picture."

Bender turned the photograph over. Snapped while half of the Athletics were playing in Orlando, it showed Bender demonstrating a follow-through to pitchers, including Joe Coleman, who had been left at the training base.

"This I must show to Jimmie [Dykes]," Bender said. "Here is definite proof that when the manager's away his pitching coach doesn't fish all the time."

Bender helped make Philadelphia a better staff as the A's lowered their team ERA by more than a full run between 1950 and 1951. He was especially good at helping Major League caliber arms fine-tune their approach, so that they could make full use of their abilities.

"Where an old-timer fits in best is with a veteran staff—with pitchers who know the mechanics of their trade thoroughly but are starting to lose their effectiveness," George Weiss said in 1951 when he was named Executive of the Year while running the New York Yankees. "By showing a pitcher of this type one or two new trick deliveries, such as a knuckler or screw ball, you can make him much more useful. And that's what the Chief seems to have done with pitchers like [Bobby] Shantz, [Bob] Hooper and [Carl] Scheib. There's no other explanation, that I can see, for their improvement."

With no pitcher was Bender's influence more evident than with lefty Bobby Shantz. In 1950, Shantz, listed at five-foot-six and 142 pounds— no one thought those dimensions artificially small for the package— went 8-14 with a 4.61 ERA. After a season with Bender he improved to 18-10 and 3.94.

Under Bender's tutelage, Shantz made another leap in 1952, going 24-7 with a 2.48 ERA, an effort that earned him the American League's Most Valuable Player Award. Though Bender took none of the credit.

"The only thing we did with Bobby was slow him down," he said. "He was in too big a hurry all the time. The only flaw with Shantz is he gets mad at himself instead of taking it out on the batters and brushing them back once in a while."

When Bender fell ill during the 1952 season the soft-spoken Shantz was distraught. He sent a letter to the hospital: "Just a few lines to let you know I have been thinking about you. . . . We all certainly do miss you,

Chief, and hope you can be back with us soon. Chief, I'd like to take this time to thank you for all of the things you taught me about pitching. I'll probably never be the pitcher you were, but I'll always be in there trying my best to do the things you taught me."

In his autobiography, Shantz acknowledged the impact Bender had on his performance. "Bender helped me develop my knuckler to the point it was second to my curveball as a stock-in-trade pitch," he said. "He also taught me to conserve my energy on the mound. I used to work too fast and I got tired too quickly. The Chief showed me how to pace myself."

When he wasn't on the field Bender served as the A's goodwill ambassador at Rotary, Kiwanis, and Lions club meetings and frequently spoke at banquets, hospitals, and schools, to athletic clubs and groups of civil servants. While serving as an Athletics scout he and George Earnshaw conducted fifteen-minute pregame World Series programs on WCAU-TV. The two former big-league stars discussed big moments in previous Series classics, including those they participated in, and worked with sportscaster Bill Sears.

Some people speak in a way that others enjoy listening to them no matter the topic. Bender had such an affable manner. Words slipped off his tongue in a way that revealed intelligence, and he had a gift for telling stories. He loved jokes, especially if he was personally involved.

At one banquet, a man who had consumed one too many martinis pestered him. Where was he from? What business was he in? What country was he born in? The fellow grilled Bender until, finally, he looked up from his rubber chicken and said, deadpan, "I sell blankets at the railroad station in Albuquerque."

Some of his more popular lines:

"I don't know why they called me a 'money pitcher.' I never got any money."

"I was sure I'd make the Hall [of Fame] sometime because I figured, sooner or later, the white man would have to give something back to the Indians."

"I don't know why I'm invited to speak at dinners, unless it's to show an Indian really talks."

After an operation in 1952: "Thank you, boys, for all the transfusions. It was wonderful. First time I ever knew a white man's blood was good for anything."

Bender would speak and show promotional films for Mack, and he talked to youngsters about the value of education. He told them that most great athletes he had known also had been exceptionally bright. He made a point to promote baseball as a means of keeping young people off the streets, of helping develop their intellect and ability to lead. After all, without baseball, how different would his life have been?

Bender encouraged kids to attend church and to embrace education. He once explained to a crowd about the boarding school outing system, that starting in the late spring American Indian students went to work, usually on farms, until the next semester started in the fall. "There were two reasons why we were sent out," Bender said. "One was to pick up a little spending money and the other was learn the ways of the white man— why, I don't know, because I've never been able to decide whether or not the white man's ways are any good for a young fellow."

Bender played the race card as a comedic prop. He wanted others to feel comfortable. He didn't start a racial crusade, didn't publicly take up any isms. The American story is a story of race, and not all those who changed the narrative for the betterment of the rest did so during the course of dramatic demonstrations. Bender inspired and changed attitudes simply by living his life. One couldn't look at him and continue to believe the stereotypes. More than anything he just wanted what most people want—to be around people, to be liked, accepted.

In 1952 he was at a party in honor of George Weiss and encountered Gene Martin. Thinking Bender wouldn't remember him, Martin, a minor league player of little renown, was about to introduce himself when Bender cut him off.

"I'd throw you two inside curves that you'd hit a mile down the right-field foul line, and then I'd fire one past you for a third strike. How are you, Gene?"

At that same gathering Bender met Yogi Berra. When they were introduced Berra asked, "Right-hander or left-hander?"

"Either hand," Bender said.

Late in life, as illness took its toll, Philadelphia A's publicity man Tommy Clark passed over Bender's name in lining up speakers for public appearances, out of respect for Bender's health. But Bender protested.

"If I'm going to die, I can do it just as well on my feet, trying to make a few friends for the club," he said. "I just figure that going out as a speaker will help and I like it."

Home. Most are born into one. May be fancy. Or falling apart. Large. Or unkind. Home is bricks and mortar and the bulletin board on which the grocery list is tacked, but its essential elements extend beyond the physical. Home is a place of human connection, and that connection provides warmth, familiarity, and a shield against the mongrels of life that nibble at the soul. At home there are people who love and accept you. The world can fall apart, but you can still walk through the front door. You can be who you are there, and that sense of belonging affords a necessary margin of error. Home is where you feel comfortable with eyes closed in the dark of night. Where life is anchored in the way a willow remains tall even after the wind blows.

Charles Bender grew up without a home, and a person without a home is a person without a place in the world. In such straits one fears more. One is more apt to worry, to feel ungrounded, unsure. The absence of home creates a shortage of hope, a fear of alienation, and makes one more likely to give credence to the opinions of others.

Shipped away from his family as a child, never to return for any meaningful length of time, never to form a lasting bond with his parents, sent to schools designed to indoctrinate, drilled by human beings who rejected his human makeup and taught him to do the same, Bender stepped into the world with a conflicted sense of who he was and what he should become. From age seven on he was told to believe certain things about his very essence—and he didn't have anyone who simply accepted him for who he was.

Bender couldn't possibly have calculated his path, and when he took the first step he probably didn't even know what he was after. But he sought what most everyone seeks—something more vital than the World Series. He spent his life searching for his place in this world. His home.

He found Marie, and no relationship could have been as meaningful. In the Philadelphia Athletics he had found lifelong friends, such as Eddie Collins, Frank Baker, Jack Coombs, Joe Bush, and Rube Oldring. He found a father figure in Connie Mack. He had a career, a sense of accomplishment, an opportunity for growth, and he performed so well that he received adulation from people he didn't even know—a level of acceptance few realize.

But so much was on the surface, so much of it was delicate, and in October 1914 something greater than a world championship was lost. In many respects, Bender's life was pulled from him like a merciless magic trick. Much of the support system he had constructed over a dozen years had been stripped away. Suddenly, Bender was no longer considered reliable. Overnight, he could no longer call on Mack. He would still have friends, but fewer of them, and those who remained were living their own lives, separate from his own. The crowd no longer roared.

What's worse, never knowing home—or having one vanish before your eyes?

The frustration, the disappointment, the loss, must have been demoralizing. This wasn't the case of a fallen hero so much as it was the story of a man whose spirit had been broken. "On the inside, I burned up," Bender said. "I couldn't eat for three hours after a game. After the 1914 season, my nerves reached such a pitch that I broke out in hives. I spent hundreds of dollars on doctors and lost two big years. Finally, [in 1918] I ran into a physician in Germantown who cured me for twenty-five cents. He gave me soda mint tablets."

There must have been years when Bender thought the search would never end. By September 4, 1952, however, he had come to know otherwise. He discovered that, in fact, he had found his place. Baseball had been the boat with which he navigated his way through unfriendly waters. Eventually, the game became more than a means. It was no warm place all those years. And the prejudice would remain for decades to come. The verbal torment did not vanish. Neither did the tacit racism. After he was voted into the Baseball Hall of Fame, *The Sporting News* said it was a "long-delayed feather for the Chief." Bender's obituary in the same publication carried the headline: "Chief Bender Answers Call to Happy Hunting Grounds."

But Charles Bender's resolve allowed him to overcome, or at least move beyond, the catty calls and the emotional strain. Strong forces had pushed him to the ground, but, just as he did as a young man following his father's swift kick, Bender always picked himself up, moved on, and didn't allow the aftertaste to leave him bitter. And, at some point, he turned around and discovered that baseball, for all its imperfections, despite the pain it caused, was waiting with its arms extended wide.

That spring *The Sporting News* and other publications called for a tribute to Bender for his some fifty years of contribution to organized baseball. With the Yankees and A's looking on, Bender stood at the center of the star-studded diamond, feet from where he fashioned a reputation as one of baseball's great clutch pitchers. Marie, who over the years had added weight but had not lost her smile, was on his arm. A three-piece hung from his frame as though he was a suit model.

At sixty-eight, Bender remained a picture of fitness, looking as though he could still throw batting practice, if not for the cancer ravaging inside. But he was not as comfortable as he looked; moments before he had dreaded the stagger he would make on his way to the center of the field. When the call came he turned and hung his cane on the rail and bit his lip. He said he was not going to let the fans see him do the dot-and-carry. The move fooled everyone, except Mrs. Bender. She strode slowly with her partner and later remarked that the only old-timer in the formulation who didn't limp was Connie Mack.

Marie was the brightest light in the park, clutching Charles as he stepped toward the microphone to deliver his remarks. He followed a small parade of well-wishers who foisted bouquets of gratitude. Among them was Shantz, that day's starting pitcher. Ironically, Shantz's opposing number was Allie Reynolds, himself dubbed Superchief, for having been born part Creek. The A's chose to have Shantz pitch that night expressly because Bender had had such an impact on him. The affection went both ways. No one, it was said, gave Bender such a lift as his pupil.

In order to pull off Chief Bender Night a committee of seventy-five had been formed that included Gov. John S. Fine and six Major League owners. Scrolls of tribute had been circulated throughout the state in hundreds of factories, department stores, fraternal organizations, clubs, American Legion posts, banks, and industrial plants. Philadelphia youngsters set up booths in the City Hall courtyard to encourage city workers and passersby to sign the scrolls. Models from a modeling school set up booths at Shibe Park. By the time Chief Bender Night was a reality, the scrolls had been signed by City Hall judges, employees in various industries, and by all Major League Baseball players.

The idea was to provide every admirer a chance to get his or her name on the scrolls, and about 150,000 signatures made the list. The scrolls read: "The undersigned are proud to add our names to this scroll of tribute to Albert (Chief) Bender, a great athlete and sportsman—a credit to baseball and an inspiration to American youth for three generations. We all join in wishing him a speedy recovery."

The scrolls were stretched across the infield by a group of models. As eyes scanned across, from a buxom brunette near third base in the direction of first, boisterous laughter was heard at the discovery that the final set of hands belonged not to a beautiful woman but rather the opposite: Philadelphia pitcher Bobo Newsom. They didn't call him Bobo because he had a fetching figure.

"If ever there was an inspiration to our youth who deserved a night, that's the Chief," said Arthur C. Kaufmann, general chairman of the Chief Bender Night committee. "Chief Bender is one of the great living symbols of the American game of baseball. He has done much to promote the game among our youth and has especially been helpful in the development of Junior Legion baseball."

Bender was handed boxes of gifts from former fellow employees of Gimbels department store, where he worked as a clothing salesman. The Athletics—no doubt this was Mack's idea—offered Bender a lifetime contract.

"Bender is a great inspiration to all of us," Cleveland president Ellie Ryan said. "He has set a fine example as a player, scout and coach. As an 'Indian,' we are proud to salute him."

The most generous gift was a check for $6,009.50, money contributed by members of both teams, and from coin containers placed in various locations all over the state of Pennsylvania in anticipation of the day's festivities. When honored, most ballplayers are given golf clubs, a trip to the Bahamas, a Cadillac. This wasn't necessarily stated, and a statement wasn't necessary, but Bender, who never earned an especially handsome paycheck, even for his era, needed the money.

He had not been allowed to retire. He sold sporting goods, televisions, insulation, and clothes—jobs that allowed him and Marie to lead lower-middle-class lives. "I'm sorry I never finished college," Bender said. "Some of my old school mates are now respected professional men." By 1952 he had depleted his bank account trying to pay his medical bills. But that's what family and friends are for. To let you know you're not alone in this world even if the candle has nearly melted. Especially then.

Bender was wired more for action than reflection. But, surely, on this day an exception was made. The day had begun hours before with a Junior Chamber of Commerce luncheon, during which Bender told the audience the honor was the nicest thing that had happened to him. It's hard to fathom that at some point during frivolity that continued until the last cheer was heard from the bleachers, that the man of the hour did not allow his mind to wander about the years.

In a few months Bender would suffer a heart attack, and in less than two years he would leave the earth. That night he formally turned his back to the mound on which he threw so many innings, many of them delighting a city that wasn't usually friendly to people of his skin color, for the last time. As he began to walk away, possibly the images sailed through his mind. Perhaps while looking against the backdrop of so many indelible scenes he reflected on an improbable, toilsome, and awesome life— a life that raised him to the height of celebrity, dragged him through the gutter of racism, placed him on a pedestal by generations of American Indians, forced him to face rare tragedy, provided winsome memories of money games, and, at last, allowed him to know the comfort of home.

Epilogue. As a boy John Burns slipped into Philadelphia Athletics games without paying. During the late innings ticket attendants were lax, and if he maneuvered his way through the gates quickly enough he could catch a glimpse of his heroes. Decades later, after he grew up, married, and started a family, Burns became closer to one of those heroes, Charles Bender, than he ever could have imagined as a sneaky kid in old Columbia Park.

Burns was born in Philadelphia in 1898, and in 1944 he bought a home and a large parcel of land in Haddon Heights, New Jersey, just across the Delaware River. The Burnses were hospitable; they often entertained friends that John had met through his work as a beer distributor. Charles and Marie Bender were among the family's guests, and the couple had dinner over at the house once in a while. Marie would always bring a large pie, and Chief, as the family called him, was the "austere" and "dignified" man who had a slow, simple, direct way of talking to them. He was not loquacious, but he was dependable and often around. Richard Burns, one of John's sons, said in the summer he would see Bender almost as often as he saw his own father.

On one section of an approximately three-acre plot, John Burns planted a large garden. Another plot sat unused, littered with trees and scrub-brush. In his later years Bender had taken up tree pruning and gardening as hobbies. But he didn't have his own slab of land, or the money to purchase one. One day Bender was helping his friend tend his garden.

"John," he said, "would you like that piece of woodland cleared off?"

"I sure would."

Using axe and saw, Bender cut the trees and pulled the stumps from the ground. He worked until he cleared close to an acre of fertile soil. Burns knew his friend was not the kind who asked for things. Bender was a willing giver, a reluctant taker. Burns later said he had that in mind when he returned his friend's favor.

"Chief," he said, "it's yours."

There was no transfer of title on the parcel of land, but that season, and for seasons thereafter, Bender planted his own garden. The Burns family, which included five children, came to call that portion of their yard "Chief's Garden." He approached gardening as he approached pitching: he was meticulous. His rows were straight and clean. There was not a weed or a plant out of place. John Burns said that Bender grew a number of different fruits and vegetables, among them blueberries, strawberries, black and red raspberries, squash, and tomatoes. Corn was a specialty. He cultivated delicious corn that was picked only at the proper moment.

"Lord help anyone who would think of pulling an ear before the designated maturity date," Burns said. Bender often joked with his friend that the white man didn't know how to eat corn. "He eat 'em too green," he'd say.

"All these things that landscape guys learned in school," said Richard Burns, who said he remembers the directions Bender gave him on how to prune a tree, "he knew."

What Bender grew Marie served on their kitchen table. What they didn't need, he gave away or sold. Although he lived in north Philadelphia, Bender seldom missed a day at the garden. He would work on it before night games or in the evenings after day games. After which he would often have a drink with John Burns. Bender's relationship with alcohol did not make public news late in his life, save for a note in a column about his decision to have a soda at a banquet. But apparently he never quit drinking. He also continued to smoke. Instead of pitching, he kept his mind busy by gardening.

While in his garden Bender communed with birds and other animals,

Bender at work in "Chief's Garden." Courtesy of Patricia Burns Ward.

including the Burns family cat. "I can see and hear him now talking to the robins and whistling to the Bobwhite in the tree," John Burns said shortly after Bender died.

Charles and Marie Bender never had children. It's not known whether they didn't want them or couldn't have them. But Bender had a gift for relating to kids, and John Burns's sons were testament to that. From his earliest walking days Michael Burns, the youngest, followed Bender around his garden, John Burns said, like a puppy follows its master. The two were inseparable pals. A few days before Bender died he received a letter from six-year-old Michael, a few words in print that covered a page: "The strawberries are good. Please get better soon. I miss you very much."

The health problems that were present throughout Bender's career were exacerbated during the final quarter of his life. Pleurisy. Shingles. Pneumonia. Gallstones. The list of illnesses he battled was more imposing than a lineup of American League stars.

In 1952 Bender underwent a serious abdominal operation. Philadelphia officials and the local American Red Cross made public pleas for blood donors for Bender, who himself had been a regular donor. He was given several transfusions, lost twenty-five pounds off his thin frame, and was weak. But, as he did while pitching, Charles Bender often quickly bounced back.

His doctors were shocked when, following a major operation, he made a remarkable comeback. They must not have known their patient didn't believe in the concept of sitting still. No hunting, the doctor said, so Bender knocked down birds by the bundle. No golf, the doctor said, so Bender only went sixteen holes at a local country club. No trapshooting, the doctor said, but Bender went to a gun club and broke 21 of 25 targets at sixteen yards. He expended energy more quickly, but he didn't let illness prevent him from living.

By the final year of his life Bender needed a thick cane to get around. He still went to the ballpark, still tried to help young pitchers. "If only I could stand up and show these fellows what I mean," Bender said. "This 'Philadelphia rheumatism' won't let me alone." Bender saw his last live baseball in March 1954 when his wife rolled him out in a wheelchair from the grandstand to the bench at West Palm Beach during A's spring training. During that last spring, Bender had to return to Philadelphia and check into the hospital.

Bing Miller, also a coach with the Athletics during Bender's tenure as pitching coach, was the last of Bender's friends to see him alive. In those years Bender was an ice cream fiend, and Miller took him a container almost every day. A few days before Bender passed, as the two were eating Miller's gift, Bender said, "I'm tired, Bingo, I'm tired."

"It's these double-headers. These double-headers are tiring you out."

"I never did like double-headers," Bender said. "And this is my last one, Bingo, old pal. I'm a good Indian. I'm going to give you back your scalp and give you the tomahawk I took it with."

Bender's final hospital stay began April 12, a day before Bobby Shantz took the mound to start the A's season, and he passed away late in the evening of May 22. The cause of death was listed as prostate cancer. He also had heart problems.

"The greatest tribute one can pay to Chief Bender—and the one he would be proudest to claim—is that he never made an enemy," said Roy Mack, general manager of the A's when Bender died. "He was everybody's favorite and everybody's friend. He will be sadly missed by all of the baseball world. There will never be another Chief Bender."

The day Marie wheeled Bender in for the final practice he would see she had proudly displayed a diamond wristwatch, pointing out the inscription on the back. It read: "To Marie from her Honey—50th Anniversary." People were surprised: You've been married fifty years?

"No," Marie said. "When he gave it to me, I told him, 'Honey, you've made a mistake. We won't be married fifty years until next October.'

"He said, 'I haven't made a mistake. I wanted you to have this now. I won't be around for the fiftieth."

Said Marie: "And how do you think he got the money to buy the watch? By saving what he sold out of the garden."

Bender was right—he would miss the fiftieth. But, said Marie, who would pass away in a nursing home in 1961 after a long illness, "I'll have my watch, little Michael's letter and my memories."

Bender's funeral, May 27, 1954, was a large affair. The Rev. William Barnes Lower, pastor emeritus of Holy Trinity Presbyterian Church, conducted services. Pallbearers were Frank Baker, Lena Blackburn, Howard

Ehmke, Hans Lobert, Bing Miller, Wally Moses, Rube Oldring, and Amos Strunk. Connie Mack was there and, the *Philadelphia Evening Bulletin* said, he was noticeably "shaken." Songs sung included "Abide with Me," "Lead to the Light" and "Schubert's Ave Maria." There was an organist and a wagon of flowers. Lower spoke on the three ideals of man—philosophy, which gives life meaning; morality, which makes life noble; and resources outside of oneself, which give life power and security. Bender had all these, he said.

Bender also had a Masonic service by the Robert Lamberton Lodge No. 487 at the Oliver H. Bair funeral home before being buried in Hillside Cemetery in Roslyn, Pennsylvania. In order to have a Masonic funeral service one must have completed a Master Mason degree and be a member in good standing of a lodge at the time of death. Lodge officers performed Bender's ceremony dressed in dark suits, white aprons, and gloves, and at the end of the service they dropped a sprig of evergreen, a symbol of eternal life, into his casket.

The imprint of Charles Bender's life lasted into the twenty-first century. His personality was infectious; once he touched your life you didn't forget it. His onetime roommate on the A's, Rube Bressler, described Bender as "one of the kindest and finest men who ever lived." Even those he never met were attracted to him. Fans wrote letters, especially when he was ill, expressing appreciation for the way he conducted his life.

Shan Buck, a twelve-year-old boy from Syracuse, wrote a letter to Marie two years after Bender passed away. Because of Bender's abilities as a pitcher in the face of racism, "I am awed with respect for him," Buck said. Marie sent a note back containing an autographed picture of the Chief. Buck was thrilled.

"Believe me, I am the happiest boy in the world," he said, and "my father is just as thrilled as I am. We had it framed and matted. It went on my wall. I am so proud of it." Buck's father also wrote a thank you: "Mrs. Buck and I know no satisfactory way of thanking you for bringing him so generously close to the great Chief."

A. G. Burgoyne Jr. from Akron, Pennsylvania, sent a letter in 1954 when Bender was in the hospital. Burgoyne had read a note in the *New York Daily News* disclosing Bender's illness. "I'm sorry to hear this sort of news regarding someone for whom I have much esteem," Burgoyne said.

"You, of course, don't know me. However, I was one of a group of convicts at the Federal Prison in Lewisburgh when you spoke there in 1946 or 1947. You didn't make a long speech and I'm sure it was off the cuff. I, however, never forgot it. I used to think of you a lot and . . . the courage which you stressed in your talk helped make my rehabilitation complete. Today I'm a respected member of my community and am regional manager of a large company. I think you played a part in this and I felt you would like to know it."

Lou Limmer was in the minor leagues when he met Bender in Lexington, North Carolina, in the mid-1940s. Bender would always wake up early and be on the field in the wee morning hours, raking the infield and the pitching mound. Fields in rural North Carolina at that level were not much softer than concrete. Rocks and pebbles were visible, but by the time Limmer arrived Bender would have made the infield flat, playable.

Bender always greeted Limmer the same way. "Boozhoo niijii," he said. *Boozhoo niijii*, pronounced "boo zhoo nee jee," French intermixed with Ojibwe that loosely translated meant "Good morning, friend." Sixty years later Limmer said, "I never forget those words."

Bender always tried to teach Limmer, a first baseman who played parts of two seasons with the A's in the early 1950s, how to hit. "He had one home run in the major leagues [actually, six] and he was trying to tell me how to hit," Limmer said. "He told me I couldn't hit the high fastball. Then I hit one on the first at bat of the season and he came up to me and told me he taught me how to hit it."

The Chief was a nice guy, Limmer said, "and that's what he wanted to be—a helluva nice guy."

He succeeded. "I can't think of a better person," former A's infielder Eddie Joost said. "I never heard a harsh word about the Chief. Everybody liked him."

Joost and Bender became friends during the later years of Bender's life and would often spend time together in spring training. Joost, who served as player-manager of the Philadelphia A's the year Bender died, would bring his sons around, and Bender would sit with the Joosts and tell stories about Indian lore and life in the big leagues when the A's were the champions of the world.

Bender made Joost smile a half-century after their last conversation when he recalled a Bender story that can't be verified. It was the sixth inning of a game at Shibe Park. Connie Mack was considering a pitching change, but after he noticed there wasn't anyone warming up in the bullpen, he sent a young ballplayer down to see what was happening. The player came back and told Mack, "No one is there." No catchers. No pitchers. No one.

"You better go back and find out what's going on," Mack supposedly said.

Turns out, as the story goes, across the street from the corner of Twenty-first and Lehigh there was a bar, and all members of that day's bullpen crew were inside, having a beer.

The memory is precarious. A middle-aged man can seemingly remember precise details of the moment as a child he was stung by a bee and yet still forget where he left the car keys fifteen minutes before he had the recollection. Perhaps the vivid memories are so only because we're fooling ourselves. The past is obscure, a convincing imposter, too often remembered differently by different people. But sometimes you don't need to be able to verify everything to find truth. Joe Astroth knows that Charles Bender's life influenced his own.

Bender taught Astroth baseball, but he also taught him life skills. Astroth said Bender always told him to "ask yourself 'why?'" When something doesn't go your way, you shouldn't find fault in others. You should look within and figure out a solution. Astroth said Bender was very bright, not just about baseball. Bender used to tell his players that "if you don't try it you'll never be able to do it," Astroth said. "Don't be afraid to make changes in your delivery. You have to seek out what's best for you. Leave your mind open."

Astroth thought of Bender more than fifty years after Bender's death when, during a holiday, he was playing around with a new DVD player. Great picture, terrific sound, but of course the time was impossible to set. "I was fooling around with the cursor and finally, there, it said 10:56. I didn't know how I did it, but it worked," he said. "At least I tried. Now I know I can figure it out because I know it can be done." He may not recall the precise words Bender uttered but he knows one reason he didn't throw his hands up and leave the DVD player blinking twelve o'clock. "It

288

was a broad statement but I practiced that all through my life" Astroth said. "He enriched my life."

Charles Bender, who in addition to being inducted in the Baseball Hall of Fame was, in 1972, inducted into the American Indian Athletic Hall of Fame, is no longer a household name. But his accomplishments have not been lost, even among people who never knew him. On a cool early-spring day in 1999, the *Anishinaabeg Today* reported, White Earth resident Paul Schultz visited Bender's grave site because "maybe his spirit would feel good about having someone stop in."

Schultz paused at Bender's grave to pay him tribute. "I offered tobacco around the headstone and gave a prayer of thanks for Chief Bender and his life, and for the inspiration that he has been to many Indian folks and many others," he said. "It felt like an honor to be there."

Dan Kratz was a child in the late 1930s living on a family farm in Bucks County. Kratz's father operated the farm, producing goods Kratz's grandfather sold on a huckster route. During the latter years of the Depression families did what they could to earn extra income, and to that end Kratz's grandfather allowed hunters to use his land. Men would pay a fee to hunt small game: rabbits, ringneck pheasants, squirrels.

Bender was one of the regulars. Dan Kratz's contacts with Bender were limited as he was not allowed to bother the hunters, in general, but a special exception was granted in the case of the Chief. Bender was always willing to give Kratz a few minutes on his way in or out. He was polite and courteous to Kratz's mother, always had a twinkle in his eye and a willing ear. Kratz was thrilled and awed.

Different than other men who used the land, Bender was respectful of the family's rules, always paying attention to the conditions of the fields before crossing them. The Kratzes didn't have to fix things after Bender left, as they often did when other hunters departed. Sometimes Bender brought an extra bird or two back from his hunt that served as that night's supper for the Kratzes. During those encounters Dan Kratz came to look up to Charles Bender. It was not a stretch to say he honored him, that he used him as a role model.

"Perhaps the greatest testimony to his powerful presence is demonstrated in that for sixty years I have expressed pride in knowing him," said Kratz, a retired pastor. "It is no accident that my colleagues are aware that Chief Bender played a part in my development."

During the last few years of his life, in the afternoons he tended Chief's Garden, Bender would eat lunch with little Michael Burns. Marie would pack her husband's lunch and, John Burns said, always included candy especially for Michael. John Burns recalled that they would sit at the edge of the garden, Bender resting on an empty beer box and Michael on a tree stump. Just the two of them—generations apart—gabbing like old buddies.

"I often wished I could listen in without them seeing me and hear what they said—the aging Indian with his years of experience and wisdom and Michael with his innocence and fresh viewpoint," John Burns said.

Michael was too young, of course, to idolize Bender for what he had been or what he had done. And Bender was not trying to impress him with stories from the World Series. But he made an impression that lasted the rest of Michael's life.

Michael Burns eventually graduated from Bradley University and spent his career in computers. Shortly before his death in 2003 he wrote a letter about Bender, calling him a "substitute grandfather," for his had passed away. "He taught me how to hold a baseball. My older brothers remember him bringing the big forty-two-inch bats for the local youth to use at the field next door," Burns said.

"Though I was a child, I say to this day that he could call the crows to his attention just as Francis of Assisi could calm a bird in his hand. He was a wonderful, wonderful man. He deserves to be remembered. In this 'modern' era of athletic heroes, the Chief should be the example, not the forgotten."

Bibliographical Essay. The early history of modern Major League Baseball is filled with funny, fantastic, and fabulous stories. Some of them are even true. In researching Charles Albert Bender's baseball career I tried to separate fact from fable—the kind of mental gymnastics I imagine every baseball biographer must perform. On one hand, players during the era were written about extensively; on the other, few sportswriters had the means (or the wherewithal) to verify facts, at least not when stories pertained to events they didn't witness. Given the nature of available resources, I have tried to be as accurate as possible. In some cases, sources used were less reliable than I would have preferred, but I have tried to point out conflicting versions of stories and have either noted or disregarded anecdotes that strained my understanding of the elusive truth. In Bender's case, the usual fog of baseball legend and lore has been layered with the reality that he lived and played in the face of untold prejudice. That he was seldom asked about the most important aspect of his life story means a full portrait is categorically impossible. I have tried simply to present the closest thing I could. Throughout the process, I was afforded many advantages. Where the book satisfies, credit should be placed on the prior research—this story was constructed on a foundation of work done by previous historians and researchers—as well as the people and institutions that provided assistance, either out of human goodness (most cases) or because I wouldn't leave them alone. This essay is intended to recognize those sources and to show my work.

Researching Bender's career meant that, like it or not, I had to develop a close, personal relationship with a microfilm reader. The drudgery was lessened because of Joe Dittmar, who studied dozens of Philadelphia newspapers, including those published during Bender's career, and created an eminently useful guide he shared without hesitation, even though we've never met. I read most historical newspapers at Rølvaag Memorial Library on St. Olaf College's comely campus, where Jill Engle and Sara Leake, members of the interlibrary loan staff, filled my requests—every last one of them. Staff members at Laurence McKinley Gould Library at Carleton College and the Northfield Public Library also provided noteworthy and regular service.

Those historical newspapers were used in almost every chapter and to a degree influenced each page. Every quote came from a newspaper, magazine, journal, dissertation, book, or, in rare instances, an interview. Every fact came from a newspaper, magazine, journal, dissertation, book, or, in rare instances, an interview. Any missteps are failures of execution, not products of invention.

Whenever possible, I relied on contemporary periodicals, which heavily influenced game accounts. At times I used the eyewitness descriptions. The most prominently used include the *Philadelphia Inquirer, Philadelphia Press, Philadelphia Evening Bulletin, Philadelphia North American, New York Times, Chicago Tribune, Boston Daily Globe, Washington Post, Carlisle American Volunteer, Carlisle Herald, Carlisle Evening Sentinel,* Carlisle Indian Industrial School student newspapers, *Harrisburg Telegraph, Baseball Magazine, Sporting Life,* and *The Sporting News.*

The bulk of information contained in the narrative about Bender's Major League pitching career and the old Philadelphia Athletics came from these contemporary newspapers and magazines. Of the rest, a substantial portion was found in clips files at one or more of the following resources: the National Baseball Hall of Fame Library, Cooperstown, New York; *The Sporting News* archives, St. Louis; the Minnesota Historical Society; Crow Wing County (Minnesota) Historical Society; Cumberland County (Pennsylvania) Historical Society; Becker County (Minnesota) Historical Society; Warroad (Minnesota) Heritage Center; Harrisburg

Historical Society; the Historical Society of Pennsylvania; the University Archives at Haskell Cultural Center and Museum, Lawrence, Kansas; the Temple University Urban Archives; the U.S. Department of the Interior Bureau of Indian Affairs Office, Bemidji, Minnesota; Hampton University Archives; and the Wichita Public Library. I learned almost immediately to appreciate the men and women who serve these and other such institutions, most of them public, throughout the country. The fact is that I could not have written this book without the help of scores of people.

I am fortunate Charles Bender played for Connie Mack and the old Philadelphia Athletics because so much of the A's rich history has been researched so capably. Not only did I find a useful team history, *The Athletics of Philadelphia: Connie Mack's White Elephants, 1901–1954*, by David M. Jordan (McFarland & Company, 1999), but when I read Bruce Kuklick's *To Every Thing A Season: Shibe Park and Urban Philadelphia, 1909–1976* (Princeton University Press, 1991), I felt lucky such a specific and important topic had already been expertly explored. Kuklick was not the only fountain of information. My correspondences with Connie Mack biographer Norman Macht, who willingly shared his expertise and research pertaining to Bender, were invaluable. Max Silberman, vice president for research at the Philadelphia Athletics Historical Society, provided prompt and expert assistance throughout. Ernie Montella is another PAHS mainstay who treated this stranger from Minnesota like a friend after only one visit. When I say I was afforded many advantages, I think of how Bender played for a team that has an active historical society devoted to it. The PAHS bills itself as the most successful organization of its kind. It's not bragging when you back it up.

Baseball statistics were taken from *Total Baseball* and the ESPN *Baseball Encyclopedia*. I also relied on the two most indispensable references in a baseball researcher's toolkit: Baseball-Reference.com, created by Sean L. Forman, which provides an astounding amount of player and team information for free; and Retrosheet.org, which provides copyrighted information gratis thanks to the work of founder Dave Smith and a cadre of volunteers. Retrosheet was especially useful for play-by-play data of Bender's World Series starts. Another Web site with baseball reference material I consulted was BaseballLibrary.com.

The overall thrust of this book, Charles Bender's complex struggle with prejudice, came from my interpretation of the historical record, which was influenced in no small way by the fine general studies of the American Indian experience that have been written throughout the years. To that end, I would have to strain some to overstate the influence Jeffrey Powers-Beck's work had on mine. Early in my research I read his article "Chief: The American Indian Integration of Baseball, 1897–1945," *American Indian Quarterly*, 2002. This piece and Powers-Beck's seminal book *The American Indian Integration of Baseball* (University of Nebraska Press, 2004) educated me about American Indians' experiences in baseball and provided numerous useful facts and astute observations about Bender that I relied on throughout the book. Those seeking information about American Indian players are advised to start by reading that primer.

Despite all of the important work available, not surprisingly, I did not find accounts of Bender's early years that were produced during the time he lived them. Among the periodic profiles written about Bender after he became a baseball star, many contained errors about his family of origin, such as saying he was "full blooded" or that he was born in Brainerd. Mostly, these appear to have been slips picked up and repeated by writers who thought they had no reason to question them. This doesn't mean, however, that all information written about Bender's early years was wholly unreliable. For the early period of his life, I used details from written interviews with Bender conducted in adulthood, where such recollections were credible. It's unlikely that Bender's memory was any better than the average human being's. Which is to say, undoubtedly it was flawed. But seldom did it seem that he made up things out of thin air. So it's likely his recollections were imprecise in the way any person's would be. Equally likely is that they were close to accurate.

Additional notes about scenes and facts that may be of interest to the reader or researcher follow for each chapter.

Chapter One

Details about the day before the 1914 World Series, including Bender's warm-up session and the scene outside Shibe Park that week, were reported in various Philadelphia newspapers. I relied most heavily on those published in the *Philadelphia North American*.

Descriptions of Bender's delivery are based on photographs as well as written accounts found in various printed materials cited in this essay. Among the useful visual aids was a short series of action photographs found in an article in the clips file at the Cumberland County Historical Society. The photos were taken to show "the pitching style" Bender used. In *A Game of Inches* (Ivan R. Dee, 2006), Peter Morris wrote that "Chief Bender was one of the first pitchers who became well known for a high leg kick."

F. C. Lane's quote about Bender came from a piece under the headline "The Greatest Pitcher on the Diamond Today" in the September 1912 issue of *Baseball Magazine.*

In addition to sources already mentioned, general information about Connie Mack and the Athletics used in this and subsequent chapters was found in *Connie Mack: Grand Old Man of Baseball,* by Fred Lieb (G. P. Putnam's Sons, 1948); *My 66 Years in Baseball,* by Connie Mack (Universal House, 1950); *Deadball Stars of the American League,* edited by David Jones (Potomac Books, 2007); and "Philadelphia Athletics: 1901–1954," a documentary found at the Philadelphia Athletics Historical Society.

Information about the Boston Braves, for this and subsequent chapters, came from contemporary newspapers in Philadelphia and Boston; *Deadball Stars of the National League,* edited by Tom Simon (Brassey's, 2004); Macht's research about the 1914 World Series; and Lieb's *The Story of the World Series* (G. P. Putnam's Sons, 1948).

The tale of Bender teasing Johnny Evers before the 1914 World Series was written about in a two-part series of columns authored by George Stallings in the January 10 and 17, 1915, editions of the *Boston Daily Globe.* These articles were also relied upon in subsequent chapters.

The section of the chapter that begins "They called him Chief" came from both my own reading of the historical record and from experts who have written about the era and the topic. Powers-Beck's work was instrumental here, including his arguments about how American Indian baseball players of the time suffered both racial and cultural prejudice, and his descriptions of how Bender and American Indians in general were characterized. A chapter called "Tinker to Evers to Chief" from a dissertation written by Patty Loew (University of Wisconsin, December 1998) called "The Lake Superior Chippewa and their Newspapers in the Unprogressive Era" also enhanced my understanding about how Bender was treated in the baseball world and how American Indians viewed him. Other useful sources on this topic include *American Indian Lives* by Nathan Aaseng (Facts on File, 1995); and *Indians in Unexpected Places*, by Philip J. Deloria (University Press of Kansas, 2004).

The Rossi quote came from *The National Game: Baseball and American Culture*, by John Rossi (Ivan R. Dee, 2000).

"I do not want my name to be presented to the public as an Indian, but as a pitcher," came from a 1905 article found in the Charles Albert Bender file at the Baseball Hall of Fame. It was also published in *Sporting Life*.

The Zuber quote came from the October 21, 1905, issue of *Sporting Life*.

The 1903 incident on the train was reported in the June 28, 1903, *North American*.

Bender's call of "Foreigners! Foreigners!" was written about frequently throughout his lifetime. Among the places found was in an undated article included in the Bender file at the Baseball Hall of Fame.

The story about the 1907 incident in which Bender was thrown out of an establishment because the proprietor apparently thought he was black was attributed to sportswriter Hugh Fullerton and published in the April 19, 1908, edition of the *Atlanta Journal Constitution*.

The observation of how children reacted to Bender in public (and how he reacted to them) came from *Baseball: The Biographical Encyclopedia*, edited by David Pietrusza, Matthew Silverman, and Michael Gershman (Total Sports, 2000).

Some of Bender's physical characteristics, found in this and subsequent chapters, were based on information contained in *Kings of the Diamond: The Immortals in Baseball's Hall of Fame*, by Lee Allen and Tom Meany (G. P. Putnam's Sons, 1965). Others were written about in contemporary newspaper coverage. An interesting note about Bender's height: It has always been written that Christy Mathewson was an imposing presence in part because of his stature and that may very well have been the case. A picture taken of Bender and Matty side by side during their trapshooting tour in 1915 reveals Bender was at least two inches taller than Matty.

Billy Evans's views on Bender were printed in columns Evans wrote that appeared in numerous periodicals, including the *New York Times*, and picked up by newspapers such as the *Carlisle Arrow*. I found copies of these articles in Bender's clips files at several places, such as the Baseball Hall of Fame and the Cumberland County Historical Society.

The story about Bender's goofy ride in Philadelphia before one of his regular season starts was reported in the *Philadelphia Press* during Bender's Major League career and found in a reprinted story in the *Carlisle Arrow*.

The paragraph in which I state that Americans enjoyed baseball's "intellectual stimulation" was influenced by *The Old Ball Game*, by Frank Deford (Atlantic Monthly Press, 2005).

My description of the advances in telegraphy that connected newspaper offices around the country and expanded baseball coverage came from a section of Loew's dissertation.

Chapter Two

The idea of Bender as a Renaissance man came from my overall review of available information on his life away from baseball. It was difficult to read a biographical sketch or a set of clips about him without learning about his long list of hobbies.

Bender's affinity for trapshooting was written about in numerous sources, including the January 1916 issue of *American Shooter* magazine. The May 10, 1915, *Carlisle Herald* contained an essay written by Bender about his feelings on the sport. An April 8, 1917, article from a Philadelphia newspaper found in Charles Albert Bender file at Temple's Urban Archives discussed Bender's abilities with a gun, saying "the big Chippewa shoots by intuition." An interview under the headline "What a Famous Pitcher Thinks of Trap Shooting," published in the April 1915 *Baseball Magazine*, and an article dated March 6, 1915, found in the Bender file in the Baseball Hall of Fame also were useful.

An article dated November 25, 1917, found at Temple's Urban Archives said how Bender and Charles H. Newcomb, since inducted into the Trapshooting Hall of Fame, were to help airmen prepare for the "great war" in the art of bringing down enemy planes.

The story about Bender shooting a vulture during spring training was found in a profile about him in the December 30, 1953, issue of *The Sporting News*.

Bender talked about how nervous he was before games in an article that appeared in *The Sporting News* on December 31, 1942.

Details about the scene in which Charley Bender waited for the train to take him to boarding school were found in direct quotes attributed to Bender in a story printed in the March 23, 1944, *Frederick Daily News.*

It's not clear whether as a boy Charles Bender would have written his name as "Charley" or "Charlie." I saw it written in documents from his childhood only as "Charles," never by his hand. Apparently, according to various biographical sketches, Bender may have signed his autograph as "Charley" Bender. Other sources consulted use "Charlie."

In a July 23, 1905, article published in the *St. Louis Post-Dispatch* Bender was quoted as saying he was born in Chippewa Falls, Wisconsin. Either this was an error on the part of the reporter or an error on Bender's part (he may not have known his precise birthplace), or it is possible he was born in Wisconsin, his mother's birth state. The latter is highly unlikely.

Information about White Earth during this time was found in *The White Earth Tragedy: Ethnicity and Dispossession at a Minnesota Anishinaabe Reservation, 1889–1920*, by Melissa L. Meyer (University of Nebraska Press, 1994), an important book and the most informative source I found about White Earth during the years that encompassed Bender's time on the reservation. I relied on this book in several sections in this and the subsequent chapter, including for the general description of White Earth, the reservation's economic conditions, and the fraud. I am also grateful to Meyer for her willingness to review facts and offer suggestions for additional research.

Research conducted by Bob Tholkes, as written in an article called "Chief Bender: The Early Years," published in the 1983 edition of the *Baseball Research Journal,* heavily influenced sections of this and subsequent chapters. It was nothing short of an indispensable resource and the foundation on which I conducted further exploration about the rough details of Bender's first years and his family. Tholkes's help was not restricted to his research; he also reviewed facts and turned over his notes without me having to ask.

Beverly Hermes helped me pick up the ball from there, as she provided important genealogical research assistance on the Bender family that was used in this and subsequent chapters. The Charles Albert Bender file at the Bureau of Indian Affairs Office, Bemidji, Minnesota, was helpful as well. Names and birth years for Bender's siblings were found in the federal Indian census, the U.S. census, and an "individual history card" contained in the Mary (Razor) Bender file, at the BIA office in Bemidji.

The Loew dissertation stated that Mary Razor Bender was a member of the White Earth Band of the Chippewa; Tholkes's article stated she was a member of the Mississippi Band.

Paulette Fairbanks Molin's assistance—her research, correspondence, and willingness to review facts about the Bender family—was particularly helpful. Molin's article "Training the Hand, the Head, and the Heart: Indian Education at Hampton Institute," published in the Fall 1988 issue of *Minnesota History* magazine, revealed details about the Bender family used in this and subsequent chapters.

Information about Mary Bender also was found in a biographical sketch produced for the Lake of the Woods Historical Society contained in a clips file at the Warroad Heritage Center.

The note about Bender throwing stones at gophers as a young boy came from papers contained in a file at the Becker County Historical Society in Detroit Lakes, Minnesota. The quote on this topic was found in multiple sources already mentioned, including the Bender file at the Baseball Hall of Fame.

For general information about American Indian boarding schools I relied on *Boarding School Seasons*, by Brenda J. Child (University of Nebraska Press, 1998). Child did not write specifically about Bender, but her work was especially useful for general descriptions about the conditions and aims of boarding schools during the time Bender attended them, for information about the Dawes Act, and conditions at White Earth.

Regarding the aims of boarding school education, in addition to sources already mentioned I consulted Wilbert H. Ahern's article "Assimilationist Racism: The Case of the 'Friends of the Indian,'" published in *The Journal of Ethnic Studies*, 1976; and *Education for Extinction*, by David Wallace Adams (University Press of Kansas, 1995).

In some ways, the Lincoln Institution is the school that time forgot, as only sketchy information is available about its abbreviated existence. This section was pieced together from numerous sources, including the charter, bylaws, and annual reports from the Educational Home in Philadelphia, 1866–1900. Tholkes provided some of these and others were found at the Historical Society of Pennsylvania. Thanks to the Free Library of Pennsylvania for supplying a copy of a chapter on the Lincoln Institution in the book *Pennsylvania's Soldiers' Orphan Schools*, published in 1876, which obviously did not shed light on Bender's time at the school but did explain the school's early mission. Short contemporary newspaper articles contained in a file at Temple's Urban Archives were useful. *The Indian Rights Association: The Herbert Welsh Years, 1882–1904*, by William T. Hagan (The University of Arizona Press, 1985), provided nuggets about the school's director and the climate surrounding American Indian education at such institutions. An article published June 29, 1900, in a Warren, Pennsylvania, newspaper provided general information about the school. An article from *Leslie's Weekly* was helpful in describing the female education at Lincoln. The National Archives has some information about the Lincoln Institution. Fran Wilcox's help in researching Lincoln is appreciated.

Bender briefly discussed his time at the Educational Home in an article that appeared in the *Roanoke World News* in 1941. This article included comments about how he made his own baseball equipment. He also talked about his early schooling in a letter written in 1942 that was found in the Bender file at the Crow Wing County Historical Society. The first article in a two-part series about Bender's life published in *The Sporting News* on December 24, 1942, was used for information about Bender's childhood. In this article Bender also discussed his time at the Educational Home and his trip back to Minnesota, where he walked to his parents' house with "the gun over my shoulder."

Among other sources consulted in this chapter were *Indians and Other Americans: Two Ways of Life Meet*, by Harold E. Fey and D'Arcy McNickle (Harper & Row, 1970); Thomas Vennum Jr.'s *Wild Rice and the Ojibway People* (Minnesota Historical Society Press, 1988), which includes a photograph of Mary Razor Bender; *Away from Home: American Indian Boarding School Experiences, 1879–2000*, edited by Margaret L. Archuleta, Brenda J. Child, and K. Tsianina Lomawaima, (Heard Museum, 2000); and *Red World and White: Memories of a Chippewa Boyhood*, by John Rogers (Chief Snow Cloud) (University of Oklahoma Press, 1973).

Chapter Three

During Charley Bender's early years, the family was not settled in a single home for long stretches, and it's not entirely clear where they were living when he returned from the Educational Home. According to information in Molin's article, at some point the family lived in a community off the reservation, and later, after Charley had left for Carlisle, Mary Bender brought her children back to White Earth. It is my understanding, based on all sources mentioned, the family was, as written, living at White Earth when he returned. But it is conceivable they were in the area but not on reservation land.

The Sporting News of December 24, 1942, was used for information about Bender's childhood, including the story of how his father kicked him in the butt and how he ran away with his brother.

Meyer's *The White Earth Tragedy* and Tholkes's "Chief Bender: The Early Years" were relied upon here as well for information about White Earth.

Pratt's comment that "Indian ways will never be good anymore" has been cited in multiple works as coming from the April 1881 *School News*, a school monthly. I have not seen the original copy.

Just as there exists outstanding sources of information about the Philadelphia Athletics, so too did I encounter a wealth of facts about the Carlisle Indian Industrial School and generous people who supplied many of them. One of the best, and one I relied on extensively, for this and subsequent chapters on Carlisle, was "Telling Stories Out of the School: Remembering the Carlisle Indian Industrial School, 1879–1918," a PhD dissertation written by Genevieve Bell (Stanford University, 1998). Bell did not write about Bender, but in her work, one of several consulted on this topic, I found general information about Carlisle, from the school's mission to its physical appearance. Bell's descriptions, background, and characterizations of Richard Henry Pratt were especially influential in this and subsequent chapters. She also provided useful guidance via e-mail.

Barb Landis, Cumberland County Historical Society, who has done extensive research on Carlisle, provided expertise that helped form this and subsequent chapters. Landis maintains an excellent Web site *(http://home.epix.net/~landis/histry.html)* about the school and the children who attended it. I am also grateful for her willingness to review facts used about the school.

The Indian Industrial School: Carlisle, Pennsylvania, 1879–1918, by Linda Witmer (Huggins Printing Company, 2002), was another fine source for general information about Richard Henry Pratt and the school he operated. Bill Crawford's *All American: The Rise and Fall of Jim Thorpe* (John Wiley & Sons, 2005) was another. Though Bender and Thorpe's time at the school did not overlap, Crawford's work provided useful general information about the school and Pop Warner.

Other sources consulted include *A Final Promise: The Campaign to Assimilate the Indians, 1880–1920,* by Frederick E. Hoxie (University of Nebraska Press, 1984); *Pratt: The Red Man's Moses,* by Elaine Goodale Eastman (University of Oklahoma Press, 1935); Powers-Beck's work; Wallace's *Education for Extinction;* and Carlisle student publications such as the *Red Man,* the *Indian Helper,* the *Arrow,* and the *Carlisle Arrow.* The latter two were published after Bender left the school but included details about his exploits.

Facts about Bender's time at the Carlisle Indian Industrial School came from copies of his student record at the Cumberland County Historical Society and the National Archives and Records Administration in Washington, D.C.

Richard Henry Pratt's quote about Carlisle's mission came from the March 18, 1898, *Indian Helper* and has been published in various sources.

Chapter Four

Kuklick measured Bender's house as seven blocks from Shibe Park.

I'm grateful for assistance provided by Jeff Purtell, a member of the Society for American Baseball Research and a golf professional, who shared research he conducted about Bender's golf game, which influenced the golf section of this chapter. He also explained to me what a cleek is. Among other sources, selected issues from 1911–1917 of *American Golfer* magazine were useful. In its February 3, 1915, edition the *Los Angeles Times* wrote that Bender had been the best golfer in the American League. Christy Mathewson's comment about Bender's golf ability came from a column Mathewson wrote in the February 24, 1916, *Boston Daily Globe.*

The story of Bender's lunch with Grantland Rice and Oswald Kirskey was written about in various sources after Bender's playing career in which he was asked to recall the 1914 World Series. Among them was a column written by Arch Ward in the May 25, 1954, *Chicago Tribune*.

Information about Shibe Park came from a variety of sources. Kuklick's *To Every Thing A Season* was heavily relied upon here. I am grateful to Kuklick personally as well, as he reviewed an early draft of sections about Shibe Park and corrected a couple of errors I had made. *Philadelphia's Old Ballparks*, by Rich Westcott (Temple University Press, 1996), also was a terrific source, and Westcott was another who generously reviewed facts. Other sources on Shibe Park include *Green Cathedrals: The Ultimate Celebration of All 273 Major League and Negro League Ballparks*, by Philip J. Lowry (Addison-Wesley, 1992); *Lost Ballparks: A Celebration of Baseball's Legendary Fields*, by Lawrence S. Ritter (Viking Studio Books, 1992); and *The New Bill James Historical Abstract*, by Bill James (Free Press, 2001).

Chapter Five

Bender's poor health was written about, usually in a general fashion, throughout his career by beat writers in Philadelphia and elsewhere, and most information in this and subsequent chapters was taken from contemporary newspaper accounts. Among other sources, Frederic Linch wrote a profile of Bender in the May 1912 *Baseball Magazine* that described some of Bender's ailments in various seasons.

Bender's endorsement of Mike Martin's Liniment was published in newspapers across the country, including the November 4, 1926, *Wisconsin Rapids Daily Herald*. The advertisement included his photograph.

The story about Bender's decision to go into isolation when ill came from an article under the headline "Bender's 'Cure'" that appeared in the July 5, 1914, *Washington Post*.

The story of Bender's stolen appendix came from reporting in Carlisle newspapers as well as an item in a January 1912 article in the *New York Herald*.

The June 6, 1909, edition of the *Washington Post* noted that Bender bet on himself during shooting matches. This same article also briefly mentioned his struggle with rheumatism.

Bender's apparent decision to leave baseball was reported in local and wire stories, including those picked up by a Carlisle newspaper found in the Charles Bender clips file at the Cumberland County Historical Society and the February 20 edition of the *Washington Post.* The Mack quote on this topic is also taken from the *Post* story.

Those wishing to learn more about the relationship between early emotional parental support and an individual's health in adulthood could consult an article titled "Emotional Support from Parents Early in Life, Aging and Health," by Benjamin A. Shaw et al., published in 2004 in the journal *Psychology and Aging.* I used the piece to form the paragraph pertaining to this topic.

Chapter Six

It's worth repeating that in regards to general information about Carlisle during Bender's time at the school, on which the mock school day in this chapter was constructed, Bell's work was especially relied on. Crawford's descriptions of life at the school also were used in this chapter.

Information about Marianne Moore and her views of Bender were written about in the February 15, 1960, *Sports Illustrated* under the headline "The Poet, The Bums and the Legendary Red Men."

The quote attributed to T. S. Eliot about Moore came from *Time* magazine, September 21, 1959.

Facts about Bender's time at the Carlisle Indian Industrial School came from copies of his student record at the Cumberland County Historical Society and the National Archives and Records Administration in Washington, D.C.

Bender's answers to the Carlisle questionnaire are found in a document labeled "Record of Graduates and Returned Students, United States Indian School, Carlisle, Pennsylvania." I found a copy of this document at the Crow Wing County Historical Society; it was useful not only in providing insight into Bender's feelings but also reveals details about his early life.

The first article in two-part series about Bender's life published in *The Sporting News* on December 24, 1942, was used for information about Bender's time at Carlisle.

Powers-Beck wrote that Bender "ostensibly" denied he faced prejudice. The quote about being treated fairly came from the October 19,

1910, *Chicago Daily News.* Other information on this topic was found in the 1983 *Baseball Research Journal.*

Brief mentions of some of Bender's behind-the-scenes efforts are made in Powers-Beck's book.

Details about the story about Bender's run in with Clark Griffith came from the May 6, 1906, *Philadelphia Inquirer* and from an article that also appeared in the *New York Times.*

Chapter Seven

Powers-Beck was the first scholar to analyze the Carlisle baseball program in depth, and I relied on his work in this chapter. Among other important aspects of his research, Powers-Beck showed that Warner deemphasized baseball and that baseball players probably did not receive the kind of coaching they would have needed to fully develop.

Pratt's comment about "greatest Christian kindness" came from the Richard Henry Pratt papers at Yale University, reprinted in various sources, including Crawford's *All American,* a book used to describe Pop Warner and the nature of Carlisle athletics during the Warner years. Crawford was also personally useful, making himself available early in my research and offering suggestions.

The story of the wild Dillsburg game was told many times over the years. The *Philadelphia Evening Bulletin* published a detailed account May 30, 1954. A copy of the letter Bender received in 1942 from the Dillsburg Baseball Club is in multiple clips files, including the Bender file at the Baseball Hall of Fame. The letter is handwritten and in certain spots is not entirely legible. Comparing the letter to reporting in newspaper accounts at the time could, if all words in the letter were made clear, reveal minor inconsistencies.

General information about the Carlisle outing program and Bender's outings were taken from the Carlisle sources previously mentioned.

Sources used for the role Pop Warner played in Bender's career were found in various sources, including the August 25, 1930, *Carlisle Evening Sentinel* and the December 28, 1927, *Evening Bulletin.* Bender's comments about Warner also were found in undated articles found at Temple's Urban Archives, including those authored by Philadelphia sportswriter James Isaminger and those published in the *Philadelphia Inquirer.* For more information about Pop Warner's views of Carlisle athletics see "Reminisces of a Football Coach," *Baseball Magazine,* January 1913.

Bender was quoted about his athletic pursuits at Carlisle in an article that appeared in the May 25, 1954, *Evening Bulletin.*

The December 24, 1942, issue of *The Sporting News* was used for information about Bender's time at Carlisle playing for Warner and his expulsion from Carlisle.

Christy Mathewson's quote about Bender's well-rounded nature came from a column Mathewson wrote in the February 24, 1916, *Boston Daily Globe.*

Joe Astroth's comments in this and subsequent chapters came from a personal interview conducted in January 2005.

Another source consulted on the topic of American Indian athletic pursuits was *To Show What an Indian Can Do: Sports at Native American Boarding Schools,* by John Bloom (University of Minnesota Press, 2000).

Chapter Eight

A lengthy article under the headline "Why the Braves Won and the Athletics Lost the Championship of the World" in the December 1914 *Baseball Magazine* was relied on for information about the 1914 World Series in this and subsequent chapters. As noted elsewhere, I am grateful to Norman Macht, who shared research he did on the 1914 World Series and the 1914 Boston Braves, research relied on heavily in this and subsequent chapters. Macht's work was especially useful in regards to George Stallings' makeup and the way he managed his team.

A picture of Mrs. Charles Bender seated next to Mrs. Walter J. Maranville during Hall of Fame induction ceremonies was published in the August 10, 1954, *New York Daily News.*

Baseball's Deadball Era is fascinating to research. I profited from the Society for American Baseball Research's Deadball Era Committee, which includes researchers who taught me things with their writings and communications, including the committee's two-volume exploration of the players of the era, *Deadball Stars of the National League* edited by Simon and *Deadball Stars of the American League,* edited by Jones.

A variety of other sources were consulted to learn about the era used in this and other chapters, including two unpublished papers by Robert H.

Schaefer: *The Legend of the Lively Ball*, dated January 2002, and *The Dawn of the Dead Ball Era*, dated May 2005. Schaefer goes into much greater detail than I have about the history of the ball, and if one is interested in the topic, his work is well worth reading. A lot of general factual information about the Deadball Era was taken from a compilation published at the Web site baseballprimer.com in 2002 (the site later changed to baseball-thinkfactory.org). Other sources relied upon: *The Glory of Their Times: The Story of the Early Days of Baseball Told by the Men Who Played It*, by Lawrence S. Ritter (William Morrow, 1992); *Never Just a Game: Players, Owners and American Baseball to 1920*, by Robert F. Burk (University of North Carolina Press, 1994); and *Our Game: An American Baseball History*, by Charles C. Alexander (Henry Holt & Company, 1991). Two numbers used about overall scoring were taken from the January 25, 2005, *Hardball Times*. James's *Abstract* provided details about Evers and Stallings.

Other sources consulted: *Batting*, by F. C. Lane (Society for American Baseball Research, 2001); *Base Ball: America's National Game, 1839–1915*, edited by Samm Coombs and Bob West (Halo Books, 1991); *Creating the National Pastime: Baseball Transforms Itself, 1903–1953*, by G. Edward White (Princeton University Press, 1996); *Early Innings: A Documentary History of Baseball, 1825–1908*, edited by Dean A. Sullivan (University of Nebraska Press, 1995); and *Baseball: The Golden Age*, by Harold Seymour (Oxford University Press, 1971).

Chapter Nine

Wordsmith William Safire wrote about the word *money* as an attributive noun in his "On Language" column in the March 13, 2005, edition of the *New York Times* under the headline "Money Quote."

Portions of sabermetrician Chris Jaffe's excellent numerical analysis of Bender's career helped form sections about Bender's outstanding 1907 run. Jaffe pointed out that the A's may have been underachieving that season and summarized Bender's totals.

Thanks to James Gerencser at the Dickinson College archives for clarifying that Bender attended the college's prep school and for assistance with the limited available materials on Bender's short time there.

Mack's comments about Bender's initial Major League contract are found in multiple sources, including Lieb's *Connie Mack*.

General information about the Harrisburg Athletic Club and Island Park came from the library files at the Historical Society of Dauphin County in Harrisburg.

Regarding Bender's signing with the A's, a short article in the November 13, 1962, *New York Times* stated that Dr. Harvey Smith, a renowned surgeon and former ballplayer, was "instrumental" in Bender's signing with the Philadelphia Athletics. This piece, written more than eight years after Bender's death, is the only mention I found of Smith's connection to Bender.

Tholkes's work was again useful in the discussion about Bender's decision to remain in the east in the fall of 1902.

Chapter Ten

The story of Bender being tagged with his nickname was told several times over the years. In another version Bender didn't know exactly who yelled out to him; it may have been Danny Hoffman or Monte Cross. An article that appeared in the May 25, 1954, *Philadelphia Evening Bulletin* quoted Bender as saying, "On and off the reservation, I was always Charles Albert Bender." The story also was written about in an article dated February 3, 1952, found Temple's Urban Archives. This article was compiled because a reader wrote in to ask whether Bender had an Indian name. His reply: "Tell the young lady she's right about how the Indians name children after things in nature. The Chippewas did it. But my father was German and he didn't go for that Little Rabbit and Running Deer Stuff. I always thought it was nonsense about the mother getting the name from the first thing she noticed after the baby was born. Before we came east there was a boy out there named Red Water. Now how could a woman see red water unless it was rum?"

Details about Bender's mannerisms early in his career, including his deliberate way of speech, were taken from contemporary press accounts, including a profile on Bender in the July 23, 1905, *St. Louis Post-Dispatch*, Philadelphia newspapers, and articles in the Baseball Hall of Fame player file and *The Sporting News* archives. Thanks to Jim Meier, who provided materials from TSN.

There is some difference of opinion as to the proper spelling of Osee

Schrecongost's name. I used what was found in *Deadball Stars of the American League,* which cites descendents and a marriage license.

Bender talked about his first spring training and told the "baseball steak" story in an article that appeared in *The Sporting News* on December 31, 1942. In this article he also discussed his first Major League game.

Bender talked how he used to study batters and pitchers during his first spring training in an article about him in the January 8, 1940, *Philadelphia Record.*

Information from Bender's rookie season was taken from the *Philadelphia Evening Bulletin*'s coverage that season. Bender also discussed his first game in an article that appeared in the *Roanoke World News* in 1941. Buck Freeman's home run off Bender in Bender's first career outing was written about in an article under the headline "Home Runs that Have Become Famous" in the July 20, 1914, daily edition of *The Star and Sentinel,* published in Pennsylvania.

Information about the Benders' marriage was taken from their marriage record. An undated article from the *Newport News Daily Press* found at the Crow Wing County Historical Society, in which Marie Bender was quoted extensively, was useful for this chapter. An article that appeared in the *Evening Bulletin* shortly after Bender's death included quotes attributed to Marie about the couple's honeymoon and activities away from the ballpark. A few notes about the early home life of Marie and Charles Bender were taken from an October 19, 1905, article in the *Carlisle American Volunteer.*

In addition to sources already mentioned regarding Connie Mack and the old Philadelphia Athletics, information about how Mack handled his players came from *Our Game: An American Baseball History,* by Charles C. Alexander (Henry Holt & Company, 1991).

Westcott was perhaps the best source about old Columbia Park. I relied on his book *Philadelphia's Old Ballparks* and an article excerpted from that volume for an edition of "Along the Elephant Trail," the newsletter of the Philadelphia Athletics Historical Society, which included Emil Beck's recollections. Other ballpark histories previously noted also were consulted.

Bender's visit home was mentioned briefly in a local newspaper clip, apparently produced years after the fact, found in Warroad. The article said that "he did not put on any great style, but made himself look just like the rest of the Indian boys." In fact, his first—and perhaps his only— visit home as a big leaguer may have been November 1904, not 1903. It is unclear, but Bender recalled it taking place in 1903.

The *Evening Bulletin* noted on May 23, 1954, that Marie was at her husband's bedside when he died.

Chapter Eleven

Information about Rube Waddell's injury and the 1905 Philadelphia Athletics, including the 1905 World Series, came from Lieb's *Connie Mack* and from correspondence with Macht.

Information about the way Bender handled pressure during the 1905 World Series was written about in *America At Ease: Some Glimpses of Our Sporting Blood at Play in the Pursuit of Happiness*, a book published in 1962. The dialogue between Bender and McGraw has been written about in numerous sources.

Information about this and subsequent World Series was found in *The Sports Encyclopedia: Baseball 2004*, edited by David Neft, Richard Cohen, and Michael Neft (St. Martin's Griffin, 2004); and *The World Series: An Illustrated History of the Fall Classic*, edited by Josh Leventhal (Tess Press, 2004).

In addition to contemporary newspapers and sources already mentioned, information about the New York Giants used in this and subsequent chapters was found in Lieb's *Connie Mack; Matty: An American Hero*, by Ray Robinson (Oxford University Press, 1993); *The Player: Christy Mathewson, Baseball, and the American Century*, by Philip Seib (Four Walls Eight Windows, 2003); *The Old Ball Game*, by Frank Deford (The Atlantic Monthly Press, 2005); *Deadball Stars of the National League*; and *John McGraw*, by Charles C. Alexander (University of Nebraska Press, 1988).

In addition, I relied on Macht's research to help form the section near the end of the chapter about the Athletics' pursuit of Mathewson and Willis.

Mack's facetious quote about the possibility of Bender and Matty pitching dual perpetual shutouts was published in, among other places, the May 28, 1954, *New York Times*.

Chapter Twelve

The two-part series of columns authored by George Stallings in the January 10 and 17, 1915, editions of the *Boston Daily Globe* were again useful here.

Those wishing to know more about Russell Ford's thoughts on the emery ball and the Boston Braves' possible use of it should see "Russell Ford Tells Inside Story of the 'Emery' Ball After Guarding His Secret for Quarter of a Century" in the April 25, 1935, issue of *The Sporting News*. Information was also found in Bill James's *Abstract*.

Information about the emery pitch came from a presentation called "A Pig in a Poke" by baseball historian Peter Morris at the Society for American Baseball Research national convention in 2004.

Information about Bender's thoughts on the spitball was found in an article that appeared in the November 22, 1950, issue of *The Sporting News*. Schaefer's *The Dawn of the Dead Ball Era* provided useful information about the spitball.

Several sources were used regarding Bender's control and his views on that topic. Evans's observations were printed in numerous periodicals. Much of the information used was from the *New York Times* column. Others were taken from a syndicated column printed in the *Frederick Daily News* (Maryland) on November 25, 1925. Several articles found in the Bender file in *The Sporting News* archives were useful in this section. Among others, Bender talked about his views on control in an article that appeared in *The Sporting News* on December 31, 1942. Information also came from undated articles found Temple's Urban Archives, including those from the *Philadelphia Evening Bulletin*. An article in the February 24, 1952, of that paper also was useful.

A profile of Hank Gowdy in the December 1914 *Baseball Magazine* was relied upon for details about Gowdy and general information about the Boston Braves and the 1914 World Series. Macht's research was also useful for information about Dick Rudolph.

Information about Louis Van Zelst came from an article written by Max Silberman in "Along the Elephant Trail." Kuklick's work was again useful here.

Information about Bender's two-homer game was found in the May 9, 1906, *Boston Daily Globe*.

Chapter Thirteen

In addition to contemporary newspapers, sources consulted about Bender's no-hitter include *The Great No-Hitters*, by Glenn Dickey (Thomas Nelson & Sons, 1976); and *The No-Hit Hall of Fame: No-Hitters of the 20th Century*, by Rich Coberly (Triple Play Publications, 1985).

Articles found in *The Sporting News* archives were useful in this chapter, including those in which both Bender and Ira Thomas discussed details about his no-hitter.

Bender talked about the game in an article that appeared in *The Sporting News* on December 31, 1942.

The note about Bender's crooked forefinger, and his belief that the middle finger is the "key finger," came from a short profile on him found *The Sporting News* archives dated September 29, 1931.

"Shut up, you'll break the spell," came from a profile on Bender in the December 30, 1953, issue of *The Sporting News*.

The October 8, 1913, *Carlisle Evening Sentinel* included a close-up photograph showing how "the Athletics' twirler holds ball for his famous drop."

Numerous sources were consulted in forming the sections on the slider. I am grateful to former big-league pitcher Dave Baldwin's consultation as Baldwin reviewed my descriptions of the pitch and showed me the error of my ways. A book I relied on heavily in this chapter was *The Neyer/James Guide to Pitchers: An Historical Compendium of Pitching, Pitchers, and Pitches*, by Rob Neyer and Bill James (Fireside, 2004), which also noted that Bender may have thrown a knuckleball. Thank you, Bill James, for corresponding with me via e-mail and reviewing facts about the history of the slider.

Regarding general information on the flight and action of the ball I used information found in "Predicting a Baseball's Path" in the May–June 2005 online issue of *American Scientist*; information about pitching and the slider was taken from *The Physics of Baseball*, by Robert K. Adair (HarperCollins, 1994).

Other sources consulted for this chapter include an article in the November 30, 1955, *The Sporting News*, which contained Bucky Walters' comments; *The Crooked Pitch*, by Martin Quigley (Algonquin Books, 1984);

and *The Story of Bobby Shantz,* by Bobby Shantz (J. B. Lippincott and Company, 1953).

Those wishing to learn more about the mysterious history of the slider are advised to read Morris's *A Game of Inches.*

Chapter Fourteen

The story about Bender using a newspaper clipping as motivation came from an article in the November 22, 1913, *Sporting Life.*

A syndicated game story reprinted in Carlisle and elsewhere following the first game of the 1910 World Series noted that "the day was ideal for baseball. One would think it was the middle of May instead of the middle of October."

Coverage in the Oct. 24, 1910, edition of *The Post-Standard,* published in Syracuse, New York, was used in this chapter.

Information about the 1910 World Series was found in Lieb's *The Story of the World Series.*

Thanks to Cindy Thomson, coauthor of *Three Finger: The Mordecai Brown Story* (University of Nebraska Press, 2006), for reviewing facts on Brown used in this chapter.

A note about American Indians who voiced their approval following the 1910 World Series was found in the coverage in the *Newark Daily Advocate.*

Chapter Fifteen

Information and quotes about Philadelphia were taken from a variety of sources, including the U.S. Geological Survey; the city's official visitors guide for fall-winter 2004–05; *Philadelphia: A 300-Year History,* by Russell F. Weigley, et al. (W. W. Norton, 1982); *Philadelphia at 300: A Time for Reflection,* by William J. Green (Day & Zimmerman, 1982); and *Philadelphia: Portrait of An American City,* by Edwin Wolf (Stackpole Books, 1975). Kuklick's *To Every Thing A Season* was also used here as was Jordan's book.

The Masonic Library and Museum of Pennsylvania provided information about Bender's involvement in the Masons; thanks to Catherine Giaimo for her assistance. I also received a helping hand from Peter J. Westbere, who has researched the topic of baseball-playing Masons. General information about Masonry was found in *The Freemasons,* by Jasper Ridley (Arcade Publishing, 2001); and the *Columbia Encyclopedia*, sixth edition (2001–05).

Chapter Sixteen

Grantland Rice said the conversation with Bender about throwing curveballs to bases took place while the two were golfing just after the 1911 World Series. The story was written about in various sources, including Rice's *The Tumult and the Shouting* (A.S. Barnes and Company, 1954), and Rice's column, included in the Bender file at the Baseball Hall of Fame. This column also included comments by Connie Mack about Bender's ability in the clutch. Arthur Daley, in a May 28, 1954, *New York Times* column, also wrote about the curveballs to bases tale.

Ty Cobb's recollection that Bender made the "greatest bit of brainwork I ever saw in a ballgame," in which Bender supposedly tricked John Meyers, was written about an April 17, 1937, article found at Temple's Urban Archives.

I am grateful to the help of Bob Gorman, who shared research he did to debunk the myth that Charles Bender's older brother, John Bender, died while pitching for the Edmonton Eskimos. Gorman's work was found in the journal *NINE*, vol. 11, 2003. There was, in fact, a short syndicated news story that was published shortly after John's death that stated he died during a game, and this short story is likely where most of the erroneous tales began. The *News and Courier* (Charleston, South Carolina) reported in its September 27, 1911 edition that John Bender died during a game as the result of a heart attack. But, as reported in the *Edmonton Journal* of September 25, he died of a heart attack at the Lewis Bros. Café a couple of weeks after the season. Information was also taken from the September 25, 1911, *Edmonton Daily Bulletin*. I am grateful to Jan Baker, who provided a copy of that hard-to-get article.

In addition to sources already mentioned, additional information about John came from Powers-Beck's research.

Information about Charles, Anna, and Elizabeth Bender's early schooling was included in "A Place Among Nations: Experiences of Indian People," by David Beaulieu, published in Clifford E. Clark Jr.'s *Minnesota in a Century of Change: The State and Its People Since 1900* (Minnesota Historical Press, 1989).

About Anna Bender's life and death I used information contained in

Molin's research and correspondence. Molin's article was relied on heavily as well. Those wishing to know more may want to consult the Anna Bender student file at Hampton University Archives, which includes "The Story of My Life," an undated manuscript. Some of these materials were found in a clips file at the Warroad Heritage Center.

In addition to Philadelphia newspapers, details about the 1911 World Series were taken from contemporary coverage from the *Cleveland Plain Dealer*, the *Chicago Tribune*, and the *New York Times*. Deford's book was also relied on for events related to Mathewson's starts and battles with Frank Baker.

The "It's the Chief!" cry came from a wire story widely published soon after the 1911 World Series, including in the *Carlisle Arrow*.

Information about how the 1911 World Series was an international spectacle came from *Our Game: An American Baseball History*, by Charles C. Alexander (Henry Holt & Company, 1991).

A significant portion of the information about Frank Baker's World Series home runs came from an excellent article written by Norman Macht in vol. 5, no. 1 of *The Inside Game*, the newsletter of SABR's Deadball Era Committee.

Bender told the story of hunting with Frank Baker in the January 6, 1940, *Philadelphia Evening Bulletin*.

Information about Bender's involvement in the Pearl Sisters vaudeville act came from *Baseball Legends and Lore*, by David Cataneo (Barnes & Noble Books, 1991).

Thanks to Edwin Thanhouser, president of the Thanhouser Company Film Preservation, who helped in the search for information about Bender's one-film movie career. Much of the information on that topic used in this chapter came from "Thanhouser Films: An Encyclopedia and History" a CD-ROM by Q. David Bowers, published by Thanhouser Company Film Preservation. Another source consulted was Hal Erickson's *Baseball in the Movies* (McFarland & Company, 1992).

Chapter Seventeen

Details about Bender's 1909 performance against the Detroit Tigers were taken from the September 19, 1909, edition of the *Philadelphia Inquirer*. Other useful facts were found in wire stories that were published widely, including the September 18 *Boston Daily Globe* and the September 19 *Washington Post*. Details about the Detroit-Philly games and Cobb's alleged incidents with Baker and Collins came from Kuklick's *To Every Thing A Season*.

Chapter Eighteen

Numerous sources were consulted regarding Bender's sharp eyesight and his ability to "steal" signs. "Chief Bender's Keen Eyes Athletics' Signal Detector" was the headline of a useful article dated April 6, 1912, which was included in the Bender file at the Baseball Hall of Fame and published in *Sporting Life* magazine. An April 1914 article in *Baseball Magazine* under the headline "Secret Factors in the Winning of a World's Championship" was relied on. Other articles on the topic include the November 6, 1915, *Fort Wayne Journal-Gazette*, and the August 27, 1917, *Fort Wayne Sentinel*, which talked about Bender's "wonderful eyes." The Meyers story about this topic came from Ritter's *The Glory of Their Times*.

The December 1914 issue of *Baseball Magazine* was very useful in this chapter, noting, among other details, that there was a "Fourth of July celebration" in the Boston dugout every time a Brave crossed the plate.

Chapter Nineteen

The story of Mack's payoff of Bender's mortgage has been told in various sources throughout the years and not always with the same details. It has been written that the exchange took place in 1911, but that is almost certainly not accurate. Mack's largesse in 1913 was likely the result of his having cut Bender's salary before the start of that season in retribution for Bender's drinking in 1912. Coverage in the *Philadelphia Evening Bulletin* and elsewhere supports 1913 as the correct year, as does an article in the March 7, 1939, *Philadelphia Evening Ledger*. Mack discussed the contract he offered Bender before the 1913 season in the March 6, 1950, *New York Times*, and included in this piece was Mack's statement that the mortgage payment story took place in 1913. It seems he was essentially making up for the miniscule 1913 contract.

Bender's quote about the differences between Connie Mack and John McGraw came from a profile about Bender in the March 4, 1941, *Richmond Times-Dispatch*.

Both the quote about Connie Mack and the Doc Cramer story came from *Baseball America: The Heroes of the Game and the Times of Their Glory*, by Donald Honig (Macmillan, 1985).

Rumors that Bender was "bought" before the 1913 World Series were published in multiple sources, including wire reports out of New York that were published in the October 8, 1913, *Minneapolis Journal* and the October 7, 1913, *Daily Northwestern*.

General information about the 1913 season came from Lieb's *Connie Mack*.

Reporting by the United Press published in various newspapers on October 7, 1913, was used to compile information about the 1913 World Series. Information about Bender's first start was also taken from wire reports published in the October 8, 1913, *Minneapolis Journal*.

Reporting in the *Sporting Life* during September, October, and November 1913 was very useful for information on Bender's exploits in the World Series.

"Real Indians Gather to See Returns of Series" was the headline of a published wire story out of Portland, Oregon, about how American Indians traveled far so they could follow Bender's exploits in the 1913 World Series. The October 10, 1913, *Indianapolis Star* was one of multiple newspapers that picked it up. Information and observations about scoreboards came from *Baseballs as History*, by Jules Tygiel (Oxford University Press, 2000).

Information about reaction to Bender's and Joe Bush's exploits during the 1913 World Series were found in a newspaper article dated October 17, 1913, contained in a clips file at the Becker County Historical Society. The article was originally published in the *Minneapolis Tribune*.

Chapter Twenty

The story of Bender choosing to ignore Connie Mack's directive that he scout the Braves was told in numerous sources over the years. In fact, not only did Mack talk about it, others, such as American League president Ban Johnson, did as well. In some versions, the exchange took place in the Philadelphia clubhouse sometime prior to Game 1. The version used is the one I found most credible. Contemporary reporting in *Sporting Life* was useful.

Rice wrote about Bender in several columns during and after Bender's Major League career, including a column that appeared in the September 2, 1915, *Boston Daily Globe*. F. C. Lane wrote about Bender, among other pitchers of the time, in a multipart series called "Pitching Science in all Its Angles" published in *Baseball Magazine* in 1913.

The exchange between Bender and Rube Bressler came from Ritter's *The Glory of Their Times*. Other comments from Bressler, including those about Connie Mack used elsewhere, came from the same source.

The story of Bender's mixup with Bobby Wallace came from the March 21, 1920, edition of the *Atlanta Constitution*. A profile on Bender that appeared in the March 2, 1913, *Minneapolis Journal* included this story.

The December 1914 issue of *Baseball Magazine* noted Bender's reaction to being taken out of the game.

Chapter Twenty-One

Norman Macht's outstanding research of the 1914 World Series was relied on for multiple sections. Jordan's book was also useful.

In addition to sources cited, information about Connie Mack's suspension of Bender in 1912 was taken from a September 7, 1912, article that appeared in the *Washington Post* under the headline "Mack Suspends Two of His Men." Reporting in the *New York Dispatch* during this time was also of use. Some of Mack's views about alcohol, including his comments about how "booze and baseball don't mix," came from a wire story that appeared in the June 14, 1913, *Fort Wayne Sentinel*.

Mack discussed problems he had with Bender and Rube Oldring in the March 6, 1950, *New York Times*. Included in this piece was Mack's recollections of the contract he offered Bender before the 1913 season.

Bender's drinking habits in the 1912 season were discussed most prominently in the *North American*'s coverage that year, from September 12 on. Other useful information was found in an article under the headline "The Fallen Stars of the 1912 Season" in the September 21, 1912, *Philadelphia Evening Telegraph*.

The note about the stipulation in Bender's contract that he would be paid a full salary as long as he "refrains from intoxicating liquors" was found at the Hall of Fame; thanks to Gabriel Schechter for providing a copy of Bender's salary history card.

Thanks to Wendy Knickerbocker, author of *Sunday at the Ballpark* (Scarecrow Press, 2000), for verifying facts about Billy Sunday, some of which were found in Seib's *The Player*.

Information about the 1914 season, the 1914 World Series, and Connie Mack's views on those topics came from an article written by Fred Lieb in the October 28, 1943, issue of *The Sporting News*.

Bender talked about the 1914 World Series in an article that appeared in *The Sporting News* on December 31, 1942.

Information about Mack's financial situation came from Kuklick's *To Every Thing a Season*.

Thanks to Wendy Knickerbocker, author of *Sunday at the Ballpark* (Scarecrow Press, 2000), for verifying facts about Billy Sunday, some of which were found in Seib's *The Player*.

Information about the 1914 World Series and the subsequent breakup of the Philadelphia A's came from Lieb's *Connie Mack*.

Several articles found *The Sporting News* archives file were useful in this chapter, including those in which Bender discussed the 1914 World Series.

The "beerless" story was told in numerous articles, including one found in the Bender file at the Baseball Hall of Fame.

Coverage in the October 10, 1914, *Trenton Evening Times*, which included wire stories, was useful about the 1914 World Series.

Wire reports published in the December 7, 1914, *Lincoln Daily News* and elsewhere included mention that Bender tanked up on "firewater" after Game 1. *Sporting Life* was also useful on this topic.

Bender's comment after hearing the news of his release was published in the November 2, 1914, *Williamsport Gazette and Bulletin*.

Chapter Twenty-Two

Information about the Federal League was found in *The Federal League of 1914–1915: Baseball's Third Major League*, by Marc Okkonen (Society for American Baseball Research, 1989) and *The New Bill James Historical Baseball Abstract*, by Bill James (Free Press, 2001).

Bender talked about his time in the Federal League in an article that appeared in *The Sporting News* on December 31, 1942.

Bender's conversation with Ty Cobb about the Federal League was reported in a column written by Cobb, or his ghostwriter, in the September 5, 1915, *Atlanta Constitution*.

An article from a Philadelphia newspaper dated April 8, 1917, found at Temple's Urban Archives discussed Bender's abilities with a gun and mentioned that he, Grover Cleveland Alexander, and police superintendent Robinson shot together at the traps one day.

Reporting on the incident in which a car driven by Bender struck and killed a man was taken exclusively from contemporary newspapers, including Philadelphia dailies, the *New York Times*, *Los Angeles Times*, and *Washington Post*. Most are cited in the narrative. Thanks to the Historical Society of Pennsylvania for providing articles from the *Philadelphia Public Ledger*.

Chapter Twenty-Three

Jaffe's work was relied upon in the sections in which Bender's statistical record is analyzed.

I am grateful to Dan Levitt, another sabermetrician and author, who reviewed many of the numbers and the analysis of those numbers contained in this chapter.

John McGraw's quote came from an article under the headline "My Thirty Years in Baseball" disseminated in 1923 by the Christy Walsh Syndicate.

The Connie Mack quote that if he could pick one pitcher for a big game "Albert would be my man" has been included in nearly every biographical profile ever written about Bender, including *Baseball: The Biographic Encyclopedia*, edited by David Pietrusza, Matthew Silverman, and Michael Gershman (Total Sports, 2000).

The story of Grover Cleveland Alexander's miraculous operation on Bender's arm was written about in the June 11, 1931, edition of the *Philadelphia Evening Bulletin* and in various other sources during Bender's retirement years.

The Bender file at Temple's Urban Archives was a very useful source of information on Bender's later years. Most of those articles are dated and all are from Philadelphia newspapers such as the *Philadelphia Inquirer* and the *Evening Bulletin*, but many are not attributed to a specific one.

Details about Bender's injury while pitching in Vineland, New York, were reported in an article dated September 18, 1919, in the Bender file at Temple's Urban Archives. The same article included details about his wife's injury. The September 19, 1919, *Boston Daily Globe* reported on the injury as well as Marie's and noted that the injury might prevent him from assisting Pat Moran's team in the World Series.

Details about the New York Yankees' acquisition of Bender was reported in a June 1918 article included in Temple's Urban Archives.

The note that James Madison Toy was probably the first American Indian in the big leagues came from Powers-Beck.

Bender discussed the Cincinnati Reds' offer in an article in the March 12, 1936, *Philadelphia Inquirer.*

Bender's bonus from Richmond was stated in the September 6, 1919, *Washington Post.*

Mention was made of Bender's pitching batting practice to the Black Sox in the September 16, 1919, *Chicago Daily Tribune.*

The August 16 *Chicago Daily Tribune* reported that Bender would report to the Reds on September 6, following the conclusion of the Virginia League season.

Several articles in Temple's Urban Archives were used about Bender's time at Hog Island.

Information about Bender's nervous breakdown was reported in the *Washington Post*, December 14–15, 1918. An article under the headline "Famous Indian Pitcher Suffers Nervous Collapse Resulting from Overwork" was found in the Temple Urban Archives file.

The story about a pitcher not accepting signals from John "Chief" Meyers was taken from Aaseng's *American Indian Lives.*

Chapter Twenty-Four

Bender's return to Carlisle was written about in various sources, including multiple articles in the *Carlisle Evening Sentinel* in late August 1930, the *Philadelphia Public Ledger* on August 29, 1930, and the East Berlin (Pennsylvania) *News Comet* on September 5, 1930. The Associated Press also disseminated information about the event.

Comments about Bender's success as an example to others were found in the October 21, 1910, *Carlisle Arrow*, which regularly published notes about Bender's Major League Baseball career.

Thanks to the Hillside Cemetery in Roslyn, Pennsylvania, for providing details about the plot Bender and Edmund Kirby jointly purchased.

A wire story published in the December 7, 1950, *Zanesville Signal*

(Ohio) briefly discussed Bender's career, including some of his stops in the minors.

Bender's dismissal from Jack Dunn's team was written about, albeit briefly, in various articles, including one dated October 23, 1923, found in Temple's Urban Archives. Another useful article came from the October 29, 1923, *Bridgeport Telegram*.

"Bender Pitches No-Hit Game" was the headline in an article found in the file in Temple's Urban Archives about Bender's no-hitter for New Haven. Other useful information was found in a profile about him in the December 30, 1953, issue of *The Sporting News* and in an article that appeared in *The Sporting News* on December 31, 1942.

Several articles found in Temple's Urban Archives contained useful information about Bender's time in the minor leagues, including details about his injury while he was with the House of David, which was published in a July 1933 *Philadelphia Evening Bulletin* article.

Details about Bender's mother's accident were taken from various contemporary newspapers and accounts written in the days following her death. Among the most useful were the local newspapers *Baudette Region* and the *Williams Northern Light*. Other sources consulted on this topic were papers and clips found at the Warroad Heritage Center and the Becker County Historical Society.

Information about Squaw Mary and Arthur Cooley was taken from stories produced for the Lake of the Woods Historical Society found in a clips file at Warroad. Molin's research was also used in this chapter.

Information about Bender's sister, Elizabeth, and her husband, Henry Roe Cloud, came from numerous sources. The Warroad clips file contained biographical information on Elizabeth; one undated article in particular was useful. It said she met Roe Cloud while teaching at Carlisle and that they married in Charles Bender's house in 1916, that she served as a nurse during World War II, went on various speaking tours for the board of missions of the Presbyterian Church, and that the Roe Clouds often visited Mary. A profile of Elizabeth written in the April 1950 issue of the *International Mothers Digest* shortly after she was named American Mother of the Year for 1950 provided useful biographical materials. The May 25, 1950, *Evening Bulletin* was also useful. Details about Elizabeth Roe Cloud's honor were also taken from reporting published widely by the Associated Press on April 28, 1950. Biographical information on Henry Roe Cloud was found in the *Dictionary of American Biography, Supplement Four, 1946–50*: "Henry Roe Cloud stands as an important transitional figure, among the best trained of the first generation of organized and educated Indian spokesmen . . . He shared with his white predecessors a belief that assimilation . . . was coming, one way or another." Additional information about the Roe Clouds and the American Indian Institute was found in clips files at the Wichita Public Library and the Wichita Sedgwick County Historical Museum Association.

Among sources on Bender's bowling ability was an article in the February 9, 1940, *Philadelphia Evening Bulletin*. There is a good photo of Bender, Jimmie Dykes, Wally Schang, Bing Miller, and Joe Bush at a bowling alley in the January 1928 *Evening Sentinel* article found at the Cumberland County Historical Society. A profile on Bender dated September 29, 1931, found in *The Sporting News* file was useful.

Bender's quote when he was fifty-four came from an article about him published in the March 5, 1938, *Philadelphia Record*.

The note about Bender's involvement in the unveiling of the new flexible safety glass came from *Time* magazine, April 10, 1939.

Chapter Twenty-Five

Information about Bender's later years was found in the Bender file at Temple's Urban Archives, including details about Chief Bender Night, Bender's comment about the nature of scouting, notes about his television career, his participation in service clubs on behalf of the Philadelphia Athletics, and barbs he used regularly during speaking engagements.

Several other sources were used to compile information about Chief Bender Night, including coverage in the *Philadelphia Inquirer*, which included a photograph of Bender standing at a microphone, Marie on his arm. Other details were found in two volumes of the "Along the Elephant Trail" newsletter from 1952. An article in the August 15, 1952, *Philadelphia Evening Bulletin* also was used.

Several articles found in *The Sporting News* archives were useful in this chapter, including one written by Dan Parker under the headline "Bender's Coaching Made the A's Pitching Staff in '51" that was stamped February 1952.

An article that appeared in the *Evening Bulletin* shortly after Bender's death discussed Bender's later years.

Useful information about Bender's later years was also found in *The Sporting News*, including articles published in the June 2, 1954, and November 22, 1950, issues.

Information about the old-timers' game in which Bender pitched for Mack's team came from Lieb's *Connie Mack*.

Bender's late-life tenure as a batting practice pitcher was discussed in numerous articles, including one found in the Baseball Hall of Fame file.

An article in the February 24, 1952, *Evening Bulletin* was useful on the topic of how Bender handled A's pitchers as pitching coach.

Coverage in the *Philadelphia Inquirer* written during Bender's tenure as pitching coach was helpful.

Bobby Shantz's relationship with Bender, including the note he sent after Bender had fallen ill, was reported in various sources, including the August 31, 1952, *Philadelphia Inquirer*.

The story of Bender meeting Yogi Berra was written about in an article published in the January 25, 1952, *New York Journal-American*.

Epilogue

I found that when you dig around in the past you meet a lot of selfless people in the present. Bob Hunter, director of the Haddon Heights Public Library, fielded an e-mail from me and instead of getting on with his busy day helped me periodically, over the course of months, to locate a member of the Burns family. I had all but abandoned the search. Thanks to Hunter I was able to speak to members of the Burns family, who enriched my understanding of Bender's later years, including Patricia Burns Ward, John Burns, and Richard Burns. Ruth Burns also provided a useful set of newspaper clippings.

However, most information used on Bender's relationship with John Burns and his family, including Bender's relationship with Michael Burns, was taken from contemporary sources, including comments John Burns made in a June 4, 1954, *Philadelphia Evening Bulletin* article.

An article that appeared in the May 24, 1954, *Evening Bulletin* shortly after Bender's death discussed time spent in Chief's Garden and Bender's later years, and included quotes from Marie used in this chapter. A June 4, 1954, article under the headline "Chief Bender was Perfectionist as a Gardener" in the same newspaper also detailed Bender's gardening skills and relationship with the Burns family.

Several articles in *The Sporting News* file were useful in this chapter, including those written about time spent in Chief's Garden and at John Burns's family home.

Details about Bender's funeral were taken from coverage in the *Evening Bulletin* and the *Philadelphia Inquirer*. Other information was found in funeral records at the Historical Society of Pennsylvania and in coverage published in the May 28, 1954, *Inquirer*. The *Evening Bulletin* was especially useful concerning details about Bender's death, his funeral, the service, and, later, Marie's death. The *Bulletin* also published the story of how Bing Miller used to take ice cream to Bender in the hospital. Information about reaction to his death, including Roy Mack's comments, was taken from an Associated Press article printed on May 24, 1954.

Thanks to the Philadelphia Athletics Historical Society for providing a copy of Bender's death certificate.

Information about Bender's funeral and his cemetery plot were found in funeral records at the Historical Society of Pennsylvania. Marie Bender's will, found in a records department at Philadelphia City Hall, was also useful, though I did not use any information directly from that document.

Bender's health problems late in life were written about in brief detail in various Philadelphia newspapers, including those found in at Temple's Urban Archives. One of the most useful was dated January 2, 1944.

The Charles Bender file at the Haskell Cultural Center and Museum in Lawrence, Kansas, contains information about Bender's induction into the American Indian Athletic Hall of Fame.

Copies of letters written by Shan Buck and A. G. Burgoyne Jr. were found at the Crow Wing County Historical Society. Paul Schultz's story came from the January 12, 2000, edition of *Anishinaabeg Today*.

Dan Kratz was interviewed in March 2005.

Eddie Joost was interviewed in January 2005.

Lou Limmer was interview in February 2005.

Thanks to Ernie St. Germaine, who taught me what *boozhoo niijii* means.

Several articles found in the Urban Archives contained useful information about Bender's illness late in life.

A letter written by Michael Burns was published in the November 2003 issue of *Native American Casino* magazine.

Other Sources

Numerous biographical sketches were useful, including Bob Warrington's biographical profile published in the November 2003 issue of *Native American Casino* magazine; an August 1956 *Baseball Magazine* profile; the *Biographical Dictionary of American Sports*, edited by David L. Porter (Greenwood Press, 2000); "Minnesota's Greatest Baseball Player," by Gary W. Clendennen, *Minnesota Monthly*, August 1983; several profiles in the Bender file at the Baseball Hall of Fame; and multiple profiles found in the Bender file in *The Sporting News* archives.

Other books consulted: *They Played the Game: The Story of Baseball Greats*, by Harry Grayson (A. S. Barnes and Company, 1944); *Baseball as History*, by Jules Tygiel (Oxford University Press, 2000); *Money Pitcher: Chief Bender and the Tragedy of Indian Assimilation*, by William C. Kashatus (Pennsylvania State University Press, 2006); *Touching Base: Professional Baseball and American Culture in the Progressive Age*, by Steven A. Reiss (Greenwood Press, 1980); *Encyclopedia of North American Indians*, by Frederick E. Hoxie (Houghton Mifflin Company, 1996); *Indian Summer: The Forgotten Story of Louis Sockalexis, the First Native American in Major League Baseball*, by Brian McDonald (Rodale, 2003); and *Koppett's Concise History of Major League Baseball*, by Leonard Koppett (Temple University Press, 1998).

Acknowledgments. In addition to the friendly faces I found along the research trail, I also received various other forms of assistance from people to whom I am beholden.

I am fortunate to regularly rub elbows—in the usual way as well as across cyberspace—with men and women who enrich my understanding of the game Charles Bender loved. If you write about baseball without a Society for American Baseball Research membership card you're disregarding the single most valuable resource available.

My work was enhanced in immeasurable ways by SABR's deep well of intellectual capital. Among those who taught me things, often without even knowing they were, include members of the Deadball Era Committee, who furthered my knowledge about the compelling period during which Bender's career unfolded. It's my good luck to be a member of the Halsey Hall Chapter, where I have learned from the likes of Dan Levitt, Bob Tholkes, and Stew Thornley—whose standards of research have been instructive (though don't think they're responsible for the book's shortcomings). At the start I asked Thornley whether the book had a chance to be published. Encouragement from the foremost historian on Minnesota baseball history never hurts a guy.

Through SABR I connected with Bill Deane, who mined for factual errors. There is no more important service to a writer of baseball history.

Other SABR members provided help without prompting, such as Rick Huhn, Bob Wilson, Cary Smith, and Dean Thilgen. Thank you, too, Jim Sexton and Mark Johnson.

Max Silberman, I owe you another cheesesteak. Or three.

I am indebted to Norman Macht's expertise about the old Philadelphia Athletics and the generous manner in which he lent it. He never refused to answer my questions, even the stupid ones.

Thanks for your thoughts, Marcie Rendon.

Every study of the Carlisle Indian School I have gotten my hands on has included a note of thanks to Barb Landis and the team at the Cumberland County Historical Society in Carlisle—I know why. Add my name to the scroll.

Thanks for the pointers, Mary Carroll Moore.

I sought out anyone who could remember being in the same room with Charles Bender. It's a small club. Thank you, Dan Kratz. Former Philadelphia Athletics Joe Astroth, Eddie Joost, and Lou Limmer also were especially helpful. Patricia Burns Ward, John Burns, and Richard Burns, thanks for your recollections.

Thanks for your helping hands, Colin Hampson, Ina Williams, Robert Rofidal, and Ted Huf.

I find baseball pleasurable for the reasons many do—is there anything better than a play at the plate?—and also because the game is a vessel of interesting ideas. So much is mystery, but there are writers who hold a lantern against the shadows, who explain the meaning of the game's numbers in a way that even my math-challenged brain can follow along. Here I am thinking of, among others, Bill James, Joe Sheehan, and those who throughout the years have contributed to SABR publications, including *The Baseball Research Journal* and *The National Pastime,* and the SABR listserv. Most of these writers and researchers wouldn't know me if I knocked on their front door, but how much I would have missed had I only read the morning newspaper. Any baseball muscle I brought to the page comes from the education I have received reading their words over time.

I am grateful to live in a place that has a resource such as the Loft Literary Center, where I sharpened my writing tools while pecking away at the manuscript.

Some advice: when you write your first book, work with a patient editor. Thanks, Rob Taylor.

I will be forever in debt to two people I could never sufficiently thank. Anything I have ever done that's any good stems from the selfless opportunities my mother and father have provided.

I am in such regular need of a psychologist that I married one. Without my wife's steady support and gentle understanding, all other forms of assistance would have been for naught.

Index.

Page numbers in italics refer to illustrations.

Index